THREE TREATISES

MARTIN LUTHER

FORTRESS PRESS

Library of Congress Catalog Card Number 73-114753
ISBN 0-8006-1639-1

Printed in the United States of America   1-1639

99 98 97 96   16 17 18 19 20 21 22 23 24

CONTENTS

ABBREVIATIONS

CIC —*Corpus Iuris Canonici*
CL   —*Luthers Werke in Auswahl*
LW —American Edition of *Luther's Works*
MA³ —*Martin Luther.* Ausgewählte Werke
MPL—*Patrologia, Series Latina* (also as Migne)
PE   —*Works of Martin Luther.* Philadelphia Edition
St. L.—*D. Martin Luthers sämmtliche Schriften*
WA – Weimar Edition of *D. Martin Luthers Werke*

FOREWORD

The year 1520 marks the watershed of the Reformation. On June 15 Pope Leo X issued the bull, *Exsurge, Domine,* giving Luther sixty days to recant or be declared a heretic. Luther officially received it on October 10. Sixty days later he wrote to a friend: "Greetings. On December 10, 1520, at nine o'clock in the morning, all the following papal books were burned in Wittenberg at the eastern gate near the Church of the Holy Cross. . . . This is the news here." Luther had publicly and ceremoniously burned the bull, canon law, and books supporting the pope. On January 3, 1521, formal excommunication was announced. What had started in 1517 as a protest against indulgences by an unknown monk, developed in 1520 into an irreconcilable conflict dividing the Western church.

These three treatises of 1520 are the heart of Luther's protest against the church of his day. The first was written in August, the second in October, and the third in November. They are about convictions causing conflict within both Protestantism and Catholicism today: the ethical responsibilities of the individual; trust in God versus trust in man's abilities; and what the freedom of the individual person means.

The unabridged text of the three treatises is reprinted from the American Edition of *Luther's Works,* whose publishers, editors, and translators hope that through this edition "the message of Luther's faith will speak more clearly to the modern church."

TO THE

CHRISTIAN NOBILITY

OF THE GERMAN NATION

Translated by Charles M. Jacobs

Revised by James Atkinson

INTRODUCTION

This treatise, one of the most significant documents produced by the Protestant Reformation, appeared at a critical point in Luther's career. The Leipzig Debate with John Eck during the summer of 1519 had projected Luther into a position of prominence and attracted support from a wide variety of partisans and sympathizers in humanist circles, episcopal courts, universities, and among the imperial knights. After his return to Wittenberg, while awaiting the decision of the several universities appointed to referee the debate, Luther resumed the whole range of his pastoral and teaching activities. In the five and one-half months after the debate he also published sixteen treatises which, though not so intended, increased his reputation as a controversial figure.

One of these treatises, *The Blessed Sacrament of the Holy and True Body of Christ, and the Brotherhoods* (1519),[1] involved him in a quarrel with the bishop of Meissen and, indirectly, with Duke George of Saxony. The settlement of this quarrel early in 1520, however, did not satisfy Elector Frederick, for he had known since the previous December that a new attack was being planned in Rome against himself and against Luther, and that this attack involved Eck, who had been summoned to Rome. By the middle of March, 1520, the condemnation of Luther's position at Leipzig by the faculties of Louvain and Cologne reached Saxony. The elector urged Luther to address a proposal of peace to his opponents, but he refused on the ground that to withdraw from a controversy would be to deny God's Word.

---

1. *LW* 35, 47-73.

Early in May, 1520, the crude Latin polemic *On the Apostolic See,* written by Augustine von Alveld, a Franciscan friar, arrived in Wittenberg. Luther did not choose to issue a personal reply, and instead assigned the task to John Lonicer, his *famulus.* But when Alveld published a similar work in German, Luther replied himself, lest the German-speaking laity be misled. In the concluding section of his reply, *On the Papacy in Rome, Against the Most Celebrated Romanist in Leipzig,*[2] Luther wrote, "Moreover, I should be truly glad if kings, princes, and all the nobles would take hold, and turn the knaves from Rome out of the country, and keep the appointment to bishoprics and benefices out of their hands. How has Roman avarice come to usurp all the foundations, bishoprics, and benefices of our fathers? Who has ever read or heard of such monstrous robbery? Do we not also have the people who need them, while out of our poverty we must enrich the assdrivers and stable boys, nay, the harlots and knaves at Rome, who look upon us as nothing else but arrant fools, and make us the objects of their vile mockery. . . . Oh, the pity that kings and princes have so little reverence for Christ, and his honor concerns them so little that they allow such heinous abominations to gain the upper hand, and look on, while at Rome they think of nothing but to continue in their madness and to increase the abounding misery, until no hope is left on earth except in the temporal authorities. About this, if this Romanist attacks me again, I will say more later. Let this suffice for a beginning."[3]

Although Alveld did not renew the attack himself, it did come. During the first week in June Luther received a copy of Prierias' *Epitome of a Reply to Martin Luther,* which contained bold assertions of papal absolutism. Al-

---

2. *LW* 39, 49-104. This reply was written during the last two weeks in May, 1520.

3. Cf. *LW* 39, 102-103.

most immediately Luther published an annotated reprint of this work.[4] In his preface to this reprint Luther wrote, "And now farewell, unhappy, hopeless, blasphemous Rome! The wrath of God has come upon you in the end, as you deserved, and not for the many prayers which are made on your behalf, but because you have chosen to grow more evil from day to day! We have cared for Babylon and she is not healed. Let us then leave her that she may be the habitation of dragons, spectres, ghosts, and witches, and true to her name of Babel, an everlasting confusion, an idol of avarice, perfidy, apostasy, of cynics, lechers, robbers, sorcerers, and endless other impudent monsters, a new pantheon of wickedness."[5]

The tenor of these words gives significance to a letter written to Spalatin just before June 8, in which Luther states, "I have a mind to issue a broadside to [Emperor] Charles and the nobility of Germany against the tyranny and baseness of the Roman curia."[6] On June 23 Luther sent the manuscript of *To the Christian Nobility* to Nicholas von Amsdorf. By August 18 the first edition of four thousand copies had come from the press of Melchior Lotther in Wittenberg. Within a week a second, somewhat enlarged, edition was being prepared.

It would appear that *To the Christian Nobility* was occasioned by the attacks of Alveld and Prierias, and was the fulfilment of Luther's thinly veiled threat in the concluding section of *On the Papacy in Rome* and of his intention expressed in the letter to Spalatin. Luther research over the last half century, however, has challenged this view.[7] Close scrutiny of the text of the treatise, of Luther's

---

4. Cf. *WA* 6, 328-348. On Prierias, cf. below, p. 124, n. 3.
5. *WA* 6, 329.
6. *WA*, Br 2, 120.
7. For details, cf. *LW* 44, 119, nn. 12, 13; 120, n. 14; 121, n. 17.

correspondence, and of other contemporary sources and documents has provided new insights.

These insights indicate that the present treatise, originally intended as a small booklet, actually came about as the result of urgent insistence from, and with the extensive co-operation of, unidentified members of the Saxon court, jurists, Wittenberg professors, and other widely respected men. In Luther these men would have a spokesman who could give to the *Gravamina* of the German nation the theological substance and expression which had been lacking previously.

Yet despite the urging and co-operation of others, *To the Christian Nobility* is the product of Luther's mind, heart, and soul. Firmly convinced of the priesthood of believers, and believing that the German nobility, as a whole, were of the same sincerity of spirit as those nobles he knew at the Saxon court, Luther, in the light of clear historical precedent, confidently conferred upon the crown and the nobility the responsibility and the right to intervene in ecclesiastical affairs to accomplish the reform of the church.

In the three sections of this treatise Luther laid the ax to the whole complex of ideas upon which the social, political, legal, and religious thought of the Western world had been developing for nearly a thousand years. The first section exposes and refutes theologically the three walls behind which the papacy was entrenched. By demolishing the first wall, the concept of spiritual and secular classes, Luther removed the medieval distinction between clergy and laity and conferred upon the state, the rulers of which (as Luther saw it) were Christians and therefore priests, the right and duty to curb evil no matter where it appeared. In rapid succession he demolishes the remaining two walls: the papal claim (most recently advanced by Alveld and Prierias) that only the pope can interpret Scripture, and that because only the pope could summon a council the decisions of a council were invalid without

5

papal sanction. Luther declares that there is no biblical ground for the papal claim of the sole right to interpret Scripture, and he asserts the necessity for Rome to listen to those who can. The third wall collapses under the barrage of Luther's attacks drawn from Scripture, church history, and the assertion that "when necessity demands it, and the pope is an offense to Christendom, the first man who is able should, as a true member of the whole body, do what he can to bring about a truly free council."

The second part of the work is a bill of particulars, a specific indictment of ecclesiastical abuses with which a general council should deal. These abuses range from the worldliness of the papacy and the curia to benefices and indulgences. For a long time it was assumed that Luther's portrayal of conditions in Rome derived from the recollection of his own stay there in 1510-1511. The evidence uncovered by modern research, however, suggests that he drew less upon his own memory than upon very recent information provided by Reuchlin's lawyer, Johann von der Wieck.

Just as specific as the indictments are the proposals for reform which constitute the final section of the work. Here Luther's proposals range from the abolition of annates and the exclusion of the church from political power to popular piety, public provision for the poor, and the relationship between church and state. The latter part of this section deals with education and the economic and social ills afflicting the German nation.

The present translation is a revision of that by Charles M. Jacobs in *PE* 2, 61-104. The German text, *An den christlichen Adel deutscher Nation von des christlichen Standes Besserung,* is in *WA* 6, (381) 404-469.

TO THE
CHRISTIAN NOBILITY
OF THE GERMAN NATION

JESUS

To the Esteemed and Reverend Master, Nicholas von Amsdorf, Licentiate of Holy Scripture, and Canon of Wittenberg, my special and kind friend, from Doctor Martin Luther.

The grace and peace of God be with you, esteemed, reverend, and dear sir and friend.

The time for silence is past, and the time to speak has come, as Ecclesiastes says [3:7]. I am carrying out our intention to put together a few points on the matter of the reform of the Christian estate, to be laid before the Christian nobility of the German nation, in the hope that God may help his church through the laity, since the clergy, to whom this task more properly belongs, have grown quite indifferent. I am sending the whole thing to you, reverend sir, [that you may give] an opinion on it and, where necessary, improve it.

I know full well that I shall not escape the charge of presumption because I, a despised, inferior person, venture to address such high and great estates on such weighty matters, as if there were nobody else in the world except Doctor Luther to take up the cause of the Christian estate and give advice to such high-ranking people. I make no apologies no matter who demands them. Perhaps I owe my God and the world another work of folly. I intend to pay my debt honestly. And if I succeed, I shall for the time being become a court jester. And if I fail, I still have one advantage—no one need buy me a cap or put scissors to my head.[1] It is a question of who will put the bells on whom.[2] I must fulfil the proverb, "Whatever the world does, a monk must be in the picture, even if he has to be painted in."[3] More than once a fool has spoken wisely, and wise men have often been arrant fools. Paul says, "He who wishes to be wise must become a fool" [I Cor. 3:18]. Moreover, since I am not only a fool, but also a sworn doctor of Holy Scripture,[4] I am glad for the opportunity to fulfil my doctor's oath, even in the guise of a fool.

I beg you, give my apologies to those who are moderately intelligent, for I do not know how to earn the grace and favor of the superintelligent. I have often sought to do so with the greatest pains, but from now on I neither desire nor value their favor. God help us to seek not our own glory but his alone. Amen.

> At Wittenberg, in the monastery of the Augustinians, on the eve of St. John Baptist [June 23] in the year fifteen hundred and twenty.

To His Most Illustrious, Most Mighty, and Imperial Majesty, and to the Christian Nobility of the German Nation, from Doctor Martin Luther.

Grace and power from God, Most Illustrious Majesty, and most gracious and dear lords.

It is not from sheer impertinence or rashness that I, one poor man, have taken it upon myself to address your worships. All the estates of Christendom, particularly in Germany, are now oppressed by distress and affliction, and this has stirred not only me but everybody else to cry out

---

1. A jocular comparison of the monk's cowl and tonsure with the jester's cap and bells.

2. I.e., who is the bigger fool.

3. *Monachus semper praesens.*

4. Luther often stressed that he had acquired his doctorate and its obligation to teach the gospel not out of his own desire but out of obedience to his superiors. Cf. *LW* 48, 6, n. 5.

8

time and 'time again and to pray for help. It has even compelled me now at this time to cry aloud that God may inspire someone with his Spirit to lend a helping hand to this distressed and wretched nation. Often the councils have made some pretense at reformation,[5] but their attempts have been cleverly frustrated by the guile of certain men, and things have gone from bad to worse. With God's help I intend to expose the wiles and wickedness of these men, so that they are shown up for what they are and may never again be so obstructive and destructive. God has given us a young man of noble birth as head of state,[6] and in him has awakened great hopes of good in many hearts. Presented with such an opportunity we ought to apply ourselves and use this time of grace profitably.

The first and most important thing to do in this matter is to prepare ourselves in all seriousness. We must not start something by trusting in great power or human reason, even if all the power in the world were ours. For God cannot and will not suffer that a good work begin by relying upon one's own power and reason. He dashes such works to the ground, they do no good at all. As it says in Psalm 33 [:16], "No king is saved by his great might and no lord is saved by the greatness of his strength." I fear that this is why the good emperors Frederick I[7] and Frederick II[8] and many other German emperors were in former times shamefully oppressed and trodden underfoot by the popes, although all the world feared the emperors. It may be that they relied on their own might more than on God, and therefore had to fall. What was it in our own times

---

5. See LW 44, 91, n. 52.

6. Charles V, who had been elected emperor in 1519 when only twenty years of age, and whom Luther appeared before at the Diet of Worms in 1521.

7. Emperor Frederick Barbarossa (1152-1190).

8. Frederick II (1212-1250), grandson of Barbarossa and last of the great Hohenstaufen emperors, died under excommunication.

9

that raised the bloodthirsty Julius II[9] to such heights? Nothing else, I fear, except that France, the Germans, and Venice relied upon themselves. The children of Benjamin slew forty-two thousand Israelites[10] because the latter relied on their own strength, Judges 30 [:21].

That it may not so fare with us and our noble Charles, we must realize that in this matter we are not dealing with men, but with the princes of hell. These princes could fill the world with war and bloodshed, but war and bloodshed do not overcome them. We must tackle this job by renouncing trust in physical force and trusting humbly in God. We must seek God's help through earnest prayer and fix our minds on nothing else than the misery and distress of suffering Christendom without regard to what evil men deserve. Otherwise, we may start the game with great prospects of success, but when we get into it the evil spirits will stir up such confusion that the whole world will swim in blood, and then nothing will come of it all. Let us act wisely, therefore, and in the fear of God. The more force we use, the greater our disaster if we do not act humbly and in the fear of God. If the popes and Romanists[11] have hitherto been able to set kings against each other by the devil's help, they may well be able to do it again if we were to go ahead without the help of God on our own strength and by our own cunning.

The Romanists have very cleverly built three walls around themselves. Hitherto they have protected themselves by these walls in such a way that no one has been able to reform them. As a result, the whole of Christendom has fallen abominably.

In the first place, when pressed by the temporal power

---

9. Pope Julius II (1503-1513) was notorious for his unscrupulous use of political power. Continually involved in war, he led his armies in person and was "the scourge of Italy."

10. Luther's memory is not accurate here. Judges speaks of twenty-two thousand.

11. Advocates of papal supremacy.

they have made decrees and declared that the temporal power had no jurisdiction over them, but that, on the contrary, the spiritual power is above the temporal. In the second place, when the attempt is made to reprove them with the Scriptures, they raise the objection that only the pope may interpret the Scriptures. In the third place, if threatened with a council, their story is that no one may summon a council but the pope.

In this way they have cunningly stolen our three rods from us, that they may go unpunished. They have ensconced themselves within the safe stronghold of these three walls so that they can practice all the knavery and wickedness which we see today. Even when they have been compelled to hold a council they have weakened its power in advance by putting the princes under oath to let them remain as they were.[12] In addition, they have given the pope full authority over all decisions of a council, so that it is all the same whether there are many councils or no councils. They only deceive us with puppet shows and sham fights. They fear terribly for their skin in a really free council! They have so intimidated kings and princes with this technique that they believe it would be an offense against God not to be obedient to the Romanists in all their knavish and ghoulish deceits.[13]

May God help us, and give us just one of those trumpets with which the walls of Jericho were overthrown[14] to blast down these walls of straw and paper in the same way and set free the Christian rods for the punishment of sin, [and]

---

12. Luther alludes to the failure of the conciliar movement to reform the church. It failed chiefly because the papacy refused to submit to the authority of the council. Moreover, the papacy refused to co-operate in convening a council unless the secular powers first swore not to deprive the pope of his authority.

13. *Spugnissen*, literally, "ghosts." The sense of the passage is that the Romanists have frightened the world with threats of purgatory and hell.

14. Cf. Josh. 6:20.

11

bring to light the craft and deceit of the devil, to the end that through punishment we may reform ourselves and once more attain God's favor.

Let us begin by attacking the first wall. It is pure invention that pope, bishop, priests, and monks are called the spiritual estate while princes, lords, artisans, and farmers are called the temporal estate. This is indeed a piece of deceit and hypocrisy. Yet no one need be intimidated by it, and for this reason: all Christians are truly of the spiritual estate, and there is no difference among them except that of office. Paul says in I Corinthians 12 [:12-13] that we are all one body, yet every member has its own work by which it serves the others. This is because we all have one baptism, one gospel, one faith, and are all Christians alike; for baptism, gospel, and faith alone make us spiritual and a Christian people.

The pope or bishop anoints, shaves heads,[15] ordains, consecrates, and prescribes garb different from that of the laity, but he can never make a man into a Christian or into a spiritual man by so doing. He might well make a man into a hypocrite or a humbug and blockhead,[16] but never a Christian or a spiritual man. As far as that goes, we are all consecrated priests through baptism, as St. Peter says in I Peter 2 [:9], "You are a royal priesthood and a priestly realm." The Apocalypse says, "Thou hast made us to be priests and kings by thy blood" [Rev. 5:9-10]. The consecration by pope or bishop would never make a priest, and if we had no higher consecration than that which pope or bishop gives, no one could say mass or preach a sermon or give absolution.

Therefore, when a bishop consecrates it is nothing else than that in the place and stead of the whole community, all of whom have like power, he takes a person and charges him to exercise this power on behalf of the others. It is like

15. I.e., confers tonsure.
16. *Olgotzen*, literally, wood images of saints; figuratively, any dull person.

ten brothers, all king's sons and equal heirs, choosing one of themselves to rule the inheritance in the interests of all. In one sense they are all kings and of equal power, and yet one of them is charged with the responsibility of ruling. To put it still more clearly: suppose a group of earnest Christian laymen were taken prisoner and set down in a desert without an episcopally ordained priest among them. And suppose they were to come to a common mind there and then in the desert and elect one of their number, whether he were married[17] or not, and charge him to baptize, say mass, pronounce absolution, and preach the gospel. Such a man would be as truly a priest as though he had been ordained by all the bishops and popes in the world. That is why in cases of necessity anyone can baptize and give absolution. This would be impossible if we were not all priests. Through canon law[18] the Romanists have almost destroyed and made unknown the wondrous grace and authority of baptism and justification. In times gone by Christians used to choose their bishops and priests in this way from among their own number, and they were confirmed in their office by the other bishops without all the fuss that goes on nowadays. St. Augustine,[19] Ambrose,[20] and Cyprian[21] each became [a bishop in this way].

Since those who exercise secular authority have been baptized with the same baptism, and have the same faith and

---

17. *Ehelich.* PE and other English translations also render this word as "married." It can, however, also mean "legitimately born." Karl Benrath notes that according to canon law only one born in wedlock may receive ordination as a priest. Cf. *LW* 44, 128, n. 17.

18. Canon law, which Luther throughout this treatise and elsewhere calls the "spiritual law," is a general name for the decrees of councils and the decisions of the popes collected in the *Corpus Iuris Canonici.* It comprised the whole body of church law and embodied the medieval theory of papal absolutism, which accounts for the bitterness with which Luther speaks of it, especially in this treatise.

19. Augustine, bishop of Hippo (395-430).

20. Ambrose, bishop of Milan (374-397), was elected to the office by the people of Milan, even though he was not yet baptized.

21. Cyprian, bishop of Carthage (247-258), was also elected by the laity.

the same gospel as the rest of us, we must admit that they are priests and bishops and we must regard their office as one which has a proper and useful place in the Christian community. For whoever comes out of the water of baptism can boast that he is already a consecrated priest, bishop, and pope, although of course it is not seemly that just anybody should exercise such office. Because we are all priests of equal standing, no one must push himself forward and take it upon himself, without our consent and election, to do that for which we all have equal authority. For no one dare take upon himself what is common to all without the authority and consent of the community. And should it happen that a person chosen for such office were deposed for abuse of trust, he would then be exactly what he was before. Therefore, a priest in Christendom is nothing else but an officeholder. As long as he holds office he takes precedence; where he is deposed, he is a peasant or a townsman like anybody else. Indeed, a priest is never a priest when he is deposed. But now the Romanists have invented *characteres indelebiles*[22] and say[23] that a deposed priest is nevertheless something different from a mere layman. They hold the illusion that a priest can never be anything other than a priest, or ever become a layman. All this is just contrived talk, and human regulation.

It follows from this argument that there is no true, basic difference between laymen and priests, princes and bishops, between religious and secular, except for the sake of office and work, but not for the sake of status. They are all of the spiritual estate, all are truly priests, bishops, and popes. But they do not all have the same work to do. Just as all priests and monks do not have the same work. This is the teaching of St. Paul in Romans 12 [:4-5] and I Corinthians 12 [:12] and in I Peter 2 [:9], as I have said above,

---

22. Cf. below, p. 242, n. 201.
23. *Schwetzen;* literally, "to chatter nonsense."

namely, that we are all one body of Christ the Head, and all members one of another. Christ does not have two different bodies, one temporal, the other spiritual. There is but one Head and one body.

Therefore, just as those who are now called "spiritual," that is, priests, bishops, or popes, are neither different from other Christians nor superior to them, except that they are charged with the administration of the word of God and the sacraments, which is their work and office, so it is with the temporal authorities. They bear the sword and rod in their hand to punish the wicked and protect the good. A cobbler, a smith, a peasant—each has the work and office of his trade, and yet they are all alike consecrated priests and bishops. Further, everyone must benefit and serve every other by means of his own work or office so that in this way many kinds of work may be done for the bodily and spiritual welfare of the community, just as all the members of the body serve one another [I Cor. 12:14-26].

Consider for a moment how Christian is the decree which says that the temporal power is not above the "spiritual estate" and has no right to punish it.[24] That is as much as to say that the hand shall not help the eye when it suffers pain. Is it not unnatural, not to mention un-Christian, that one member does not help another and prevent its destruction? In fact, the more honorable the member, the more the others ought to help. I say therefore that since the temporal power is ordained of God to punish the wicked and protect the good, it should be left free to perform its office in the whole body of Christendom without restriction and without respect to persons, whether it affects pope, bishops, priests, monks, nuns, or anyone else. If it were right to say that the temporal power is inferior to all the spiritual estates (preacher, confessor, or any

---

24. The sharp distinction drawn by the Roman church between clergy and laity made possible the contention that the clergy was exempt from the jurisdiction of the civil courts.

spiritual office), and so prevent the temporal power from doing its proper work, then the tailors, cobblers, stonemasons, carpenters, cooks, innkeepers, farmers, and all the temporal craftsmen should be prevented from providing pope, bishops, priests, and monks with shoes, clothes, house, meat and drink, as well as from paying them any tribute. But if these laymen are allowed to do their proper work without restriction, what then are the Romanist scribes doing with their own laws, which exempt them from the jurisdiction of the temporal Christian authority? It is just so that they can be free to do evil and fulfil what St. Peter said, "False teachers will rise up among you who will deceive you, and with their false and fanciful talk, they will take advantage of you" [II Pet. 2:1-3].

For these reasons the temporal Christian authority ought to exercise its office without hindrance, regardless of whether it is pope, bishop, or priest whom it affects. Whoever is guilty, let him suffer. All that canon law has said to the contrary is the invention of Romanist presumption. For thus St. Paul says to all Christians, "Let every soul (I take that to mean the pope's soul also) be subject to the temporal authority; for it does not bear the sword in vain, but serves God by punishing the wicked and benefiting the good" [Rom. 13:1, 4]. St. Peter, too, says, "Be subject to all human ordinances for the sake of the Lord, who so wills it" [I Pet. 2:13, 15]. He has also prophesied in II Peter 2 [:1] that such men would arise and despise the temporal authority. This is exactly what has happened through the canon law.

So, then, I think this first paper wall is overthrown. Inasmuch as the temporal power has become a member of the Christian body it is a spiritual estate, even though its work is physical.[25] Therefore, its work should extend without hindrance to all the members of the whole body to punish and

---

25. I.e., temporal.

use force whenever guilt deserves or necessity demands, without regard to whether the culprit is pope, bishop, or priest. Let the Romanists hurl threats and bans about as they like. That is why guilty priests, when they are handed over to secular law, are first deprived of their priestly dignities.[26] This would not be right unless the secular sword previously had had authority over these priests by divine right. Moreover, it is intolerable that in canon law so much importance is attached to the freedom, life, and property of the clergy, as though the laity were not also as spiritual and as good Christians as they, or did not also belong to the church. Why are your life and limb, your property and honor, so cheap and mine not, inasmuch as we are all Christians and have the same baptism, the same faith, the same Spirit, and all the rest? If a priest is murdered, the whole country is placed under interdict.[27] Why not when a peasant is murdered? How does this great difference come about between two men who are both Christians? It comes from the laws and fabrications of men.

Moreover, it can be no good spirit which has invented such exceptions and granted sin such license and impunity. For if it is our duty to strive against the words and works of the devil and to drive him out in whatever way we can, as both Christ and his apostles command us, how have we gotten into such a state that we have to do nothing and say nothing when the pope or his cohorts undertake devilish words and works? Ought we merely out of regard for these people allow the suppression of divine commandments and truth, which we have sworn in baptism to sup-

26. Church authorities insisted that clergy charged with infractions of laws of the state first be tried in ecclesiastical courts. Priests found guilty were deprived of their priesthood and surrendered to the temporal authorities.

27. The interdict prohibits the administration of the sacraments and other rites of the church within a given territory. At the height of papal power it was an effective means of bringing rulers to terms. Interdicts of local extent were quite frequent. Their use for trifling infractions of church law was protested at diets in 1521 and 1524.

port with life and limb? Then we should have to answer for all the souls that would thereby be abandoned and led astray!

It must, therefore, have been the chief devil himself who said what is written in the canon law, that if the pope were so scandalously bad as to lead crowds of souls to the devil, still he could not be deposed.[28] At Rome they build on this accursed and devilish foundation, and think that we should let all the world go to the devil rather than resist their knavery. If the fact that one man is set over others were sufficient reason why he should not be punished, then no Christian could punish another, since Christ commanded that every man should esteem himself as the lowliest and the least [Matt. 18:4].

Where sin is, there is no longer any shielding from punishment. St. Gregory writes that we are indeed all equal, but guilt makes a man inferior to others.[29] Now we see how the Romanists treat Christendom. They take away its freedom without any proof from Scripture, at their own whim. But God, as well as the apostles, made them subject to the temporal sword. It is to be feared that this is a game of the Antichrist,[30] or at any rate that his forerunner has appeared.

The second wall is still more loosely built and less substantial. The Romanists want to be the only masters of Holy Scripture, although they never learn a thing from the

---

28. The statement is found in the *Decreti Prima Pars,* dist. XL, C. VI, *Si papa. CIC* 1, 146. In his *Epitome* Prierias had quoted this canon against Luther: "A *Pontifex indubitatus* [i.e., a pope not accused of heresy or schism] cannot lawfully be deposed or judged either by a council or by the whole world, even if he is so scandalous as to lead people with him by crowds into the possession of hell." Luther's comment is, "Be astonished, O heaven; shudder, O earth! Behold, O Christians, what Rome is!" *WA* 6, 336.

29. Gregory the Great (590-604), in *Regula pastoralis,* II, 6. *MPL* 77, 34.

30. Antichrist is the incarnation of all that is hostile to Christ and his kingdom and whose appearance is prophesied in II Thess. 2:3-10; I John 2:18, 22; 4:3; and Revelation 13.

Bible all their life long. They assume the sole authority for themselves, and, quite unashamed, they play about with words before our very eyes, trying to persuade us that the pope cannot err in matters of faith,[31] regardless of whether he is righteous or wicked. Yet they cannot point to a single letter.[32] This is why so many heretical and un-Christian, even unnatural, ordinances stand in the canon law. But there is no need to talk about these ordinances at present. Since these Romanists think the Holy Spirit never leaves them, no matter how ignorant and wicked they are, they become bold and decree only what they want. And if what they claim were true, why have Holy Scripture at all? Of what use is Scripture? Let us burn the Scripture and be satisfied with the unlearned gentlemen at Rome who possess the Holy Spirit! And yet the Holy Spirit can be possessed only by pious hearts. If I had not read the words with my own eyes,[33] I would not have believed it possible for the devil to have made such stupid claims at Rome, and to have won supporters for them.

But so as not to fight them with mere words, we will quote the Scriptures. St. Paul says in I Corinthians 14 [:30], "If something better is revealed to anyone, though he is already sitting and listening to another in God's word, then the one who is speaking shall hold his peace and give place." What would be the point of this commandment

---

31. The doctrine of papal infallibility was never officially sanctioned in the Middle Ages, but the claim was repeatedly made by the champions of papal power. In his attack on the *Ninety-five Theses* (*Dialogus de potestate Papae*, 1517) Prierias had asserted, "The supreme pontiff cannot err when giving a decision as pontiff, i.e., when speaking officially [*ex officio*]"; and also, "Whoever does not rest upon the teaching of the Roman church and the supreme pontiff as an infallible rule of faith, from which even Holy Scripture draws its vigor and authority, is a heretic." In the *Epitome* Prierias had said, "Even though the pope as an individual [*singularis persona*] can do wrong and hold a wrong faith, nevertheless as pope he cannot give a wrong decision (*WA* 6, 337). Cf. *LW* 44, 133, n. 31.

32. I.e., a single letter of Scripture to support their claim.

33. In the *Epitome* of Prierias.

if we were compelled to believe only the man who does the talking, or the man who is at the top? Even Christ said in John 6 [:45] that all Christians shall be taught by God. If it were to happen that the pope and his cohorts were wicked and not true Christians, were not taught by God and were without understanding, and at the same time some obscure person had a right understanding, why should the people not follow the obscure man? Has the pope not erred many times? Who would help Christendom when the pope erred if we did not have somebody we could trust more than him, somebody who had the Scriptures on his side?

Therefore, their claim that only the pope may interpret Scripture is an outrageous fancied fable. They cannot produce a single letter [of Scripture] to maintain that the interpretation of Scripture or the confirmation of its interpretation belongs to the pope alone. They themselves have usurped this power. And although they allege that this power was given to St. Peter when the keys were given him, it is clear enough that the keys were not given to Peter alone but to the whole community. Further, the keys were not ordained for doctrine or government, but only for the binding or loosing of sin.[34] Whatever else or whatever more they arrogate to themselves on the basis of the keys is a mere fabrication. But Christ's words to Peter, "I have prayed for you that your faith fail not" [Luke 22:32], cannot be applied to the pope, since the majority of the popes have been without faith, as they must themselves confess. Besides, it is not only for Peter that Christ prayed, but also for all apostles and Christians, as he says in John 17 [:9, 20],

---

34. Matt. 16:19, 18:18, and John 20:23. Throughout his career Luther dealt with the office of the keys. He first mentioned it in 1517 in his *Ninety-five Theses* (LW 31, 27, 31) and devoted a substantial portion of his last treatise, *Against the Roman Papacy, An Institution of the Devil* (1545) to a discussion of the keys (LW 41, 315–320 *passim*). His clearest and most extensive treatment was set forth in his 1530 treatise *The Keys* (LW 40, 321–377).

"Father, I pray for those whom thou hast given me, and not for these only, but for all who believe on me through their word." Is that not clear enough?

Just think of it! The Romanists must admit that there are among us good Christians who have the true faith, spirit, understanding, word, and mind of Christ. Why, then, should we reject the word and understanding of good Christians and follow the pope, who has neither faith nor the Spirit? To follow the pope would be to deny the whole faith[35] as well as the Christian church. Again, if the article, "I believe in one holy Christian church," is correct, then the pope cannot be the only one who is right. Otherwise, we would have to confess,[36] "I believe in the pope at Rome." This would reduce the Christian church to one man, and be nothing else than a devilish and hellish error.

Besides, if we are all priests, as was said above, and all have one faith, one gospel, one sacrament,[37] why should we not also have the power to test and judge what is right or wrong in matters of faith? What becomes of Paul's words in I Corinthians 2 [:15], "A spiritual man judges all things, yet he is judged by no one"? And II Corinthians 4 [:13], "We all have one spirit of faith"? Why, then, should not we perceive what is consistent with faith and what is not, just as well as an unbelieving pope does?

We ought to become bold and free on the authority of all these texts, and many others. We ought not to allow the Spirit of freedom (as Paul calls him [II Cor. 3:17]) to be frightened off by the fabrications of the popes, but we ought to march boldly forward and test all that they do, or leave undone, by our believing understanding of the Scriptures. We must compel the Romanists to follow not their own interpretation but the better one. Long ago Abraham had to

---

35. Literally, "the creed," referring to the Apostles' Creed.
36. *Beten;* literally, "to pray."
37. Luther means baptism. See p. 127.

listen to Sarah, although she was in more complete subjection to him than we are to anyone on earth [Gen. 21:12]. And Balaam's ass was wiser than the prophet himself [Num. 22:21-35]. If God spoke then through an ass against a prophet, why should he not be able even now to speak through a righteous man against the pope? Similarly, St. Paul rebukes St. Peter as a man in error in Galatians 2 [:11-12]. Therefore, it is the duty of every Christian to espouse the cause of the faith, to understand and defend it, and to denounce every error.

The third wall falls of itself when the first two are down. When the pope acts contrary to the Scriptures, it is our duty to stand by the Scriptures, to reprove him and to constrain him, according to the word of Christ, Matthew 18 [:15-17], "If your brother sins against you, go and tell it to him, between you and him alone; if he does not listen to you, then take one or two others with you; if he does not listen to them, tell it to the church; if he does not listen to the church, consider him a heathen." Here every member is commanded to care for every other. How much more should we do this when the member that does evil is responsible for the government of the church, and by his evil-doing is the cause of much harm and offense to the rest! But if I am to accuse him before the church, I must naturally call the church together.

The Romanists have no basis in Scripture for their claim that the pope alone has the right to call or confirm a council.[38] This is just their own ruling, and it is only valid as long as it is not harmful to Christendom or contrary to the laws of God. Now when the pope deserves punish-

---

38. On November 28, 1518, Luther appealed his cause from the decision of the pope, which he could foresee would be adverse, to the decision of a council to be held at some future time. In the *Epitome* Prierias discusses this appeal, asserting that "when there is one undisputed pontiff, it belongs to him alone to call a council," and that "the decrees of councils neither bind nor hold unless they are confirmed by authority of the Roman Pontiff." WA 6, 335.

ment, this ruling no longer obtains, for not to punish him by authority of a council is harmful to Christendom.

Thus we read in Acts 15 that it was not St. Peter who called the Apostolic Council but the apostles and elders. If then that right had belonged to St. Peter alone, the council would not have been a Christian council, but a heretical *conciliabulum*.[39] Even the Council of Nicaea, the most famous of all councils, was neither called nor confirmed by the bishop of Rome, but by the emperor Constantine.[40] Many other emperors after him have done the same, and yet these councils were the most Christian of all.[41] But if the pope alone has the right to convene councils, then these councils would all have been heretical. Further, when I examine the councils the pope did summon, I find that they did nothing of special importance.

Therefore, when necessity demands it, and the pope is an offense to Christendom, the first man who is able should, as a true member of the whole body, do what he can to bring about a truly free council. No one can do this so well as the temporal authorities, especially since they are also fellow-Christians, fellow-priests, fellow-members of the spiritual estate, fellow-lords over all things. Whenever it is necessary or profitable they ought to exercise the office and work which they have received from God over everyone. Would it not be unnatural if a fire broke out in a city and everybody were to stand by and let it burn on and on and consume everything that could burn because nobody had the authority of the mayor, or because, perhaps, the fire broke out in the mayor's house? In such a situation is it not the duty of every citizen to arouse and summon the rest? How much more should this be done in the spiritual city of Christ if a fire of offense breaks out,

---

39. A mere gathering of people as opposed to a *concilium*, i.e., a valid council.

40. In 325. Luther's contention is historically correct.

41. Luther is referring to the first four ecumenical councils: Nicaea, Constantinople (381), Ephesus (431), and Chalcedon (451).

whether in the papal government, or anywhere else! The same argument holds if an enemy were to attack a city. The man who first roused the others deserves honor and gratitude. Why, then, should he not deserve honor who makes known the presence of the enemy from hell and rouses Christian people and calls them together?

But all their boasting about an authority which dare not be opposed amounts to nothing at all. Nobody in Christendom has authority to do injury or to forbid the resisting of injury. There is no authority in the church except to promote good. Therefore, if the pope were to use his authority to prevent the calling of a free council, thereby preventing the improvement of the church, we should have regard neither for him nor for his authority. And if he were to hurl his bans and thunderbolts, we should despise his conduct as that of a madman. On the contrary, we should excommunicate him and drive him out as best we could, relying completely upon God. This presumptuous authority of his is nothing. He does not even have such authority. He is quickly defeated by a single text of Scripture, where Paul says to the Corinthians, "God has given us authority not to ruin Christendom, but to build it up" [II Cor. 10:8]. Who wants to leap over the hurdle of this text? It is the power of the devil and of Antichrist which resists the things that serve to build up Christendom. Such power is not to be obeyed, but rather resisted with life, property, and with all our might and main.

Even though a miracle were to be done against the temporal authority on the pope's behalf, or if somebody were struck down by the plague—which they boast has sometimes happened—it should be considered as nothing but the work of the devil designed to destroy our faith in God. Christ foretold this in Matthew 24 [:24], "False Christs and false prophets shall come in my name, who shall perform signs and wonders in order to deceive even the elect." And Paul says in II Thessalonians 2 [:9] that

Antichrist shall, through the power of Satan, be mighty in false wonders.

Let us, therefore, hold fast to this: no Christian authority can do anything against Christ. As St. Paul says, "We can do nothing against Christ, only for Christ" [II Cor. 13:8]. But if an authority does anything against Christ, then that authority is the power of Antichrist and of the devil, even if it were to deluge us with wonders and plagues. Wonders and plagues prove nothing, especially in these evil latter days. The whole of Scripture foretells such false wonders. This is why we must hold fast to the word of God with firm faith, and then the devil will soon drop his miracles!

With this I hope that all this wicked and lying terror with which the Romanists have long intimidated and dulled our conscience has been overcome, and that they, just like all of us, shall be made subject to the sword. They have no right to interpret Scripture merely by authority and without learning.[42] They have no authority to prevent a council, or even worse yet at their mere whim to pledge it, impose conditions on it, or deprive it of its freedom. When they do that they are truly in the fellowship of Antichrist and the devil. They have nothing at all of Christ except the name.

We shall now look at the matters which ought to be properly dealt with in councils, matters with which popes, cardinals, bishops, and all scholars ought properly to be occupied day and night if they loved Christ and his church. But if this is not the case, let ordinary people[43] and the temporal authorities do it without regard to papal bans and fulminations, for an unjust ban is better than ten just and proper absolutions, and one unjust, improper absolution

---

42. *Kunst;* literally, "skill."

43. *Der hauff;* literally, rank and file Christians without authority in the church.

is worse than ten just bans.[44] Therefore, let us awake, dear Germans, and fear God more than man [Acts 5:29], lest we suffer the same fate of all the poor souls who are so lamentably lost through the shameless, devilish rule of the Romanists. The devil grows stronger[45] every day, if such a thing were possible, if such a hellish regime could grow any worse—a thing I can neither conceive nor believe.

1. It is horrible and shocking to see the head of Christendom, who boasts that he is the vicar of Christ and successor of St. Peter, going about in such a worldly and ostentatious style that neither king nor emperor can equal or approach him. He claims the title of "most holy" and "most spiritual," and yet he is more worldly than the world itself. He wears a triple crown,[46] whereas the highest monarchs wear but one. If that is like the poverty of Christ and of St. Peter, then it is a new and strange kind of likeness! When anybody says anything against it, the Romanists bleat, "Heresy!" They refuse to hear how un-Christian and ungodly all this is. In my opinion, if the pope were to pray to God with tears, he would have to lay aside his triple crown, for the God we worship cannot put up with pride. In fact, the pope's office should be nothing else but to weep and pray for Christendom and to set an example of utter humility.

Be that as it may, this kind of splendor is offensive, and the pope is bound for the sake of his own salvation to set it aside. It was because of this kind of thing that St. Paul said, "Abstain from all practices which give offense"

---

44. That is, if the ecclesiastical hierarchy will not do its duty and convene a council, then the secular authorities and ordinary Christians must take the matter in hand despite ecclesiastical sanctions. To come under one such sanction for the sake of this good cause is better than to receive ten absolutions.

45. *Zunympt;* literally, "grows larger" or "increases."

46. The papal crown dates from the eleventh century; the triple crown or tiara, from the fourteenth. It signified the superiority of the pope over temporal rulers.

[I Thess. 5:22], and in Romans 12 [:17], "We should do good, not only in the sight of God, but also in the sight of all men." An ordinary bishop's mitre ought to be good enough for the pope. It is in wisdom and holiness that he should be above his fellows. He ought to leave the crown of pride to Antichrist, as his predecessors did centuries ago. The Romanists say he is a lord of the earth. That is a lie! For Christ, whose vicar and vicegerent he claims to be, said to Pilate, "My kingdom is not of this world" [John 18:36]. No vicar's rule can go beyond that of his lord. Moreover, he is not the vicar of Christ glorified but of Christ crucified. As Paul says, "I was determined to know nothing among you save Christ, and him only as the crucified" [I Cor. 2:2], and in Philippians 2 [:5-7], "This is how you should regard yourselves, as you see in Christ, who emptied himself and took upon himself the form of a servant." Or again in I Corinthians 1 [:23], "We preach Christ, the crucified." Now the Romanists make the pope a vicar of the glorified Christ in heaven, and some of them have allowed the devil to rule them so completely that they have maintained that the pope is above the angels in heaven and has them at his command.[47] These are certainly the proper works of the real Antichrist.

Of what use to Christendom are those people called cardinals? I shall tell you. Italy and Germany have many rich monasteries, foundations,[48] benefices, and livings. No better way has been discovered of bringing all these to Rome than by creating cardinals and giving them bishoprics, monasteries, and prelacies for their own use[49] and so overthrowing the worship of God. You can see that

---

47. Cf. below, p. 207, n. 148. Cf. also *LW* 44, 140, n. 48.

48. *Stift;* i.e., endowed institutions.

49. For example, Pope Julius II, when a cardinal, held the revenues of the archbishopric of Avignon, the bishoprics of Bologna, Lausanne, Coutances, Viviers, Mende, Ostia, and Velletri, and the abbacies of Nonantola and Grottaferrata.

Italy is now almost a wilderness: monasteries in ruins, bishoprics despoiled, the prelacies and the revenues of all the churches drawn to Rome, cities decayed, land and people ruined because services are no longer held and the word of God is not preached. And why? Because the cardinals must have the income! No Turk could have devastated Italy and suppressed the worship of God so effectively!

Now that Italy is sucked dry, the Romanists are coming into Germany.[50] They have made a gentle beginning. But let us keep our eyes open! Germany shall soon be like Italy. We have a few cardinals already. The "drunken Germans" are not supposed to understand what the Romanists are up to until there is not a bishopric, a monastery, a living, a benefice, not a red cent left. Antichrist must seize the treasures of the earth, as it is prophesied [Dan. 11:39, 43]. It works like this: they skim the cream off the bishoprics, monasteries, and benefices, and because they do not yet venture to put them all to shameful use, as they have done in Italy, they in the meantime practice their holy cunning and couple together ten or twenty prelacies. They then tear off a little piece each year so as to make quite a tidy sum after all. The priory of Würzburg yields a thousand gulden; the priory of Bamberg also yields a sum; Mainz, Trier, and others. In this way one thousand or ten thousand gulden may be collected, so that a cardinal could live like a wealthy monarch at Rome.

When we have got that, we shall appoint thirty or forty cardinals in one day.[51] We shall give to one of them Mount

---

50. The complaint that the cardinals were provided with incomes by appointment to German benefices goes back to the Council of Constance (1414-1418). Cf. Luther's complaint in *Treatise on Good Works. LW* 44, 89. Cf. below, p. 30, n. 56.

51. Luther puts these words into the mouths of the Romanists, hence the change from "they" to "we." The creation of cardinals was a lucrative matter for the popes. On July 31, 1517, Pope Leo X created thirty-one cardinals. He is reported to have received 300,000 ducats from the appointees. *WA* 6, 417, n. 1.

St. Michael near Bamberg,[52] along with the bishopric of Würzburg, attach a few rich benefices to them until churches and cities are destitute, and then we will say, "We are Christ's vicars, and shepherds of Christ's sheep. The foolish, drunken Germans will just have to put up with it."

My advice is to make fewer cardinals, or to let the pope support them at his own expense. Twelve of them would be enough, and each of them might have an income of a thousand gulden.[53] How is it that we Germans must put up with such robbery and extortion of our goods at the hands of the pope? If the kingdom of France has prevented it,[54] why do we Germans let them make such fools and apes of us? We could put up with all this if they stole only our property, but they lay waste to the churches in so doing, rob Christ's sheep of their true shepherds, and debase the worship and word of God. If there were not a single cardinal, the church would not perish. The cardinals do nothing to serve Christendom. They are only interested in the money side of bishoprics and prelacies, and they wrangle about them just as any thief might do.

3. If ninety-nine per cent of the papal court[55] were abolished and only one per cent kept, it would still be large enough to give answers in matters of faith. Today, however, there is such a swarm of parasites in that place called Rome, all of them boasting that they belong to the pope,

---

52. A Benedictine monastery on Mount St. Michael (*Mönchberg*).

53. The Council of Constance had suggested a yearly salary of three to four thousand gulden for cardinals.

54. In the fourteenth century England and France enacted laws protecting themselves against these practices. Cf. *LW* 44, 142, n. 56.

55. According to a document printed in Rome in 1545 and found among the belongings of John Eck, there were 949 curial positions obtained by paying a fee. This figure does not include officials who administered the city of Rome and the papal states, or members of the "papal household." The Diet of Worms in 1521 complained that the increase of these offices had added greatly to the financial burdens of the German church. Cf. *LW* 44, 142, n. 57.

that not even Babylon saw the likes of it. There are more than three thousand papal secretaries alone. Who could count the other officials? There are so many offices that one could scarcely count them. These are all the people lying in wait for the endowments and benefices of Germany as wolves lie in wait for the sheep. I believe that Germany now gives much more to the pope at Rome than it used to give to the emperors in ancient times. In fact, some have estimated that more than three hundred thousand gulden a year find their way from Germany to Rome. This money serves no use or purpose. We get nothing for it except scorn and contempt. And we still go on wondering why princes and nobles, cities and endowments, land and people, grow poor. We ought to marvel that we have anything left to eat!

Since we have now come to the heart of the matter, we will pause a little and let it be seen that the Germans are not quite such crass fools that they do not see or understand the sharp practices of the Romanists. I do not at the moment complain that God's command and Christian law are despised at Rome, for the state of Christendom is such—Rome in particular—that we may not complain of such exalted matters now. Nor am I complaining that natural law, or secular law, or even reason count for nothing. My complaint goes deeper than that. I complain that the Romanists do not keep their own self-devised canon law, though it is in fact just tyranny, avarice, and temporal splendor rather than law. That I shall now show you.

In former times German emperors and princes permitted the pope to receive annates from all the benefices of the German nation. This sum amounts to one half of the revenue of the first year from every single benefice.[56] This

---

56. The annates were originally the various incomes a bishop received from vacant benefices in his diocese. The term was extended to include payments made to the curia by bishops and abbots at the time of their accession. These charges soon became a fixed tax on all church offices which be-

permission was given, however, so that by means of these large sums of money the pope might raise funds to fight against the Turks and infidels in defense of Christendom, and, so that the burden of war might not rest too heavily upon the nobility, the clergy too should contribute something toward it. The popes have so far used the splendid and simple devotion of the German people—they have received this money for more than a hundred years and have now made it an obligatory tax and tribute, but they have not only accumulated no money, they have used it to endow many posts and positions at Rome and to provide salaries for these posts, as though the annates were a fixed rent.

When they pretend that they are about to fight the Turks, they send out emissaries to raise money. They often issue an indulgence[57] on the same pretext of fighting the Turks. They think that those half-witted Germans will always be gullible, stupid fools, and will just keep handing over money to them to satisfy their unspeakable greed. And they think this in spite of the fact that everybody knows that not a cent of the annates, or of the indulgence money, or of all the rest, is spent to fight the Turk. It all goes into their bottomless bag. They lie and deceive. They make laws and they make agreements with us, but they do not intend to keep a single letter of them. Yet all this is done in the holy names of Christ and St. Peter.

Now in this matter the German nation, bishops and princes, should consider that they, too, are Christians. They should rule the people entrusted to them in temporal and spiritual matters and protect them from these

---

came vacant, and claims against overassessment and extortion were frequent. The Council of Constance (1415) restricted annates, and the Council of Basel resolved to abolish them (1439), but could not enforce its decision. They were protested at the Diet of Worms in 1521. Cf. *LW* 44, 144, n. 58.

57. The Crusades indulgence was established by Urban II (1088-1099) and granted to those who went to Palestine. In 1198 Innocent III extended it to include those who supported the Crusades in other than military ways.

rapacious wolves in sheep's clothing who pretend to be their shepherds and rulers. And since the annates have been so shockingly abused, and not even kept for their original agreed purpose, [the bishops and princes] should not allow their land and people to be so pitilessly robbed and ruined contrary to all law. By decree either of the emperor or of the whole nation the annates should either be kept here at home or else abolished again. Since the Romanists do not keep to their agreement, they have no right to the annates. Therefore, the bishops and princes are responsible for punishing such thievery and robbery, or even preventing it, as the law requires.

In such a matter they ought to help the pope and strengthen his hand. Perhaps he is too weak to prevent such abuse single-handedly. Or, in those cases where he wants to defend and maintain this state of affairs, they ought to resist him and protect themselves from him as they would from a wolf or a tyrant, for he has no authority to do evil or fight on its behalf. Even if it were ever desirable to raise such funds for fighting the Turk, we ought to have enough sense at least to see that the German nation could be a better custodian of these funds than the pope. The German nation itself has enough people to wage the war if the money is available. It is the same with the annates as it has been with many other Romanist pretenses.

Then, too, the year has been so divided between the pope and the ruling bishops and chapters that the pope has six months in the year (every other month) in which to bestow the benefices which become vacant in his months.[58] In this way almost all the best benefices have

---

58. This whole section deals with the "right of reservation," i.e., the alleged right of the pope to fill vacant church positions by appointment. The papal theory held that the right of appointment belonged to the pope, who in some cases yielded the right to others. The rule of the "papal months" provided that livings (except those of cathedrals and the chief posts in monasteries) which became vacant in February, April, June, August, Oc-

fallen into the hands of Rome, especially the very best livings and dignities.[59] And when they once fall into the hands of Rome, they never come out of them again, though a vacancy may never occur again in the pope's month. In this way the chapters are cheated. This is plain robbery, and the intention is to let nothing escape. Therefore, it is high time to abolish the "papal months" altogether. Everything that has been taken to Rome in this way must be restored. The princes and nobles ought to take steps for the restitution of the stolen property, punish the thieves, and deprive of privilege those who have abused that privilege. If it is binding and valid for the pope, on the day after his election, to make regulations and laws in his chancery[60] by which our endowed chapters and livings are stolen from us—a thing he has absolutely no right to do—then it should be still more valid for Emperor Charles, on the day after his coronation,[61] to make rules and laws that not another benefice or living in all Germany should be allowed to pass into the hands of Rome by means of the "papal months." The livings which have already fallen into the hands of Rome should be restored and redeemed from these Romanist robbers. Charles V has the right to do this by virtue of his authority as ruler.

But now this Romanist See of avarice and robbery has not had the patience to wait for the time when all the benefices would fall to it one by one through this device of the "papal months." Rather, urged on by its insatiable appetite to get them all in its hands as speedily as possible,

tober, and December should be filled by the ordinary methods—election, presentation, and appointment by the bishop, etc. Vacancies occurring in the other months were to be filled by the pope.

59. A dignity or prelacy was originally an ecclesiastical office in which jurisdiction was exercised in the name of the incumbent. Cf. *LW* 44, 146, n. 62.

60. Luther refers to policies governing the conferring of reserved benefices, etc. The pope usually established these policies just after his ascension to the papal throne. The Germans had protested the arbitrariness of these regulations and insisted that they be fixed by legislation. Cf. *LW* 44, 146, n. 63.

61. Charles V had not yet been crowned emperor when this treatise was written.

the Romanist See has devised a scheme whereby, in addition to the "annates" and "papal months," the benefices and livings should fall to Rome in three ways.

First, if anyone who holds a "free" living[62] should die in Rome or on a journey to Rome, his living becomes the property in perpetuity of the Romanist—I ought to say roguish—See.[63] But the Romanists do not want to be called robbers on this account, though they are guilty of robbery of a kind never heard of or read about before.

Second, if anyone belonging to the household of the pope or cardinals holds or takes over a benefice, or if anyone who had previously held a benefice subsequently enters the household of the pope or cardinals, [his living becomes the property in perpetuity of the Romanist See].[64] But who can count the household of the pope and cardinals? If he only goes on a pleasure ride, the pope takes with him three or four thousand on mules, all emperors and kings notwithstanding! Christ and St. Peter went on foot so that their successors might have all the more pomp and splendor. Now Avarice has cleverly thought out another scheme, and arranges it so that many even outside Rome have the name "member of the papal household" just as if they were in Rome. This is done for the sole purpose that, by the simple use of that pernicious phrase "member of the pope's household," all benefices may be brought to Rome and tied there for all time. Are not these vexatious and devilish little inventions? Let us beware! Soon Mainz, Magdeburg, and Halberstadt will quietly slip into the hands of Rome, and then the cardinalate will cost a pretty penny![65] After that they will make all the German bishops cardinals, and then there will be nothing left.

---

62. A living not hitherto filled by papal appointment.

63. A rule found in the Concordat of Vienna. Cf. WA 6, 420, n. 3.

64. Everyone to whom the name "papal servant" could be made to apply. Luther later refers to them as "courtesans."

65. In 1513 Prince Albert of Brandenburg was made archbishop of Magdeburg. Later that same year he became administrator of Halberstadt. The next

Third, when a dispute has started at Rome over a benefice.[66] In my opinion this is the commonest and widest road to bring livings into the hands of Rome. Even when there is no dispute here, countless knaves will be found at Rome who will unearth a dispute and snatch the benefices at will. Thus many a good priest must lose his living or pay a sum of money to avoid having his benefice disputed. Such a living, rightly or wrongly contested, becomes the property of the Roman See forever. It would be no wonder if God would rain fire and brimstone from heaven and sink Rome in the abyss, as he did Sodom and Gomorrah of old [Gen. 19:24]. Why should there be a pope in Christendom if his power is used for nothing else than for such gross wickedness and to protect and practice it? O noble princes and lords, how long will you leave your lands and your people naked and exposed to such ravening wolves?

Since even these practices were not enough, and Avarice grew impatient at the long time it took to get hold of all the bishoprics, my lord Avarice devised the fiction that the bishoprics should be nominally abroad but that their origin and foundation is at Rome. Furthermore, no bishop can be confirmed unless he pays a huge sum for his pallium[67] and binds himself with solemn oaths to the personal service of the pope. That explains why no bishop dares to act against the pope. That is what the Romanists were seeking when they imposed the oath. It also explains why all the richest bishoprics have fallen into debt and ruin. I am told that Mainz pays twenty thousand gulden.[68] That is the Romanists all over! To be sure, they decreed a long time ago in canon law that the pallium should be given

year he became archbishop of Mainz as well and in 1518 was made a cardinal. The expenses attending this pluralism were defrayed by the sale of indulgences.

66. This rule is also mentioned in the Concordat of Vienna.

67. A wool shoulder cape, the emblem of the archbishop's office. Luther's contentions are correct. Cf. LW 44, 148, n. 71.

68. Cf. p. 34, n. 65.

without cost, that the number in the pope's household be reduced, disputes[69] lessened, and the chapters and bishops allowed their liberty. But this did not bring in money. So they turned over a new leaf and have taken all authority away from the bishops and chapters. These sit there like ciphers, and have neither office nor authority nor work. Everything is controlled by those arch-villains at Rome, almost right down to the office of sexton and bell-ringer. Every dispute is called to Rome,[70] and everyone does just as he pleases, under cover of the pope's authority.

What has happened in this very year? The bishop of Strassburg[71] wanted to govern his chapter properly and reform it in matters of worship. With this end in view he established certain godly and Christian regulations. But our dear friend the pope and the Holy Roman See wrecked and damned this holy and spiritual ordinance, all at the instigation of the priests. This is called feeding the sheep of Christ![72] That is how priests are strengthened against their own bishop, and how their disobedience to divine law is protected! Antichrist himself, I hope, will not dare to shame God so openly. There is your pope for you! Just as you have always wanted! Why did the pope do this? Ah! If one church were reformed that would be a dangerous breakthrough. Rome might have to follow suit. Therefore, it is better that no priest be allowed to get along with another and, as we have grown accustomed to seeing right up to the present day, that kings and princes should be set at odds. It is better to flood the world with Christian blood, lest the unity of Christians compel the Holy Roman See to reform itself!

So far we have been getting an idea of how they deal with benefices which become vacant and free. But for

---

69. I.e., the contesting of benefices.
70. For adjudication.
71. Wilhelm III, count of Honstein, was bishop from 1506 to 1541.
72. Cf. John 21:15-17.

tenderhearted Avarice the free vacancies are too few. Therefore, he has kept a very close watch even on those benefices still occupied by their incumbents, so that these too can be made free, even though they are not now free. He does this in several ways.

First, Avarice lies in wait where fat prebends or bishoprics are held by an old or sick man, or even by one with an alleged disability. The Holy See gives a coadjutor, that is, an assistant, to an incumbent of this kind. This is done without the holder's consent or gratitude, and for the benefit of the coadjutor, because he is a member of the pope's "household," or because he has paid for it or has otherwise earned it by some sort of service to Rome. In this case the free rights of the chapter or the rights of the incumbent are disregarded, and the whole thing falls into the hands of Rome.

Second, there is the little word "commend." This means the pope puts a cardinal, or another of his underlings, in charge of a rich, prosperous monastery,[73] just as if I were to give you a hundred gulden to keep. This does not mean to give the monastery or bestow it. Nor does it mean abolishing it or the divine service. It means quite simply to give it into his keeping. Not that he to whom it is entrusted is to care for it or build it up, but he is to drive out the incumbent, receive the goods and revenues, and install some apostate, renegade monk[74] or another, who accepts five or six gulden a year and sits all day long in the church selling pictures and images to the pilgrims, so that neither prayers nor masses are said in that place any more. If this were to be called destroying monasteries and abolishing

---

73. The recipient was not obligated to exercise the duties attached to the benefice. Even Duke George of Saxony, an opponent of the Reformation, complained in 1521 about such commendations. Cf. LW 44, 150, n. 78.

74. An apostate monk was one who left his monastery without permission and functioned as a secular priest (MA³ 2, 395). They wandered from place to place, often wearing the garb and exercising the rights and privileges of their order. They were a nuisance because they often disrupted parish life.

the worship of God, then the pope would have to be called a destroyer of Christendom and an abolisher of divine worship. He certainly does well at it! But this would be harsh language for Rome, so they have to call it a "commend," or a command to take over the charge of the monastery. The pope can make "commends" of four or more of these monasteries in one year, any single one of which may have an income of more than six thousand gulden. This is how the Romanists increase the worship of God and maintain the monasteries! Even the Germans are beginning to find that out!

Third, there are some benefices they call *incompatabilia*,[75] which, according to the ordinances of canon law, cannot be held at the same time, such as two parishes, two bishoprics, and the like. In these cases the Holy Roman See of Avarice evades canon law by making glosses[76] to its own advantage, called *unio* and *incorporatio*. This means that the pope incorporates many *incompatabilia* into one single unity, so that each is a part of every other and all of them together are looked upon as one benefice. They are then no longer *incompatabilia*, and the holy canon law is satisfied because it is no longer binding, except upon those who do not buy these glosses from the pope or his *datarius*.[77] The *unio*, that is, the uniting, is very similar. The pope combines many such benefices like a bundle of sticks, and they are all regarded as one benefice. There is at present a certain court follower in Rome who alone holds twenty-two parishes, seven priories, as well as forty-four benefices. All these are held by the help of that masterly gloss, which declares that this is not against canon law. What the cardinals and other prelates

---

75. Offices which cannot be united in the hands of one man.

76. Glosses are more or less authoritative comments on canon law. Their chief aim is to show how the law applies to practical cases. Cf. *LW* 44, 151, n. 82.

77. The bureau that granted dispensations and was responsible for the issuing, registration, and dating of papal appointments. A fee had to be paid for its services.

get out of it is anybody's guess. And this is the way the Germans are to have their purses emptied and their itch scratched.[78]

Another of these glosses is the *administratio*. This means a man may hold, in addition to his bishopric, some abbacy or dignity and all its emoluments, without having the title attached to it. He is simply called the "administrator."[79] At Rome it is sufficient to change a word or two but leave the actuality what it was before. It is as if I were to teach that we were now to call the brothelkeeper the mayor's wife. She still remains what she was before. This kind of Romish regime Peter foretold in II Peter 2 [:1, 3], "False teachers will come who will deal with you in greed and lying words for their gain."

Our worthy Roman Avarice has devised another technique. He sells or disposes of livings on the condition that the vendor or disposer retains reversionary rights to them. In that event, when the incumbent dies the benefices automatically revert to him who had sold, disposed, or surrendered them in the first instance. In this way they have made hereditary property out of the benefices. Nobody else can come into possession of them except the man to whom the seller is willing to dispose of them, or to whom he bequeaths his rights at death. Besides, there are many who transfer to another the mere title to a benefice, but from which the titleholder does not draw a cent. Today, too, it has become an established custom to confer a benefice on a man while reserving a portion of the annual income for oneself.[80] This used to be called si-

---

78. I.e., have their pride deflated. Court follower Johannes Zink received 56 appointments between 1513 and 1521. Johannes Ingenwinkel received 106 appointments between 1496 and 1521.

79. Cardinal Albrecht of Mainz had the title of Administrator of Halberstadt.

80. The complaint was made at Worms in 1521 that it was impossible for a German to secure a clear title to a benefice from Rome unless he applied for it in the name of an Italian, who demanded a lump sum, a yearly pension, or a percentage of the income in return for the use of his name.

mony.[81] There are many more things of this sort than can be counted. They treat benefices more shamefully than the heathen soldiers treated Christ's clothes at the foot of the cross.[82]

But all that has been said up till now has been going on for so long that it has become established custom. Yet Avarice has devised one more thing, which I hope may be his last and choke him. The pope has a noble little device called *pectoralis reservatio,* meaning mental reservation, and *proprius motus,* meaning the arbitrary will of his authority.[83] It goes like this. A certain man goes to Rome and succeeds in procuring a benefice. It is duly signed and sealed in the customary manner. Then another candidate comes along, who brings money or else has rendered services to the pope, which we shall not mention here, and desires the same benefice of the pope. The pope then gives it to him and takes it away from the other.[84] If anybody complains that this is not right, then the Most Holy Father has to find some excuse lest he be accused of a flagrant violation of the [canon] law. He then says that he had mentally reserved that particular benefice to himself and had retained full rights of disposal over it, although he had neither given it a thought in his life nor even heard of it. In this way he has now found his usual little gloss. As pope he can tell lies, deceive, and make everybody look like a fool. And all this he does openly and unashamedly. And yet he still wants to be the head of Christendom, but lets himself be ruled by the evil spirit in obvious lies.

The arbitrary and deceptive reservation of the pope

---

81. Simony (Acts 8:18-20) is the ecclesiastical name for buying or procuring of an office in the church for money, favor, or any consideration or reward.

82. Cf. Matt. 27:35.

83. Since the pope ultimately held all rights of appointment, any case could be made an exception to the usual regulations, if the canonists' theory is supported, and in these cases the matter was "reserved in the heart of the pope," and the appointment then made "on his own motion."

84. An instance of this giving and taking back was cited at Worms in 1521.

only creates a state of affairs in Rome that defies description. There is buying, selling, bartering, changing, trading, drunkenness, lying, deceiving, robbing, stealing, luxury, harlotry, knavery, and every sort of contempt of God. Even the rule of the Antichrist could not be more scandalous. Venice, Antwerp, and Cairo have nothing on this fair at Rome and all that goes on there.[85] In these places there is still some regard for right and reason, but in Rome the devil himself is in charge. And out of this sea the same kind of morality flows into all the world. Is it any wonder that people like this are terrified of reformation and of a free council, and prefer rather to set all the kings and princes at enmity lest in their unity they should call a council? Who could bear to have such villainy brought to light?

Finally, the pope has built his own store for all this noble commerce, that is, the house of the *datarius* in Rome. All who deal in benefices and livings must go there. Here they have to buy their glosses, and transact their business, and get authority to practice such arch-knavery. There was a time when Rome was still gracious. In those days people had to buy justice or suppress it with money. But Rome has become so expensive today that it allows no one to practice knavery unless he has first bought the right to do so. If that is not a brothel above all imaginable brothels, then I do not know what brothels are.

If you have money in this establishment you can obtain all these things we have just discussed. Indeed, not just these! Here usury becomes honest money, the possession of property acquired by theft or robbery is legalized. Here vows are dissolved; monks are granted liberty to leave their orders. Here marriage is on sale to the clergy. Here bastards can be legitimized. Here all dishonor and shame can be made to look like honor and glory. Here every kind

---

85. These three great centers of foreign trade were notorious.

of iniquity and evil is knighted or raised to nobility. Here marriage is permitted which is within the prohibited relationships or otherwise forbidden. O what assessing and fleecing goes on there! It seems as though canon law were instituted solely for the purpose of making a great deal of money. Whoever would be a Christian has to buy his way out of its provisions.[86] In fact, here the devil becomes a saint, and a god as well. What cannot be done anywhere else in heaven or on earth, can be done in this place. They call these things *compositiones!* Compositions indeed! Better named confusions.[87] They put nothing together, but break everything all up! Compared with the exactions of this bureau, the Rhine toll[88] is but a drop in the bucket.

Let no one accuse me of exaggeration. It is all so open that even in Rome they have to admit that the state of affairs is more revolting and worse than anyone can say. I have not yet stirred the real hellish broth of their personal vices—nor do I want to. I speak only of general, current matters, and still words fail me. The bishops, priests, and above all the doctors in the universities ought to have done their duty and with common accord written against such goings-on and cried out against them. This is what they are paid to do! Just turn the page over, and then you'll find out.[89]

One final word remains, and I am bound to say it. Since this boundless Avarice is not satisfied with all this wealth, wealth with which three great kings would be content, he now begins to transfer this trade and sell it to the Fuggers of Augsburg.[90] The lending, trading, and buying of bish-

---

86. I.e., buy exemptions from canon law in the form of dispensations.

87. Fees paid for dispensations were called *compositiones.* Luther makes a pun on *compositiones* and *confusiones.* Cf. WA 6, 426, n. 1.

88. Levied by the Rhine castle "robber barons" on passing merchants.

89. Cf. CL 1, 383, which interprets this obscure expression to mean "the opposite is the case."

90. The greatest international bankers of the sixteenth century and bankers to the curia. They were zealous Romanists and supported Eck against Luther.

oprics and benefices, and the commerce in ecclesiastical holdings, have now come to the right place. Now spiritual and secular goods have become one. I would now like to hear of somebody clever enough to imagine what Roman Avarice could do more than what it has already done, unless perhaps Fugger were to transfer or sell this present combination of two lines of business to somebody else. I really think it has just reached the limit.

As for what they have stolen in all lands, and still steal and extort, through indulgences, bulls, letters of confession,[91] butter letters,[92] and other *confessionalia*[93]—all this is just patchwork. It is like casting one devil into hell. Not that these bring in little money, for a powerful king could well support himself on such proceeds, but it is not to be compared with the streams of treasure referred to above. I shall say nothing at present about where this indulgence money has gone. I shall have more to say about that later. The Campoflore[94] and the Belvindere[95] and certain other places probably know something about that.

Since, then, such devilish rule is not only barefaced robbery, deceit, and the tyranny of hell's portals, but ruinous to the body and soul of Christendom, it is our duty to exercise all diligence to protect Christendom from such misery and destruction. If we want to fight against the Turks, let us begin here where they are worst of all.

They made the financial arrangements between the pope and Albrecht of Mainz which occasioned the indulgence controversy of 1517.

91. Certificates which entitled the holder to choose his own confessor and authorized the confessor to absolve him from certain "reserved" sins.

92. *Butterbriefe* were dispensations permitting the eating of eggs and milk products. Cf. *LW* 44, 155, n. 102.

93. *Confessionalia* is used here in the broad sense, and means dispensations of all sorts, including those relating to penance.

94. The Campo di Fiore, a Roman marketplace, was restored and adorned at great expense by Eugene IV (1431-1447) and his successors.

95. A part of the Vatican palace notorious as the banquet hall of Alexander VI (1492-1503). Julius II (1503-1513) turned it into a museum to house his collection of ancient works of art.

If we are right in hanging thieves and beheading robbers, why should we let Roman Avarice go free? He is the worst thief and robber that has ever been or could ever come into the world, and all in the holy name of Christ and St. Peter! Who can put up with it a moment longer and say nothing? Almost everything Avarice possesses has been gotten by theft and robbery. It has never been otherwise, as all the history books prove. The pope never purchased such extensive holdings that the income from his *officia*[96] should amount to one million ducats, over and above the gold mines we have just been discussing and the income from his lands. Nor did Christ and St. Peter bequeath it to him. Neither has anyone given or lent it to him. Neither is it his by virtue of ancient rights or usage. Tell me, then, from what source he could have got it? Learn a lesson from this, and watch carefully what they are after and what they say when they send out their legates to collect money to fight the Turks.

Now, although I am too insignificant a man to make propositions for the improvement of this dreadful state of affairs, nevertheless I shall sing my fool's song through to the end and say, so far as I am able, what could and should be done, either by the temporal authority or by a general council.

1. Every prince, every noble, every city should henceforth forbid their subjects to pay annates to Rome and should abolish them entirely. The pope has broken the agreement and made the annates a robbery to the injury and shame of the whole German nation. He gives them to his friends, sells them for huge sums of money, and uses them to endow offices. In so doing he has lost his right to them and deserves punishment. Consequently the temporal authority is under obligation to protect the innocent and prevent injustice, as Paul teaches in Romans 13,

---

96. The host of positions for sale having substantial incomes.

and St. Peter in I Peter 2 [:14], and even the canon law in Case 16, Question 7, in the *de filiis* clause.[97] Thus it has come about that they say to the pope and his crowd, *"Tu ora*, thou shalt pray"; to the emperor and his servants, *"Tu protege*, thou shalt protect"; to the common man, *"Tu labora*, thou shalt work," not however as though everyone were not to pray, protect, and work. For the man who is diligent in his work prays, protects, and works in all that he does. But everyone should have his own special work assigned him.

2. Since the pope with his Romanist practices—his commends, coadjutors, reservations, *gratiae expectativae*,[98] papal months, incorporations, unions, pensions, pallia, chancery rules, and such knavery—usurps for himself all the German foundations without authority and right, and gives and sells them to foreigners at Rome who do nothing for Germany in return, and since he robs the local bishops of their rights and makes mere ciphers and dummies of them, and thereby acts contrary to his own canon law, common sense, and reason, it has finally reached the point where the livings and benefices are sold to coarse, unlettered asses and ignorant knaves at Rome out of sheer greed. Pious and learned people do not benefit from the service or skill of these fellows. Consequently the poor German people must go without competent and learned prelates and go from bad to worse.

For this reason the Christian nobility should set itself against the pope as against a common enemy and destroyer of Christendom for the salvation of the poor souls who perish because of this tyranny. The Christian nobility

---

97. Not *de filiis,* but *Filiis vel nepotibus.* The clause provides that in case the income from endowments bequeathed to the church is misused, and appeals to the bishop and archbishop fail to correct the misuse, the heirs may appeal to the royal courts. Luther wants to apply this principle to the annates.

98. Promises to bestow livings not yet vacant. Complaints of the evils arising out of the practice were heard continually after 1416.

should ordain, order, and decree that henceforth no further benefice shall be drawn into the hands of Rome, and that hereafter no appointment shall be obtained there in any manner whatsoever, but that the benefices should be dragged from this tyrannical authority and kept out of his reach. The nobility should restore to the local bishops their right and responsibility to administer the benefices in the German nation to the best of their ability. And when a lackey comes along from Rome he should be given a strict order to keep out, to jump into the Rhine or the nearest river, and give the Romish ban with all its seals and letters a nice, cool dip. If this happened they would sit up and take notice in Rome. They would not think that the Germans are always dull and drunk, but have really become Christian again. They would realize that the Germans do not intend to permit the holy name of Christ, in whose name all this knavery and destruction of souls goes on, to be scoffed and scorned any longer, and that they have more regard for God's honor than for the authority of men.

3. An imperial law should be issued that no bishop's cloak and no confirmation of any dignity whatsoever shall henceforth be secured from Rome, but that the ordinance of the most holy and famous Council of Nicaea[99] be restored. This ordinance decreed that a bishop shall be confirmed by the two nearest bishops or by the archbishop. If the pope breaks the statutes of this and of all other councils, what is the use of holding councils? Who has given him the authority to despise the decisions of councils and tear them to shreds like this?

This is all the more reason for us to depose all bishops, archbishops, and primates and make ordinary parsons of them, with only the pope as their superior, as he now is. The pope allows no proper authority or responsibility to

---

99. Luther refers to canon 4 of this council.

the bishops, archbishops, and primates. He usurps everything for himself and lets them keep only the name and
the empty title. It has even gone so far that by papal exemption[100] the monasteries, abbots, and prelates as well
are excepted from the regular authority of the bishops.
Consequently there is no longer any order in Christendom.
The inevitable result of all this is what has happened
already: relaxation of punishment, and license to do evil
all over the world. I certainly fear that the pope may
properly be called "the man of sin" [II Thess. 2:3]. Who
but the pope can be blamed for there being no discipline,
no punishment, no rule, no order in Christendom? By his
usurpation of power he ties the prelates' hands and takes
away their rod of discipline. He opens his hands to all
those set under him, and gives away or sells their release.[101]

Lest the pope complain that he is being robbed of his
authority, it should be decreed that in those cases where
the primates or the archbishops are unable to settle a case,
or when a dispute arises between them, then the matter
should be laid before the pope, but not every little thing.
It was done this way in former times, and this was the
way the famous Council of Nicaea[102] decreed. Whatever
can be settled without the pope, then, should be so settled
so that his holiness is not burdened with such minor matters, but gives himself to prayer, study, and the care of
all Christendom. This is what he claims to do. This is what
the apostles did. They said in Acts 6 [:2-4], "It is not right
that we should leave the word of God and serve tables,
but we will hold to preaching and prayer, and set others
over that work." But now Rome stands for nothing else

---

100. "Exemption" was a constant subject of complaint by the bishops, and
the Fifth Lateran Council passed a decree (1516) abolishing all monastic
exemptions. This decree seems not to have been effective.

101. I.e., release from their lawful superiors.

102. A reference to canon 5 of the Council of Sardica (343), which was later
incorporated in canon law as a canon of Nicaea.

than the despising of the gospel and prayer, and for the serving of tables, that is, temporal things. The rule of the apostles and of the pope have as much in common as Christ has with Lucifer, heaven with hell, night with day. Yet the pope is called "Vicar of Christ" and "Successor to the Apostles."

4. It should be decreed that no temporal matter is to be referred to Rome, but that all such cases shall be left to the temporal authority, as the Romanists themselves prescribe in that canon law of theirs, which they do not observe. It should be the pope's duty to be the most learned in the Scriptures and the holiest (not in the name only but in fact) and to regulate matters which concern the faith and holy life of Christians. He should hold the primates and archbishops to this task, and help them in dealing with these matters and taking care of these responsibilities. This is what St. Paul teaches in I Corinthians 6 [:7], and he takes the Corinthians severely to task for their concern with worldly things. That such matters are dealt with in Rome causes unbearable grief in every land. It increases the costs, and, moreover, these judges do not know the usage, laws, and customs of these lands, so that they often do violence to the facts and base their decisions on their own laws and precedents. As a result the contesting parties often suffer injustice.

In addition, the horrible extortion practiced by the judges in the bishops' courts[103] must be forbidden in every diocese so that they no longer judge anything except matters of faith and morals, and leave matters of money and property, life and honor, to the temporal judges. The temporal authorities, therefore, should not permit sentences of excommunication and exile to be passed where faith and morality are not involved. Spiritual authorities

---

103. The complaint was that these judges assumed jurisdiction over cases belonging in the secular courts and enforced their decisions through ecclesiastical censure. The *Gravamina* of 1521 specify these charges.

should rule over matters which are spiritual; this is just a matter of common sense. But spiritual matters are not money or material things; they are faith and good works.

Nevertheless, it might be granted that cases concerning benefices or livings be tried before bishops, archbishops, and primates. Therefore, to settle disputes and disagreements, it might be possible for the primate of Germany to hold a general consistory court with its auditors and chancellors.[104] This court should have control of the *signaturae gratiae* and *signaturae justitiae*,[105] which are now controlled at Rome, and to this court of appeal the cases in Germany would normally be brought and tried. These courts ought not to be paid for by chance presents and gifts, as is the practice at Rome, by which they have grown accustomed to selling justice and injustice. They are forced to do this at Rome because the pope does not pay them a salary, but lets them grow fat from gifts. The fact is that at Rome no one bothers now about what is right or wrong, only about what is money and what is not. This court, however, might be paid from the annates, or in some other way devised by those who are more clever and more experienced in these things than I. All I seek to do is to arouse and set to thinking those who have the ability and inclination to help the German nation to be free and Christian again after the wretched, heathenish, and un-Christian rule of the pope.

5. Reservations should no longer be valid, and no more benefices should be seized by Rome, even if the incumbent dies, or there is a dispute, or even if the incumbent is a member of the pope's household or on the staff of a

---

104. This idea is not original with Luther. Jacob Wimpheling, the Alsatian-born humanist and German patriot. had made just such a suggestion to the emperor in 1510. Its effect would have been substantial independence of the German church from Roman control.

105. Bureaus through which the pope regulated matters of administration belonging to his own special prerogative.

cardinal. And it must be strictly forbidden and prevented for any member of the papal court to contest any benefice whatsoever, to summon pious priests to court, harass them, or force them into lawsuits. If, in consequence of this prohibition, any ban or ecclesiastical pressure should come from Rome, it should be disregarded, just as though a thief were to put a man under the ban because he would not let him steal. Indeed, they should be severely punished for blasphemous misuse of the ban and the divine name to strengthen their hand at robbery. They want to drive us with their threats, which are only lies and fabrications, to the point where we put up with, yes, even praise, such blasphemy of God's name and such abuse of spiritual authority. They want to force us to be partakers in their rascality in the sight of God. We are responsible before God to oppose them, as St. Paul in Romans 1 [:32] reproves as worthy of death not only those who do such things, but also those who approve and permit them to be done. Most unbearable of all is the lying *reservatio pectoralis*,[106] whereby Christendom is so scandalously and openly put to shame and scorn because its head deals with open lies and for filthy lucre unashamedly deceives and fools everybody.

6. The *casus reservati*, reserved cases,[107] should also be abolished. They are not only the means of extorting much money from the people, but by means of them the ruthless tyrants ensnare and confuse many tender consciences, intolerably injuring their faith in God. This is especially true of the ridiculous, childish cases they make such a fuss about in the bull *Coena domini*,[108] sins which should not even be called everyday sins, much less so great that the pope cannot remit them by indulgence. Examples of these

---

106. Cf. p. 40, n. 83.

107. Specifically those cases in which only the pope could absolve. Cf. p. 212, n. 151.

108. Cf. below, p. 213, n. 152.

sins are hindering a pilgrim on his way to Rome, supplying weapons to the Turk, or counterfeiting papal letters.[109] They make fools of us with such crude, silly, clumsy goings-on! Sodom and Gomorrah, and all those sins which are or may be committed against the commandments of God, are not reserved cases. But what God has never commanded, what they themselves have imagined—these must be reserved cases. The only reason for all this is to make sure that no one will be prevented from bringing money to Rome, so that the Romanists may live in the lap of luxury, safe from the Turks, and by their wanton, worthless bulls and letters keep the world subjected to their tyranny.

Every priest simply ought to know, and a decree publicly made, that no secret, undenounced sin constitutes a reserved case; and that every priest has the power to remit every sin no matter what it is. Where sins are secret, neither abbot, bishop, nor pope has the power to reserve one to himself. If they did that, their action would be null and void. They ought even to be punished as men who without any right at all presume to make judgments in God's stead, and thereby ensnare and burden poor and ignorant consciences. In those cases, however, where open and notorious sins are committed, especially sins against God's commandment, then there are indeed grounds for reserved cases. But even then there should not be too many of them, and they should not be reserved arbitrarily and without cause. For Christ did not set tyrants in his church, but shepherds, as Peter said in the last chapter of his first epistle [I Pet. 5:2-3].

7. The Roman See should do away with the *officia,* and cut down the creeping, crawling swarm of vermin at Rome, so that the pope's household can be supported out of the pope's own pocket. The pope should not allow his court

---

109. A papal decree of equal authority with the bull, but differing from it in form and usually dealing with matters of lesser importance.

to surpass the courts of all kings in pomp and extravagance, because this kind of thing not only has never been of any use to the cause of the Christian faith, but has kept the courtesans from study and prayer until they are hardly able to speak about the faith at all. This they proved quite flagrantly at this last Roman council,[110] in which, among many other childish and frivolous things, they decreed that the soul of man is immortal and that every priest must say his prayers once a month unless he wants to lose his benefice. How can the affairs of Christendom and matters of faith be settled by men who are hardened and blinded by gross avarice, wealth, and worldly splendor, and who now for the first time decree that the soul is immortal? It is no small shame to the whole of Christendom that they deal so disgracefully with the faith at Rome. If they had less wealth and pomp, they could pray and study more diligently to be worthy and diligent in dealing with matters of faith, as was the case in ancient times when bishops did not presume to be the kings of kings.

8. The harsh and terrible oaths which the bishops are wrongfully compelled to swear to the pope should be abolished. These oaths bind the bishops like servants, and are decreed in that arbitrary, stupid, worthless, and unlearned chapter, *Significasti*.[111] Is it not enough that they burden us in body, soul, and property with their countless foolish laws by which they weaken faith and waste Christendom, without also making a prisoner of the bishop both as a person as well as in his office and function? In addition, they have also assumed the investiture,[112] which in ancient times was the right of the German emperor, and

---

110. The Fifth Lateran Council (1512-1517), convened by Pope Julius II. The main item on the agenda was the reformation of the church.

111. *Decretalium D. Gregorii Papae IX*, lib. i, tit. VI, C. IV (*CIC* 2, cols. 49-50). This chapter forbids the bestowing of the pallium on an archbishop-elect until he first shall have sworn allegiance to the Holy See.

112. The ceremony inducting church officials into offices to which revenues and certain temporal powers were attached. Cf. *LW* 44, 164, n. 125.

in France and other countries investiture still belongs to the king. They had great wars and disputes with the emperors about this matter until finally they had the brazen effrontery to take it over, and have held it until now; just as though the Germans more than all other Christians on earth had to be the country bumpkins of the pope and the Romanist See and do and put up with what no one else will either put up with or do. Since this is sheer robbery and violence, hinders the regular authority of the bishop, and injures poor souls, the emperor and his nobles are duty-bound to prevent and punish such tyranny.

9. The pope should have no authority over the emperor, except the right to anoint and crown him at the altar just as a bishop crowns a king.[113] We should never again yield to that devilish pride which requires the emperor to kiss the pope's feet, or sit at his feet, or, as they say, hold his stirrup or the bridle of his mule when he mounts to go riding. Still less should he do homage and swear faithful allegiance to the pope as the popes brazenly demand as though they had a right to it. The chapter *Solite*,[114] which sets papal authority above imperial authority, is not worth a cent, and the same goes for all those who base their authority on it or pay any deference to it. For it does nothing else than force the holy words of God, and wrest them out of their true meaning to conform to their own fond imaginations, as I have shown in a Latin treatise.[115]

This most extreme, arrogant, and wanton presumption of the pope has been devised by the devil, who under cover of this intends to usher in the Antichrist and raise the pope above God, as many are now doing and even have already done. It is not proper for the pope to exalt himself above the temporal authorities, except in spiritual offices such as

---

113. Cf. below, p. 131, n. 25.
114. *Decretalium D. Gregorii Papae IX*, lib. i., tit. XXXIII, C. VI. *CIC* 2, col. 196.
115. *On the Power of the Pope (De potestate papae)* (1520). *WA* 2, 217.

preaching and giving absolution. In other matters the pope is subject to the crown, as Paul and Peter teach in Romans 13 [:1-7] and I Peter 2 [:13], and as I have explained above.[116]

The pope is not a vicar of Christ in heaven, but only of Christ as he walked the earth. Christ in heaven, in the form of a ruler, needs no vicar, but sits on his throne and sees everything, does everything, knows everything, and has all power. But Christ needs a vicar in the form of a servant, the form in which he went about on earth, working, preaching, suffering, and dying. Now the Romanists turn all that upside down. They take the heavenly and kingly form from Christ and give it to the pope, and leave the form of a servant to perish completely. He might almost be the Counter-Christ, whom the Scriptures call Antichrist, for all his nature, work, and pretensions run counter to Christ and only blot out Christ's nature and destroy his work.

It is also ridiculous and childish for the pope, on the basis of such perverted and deluded reasoning, to claim in his decretal *Pastoralis*[117] that he is rightful heir to the empire in the event of a vacancy. Who has given him this right? Was it Christ when he said, "The princes of the Gentiles are lords, but it shall not be so among you" [Luke 22:25-26]? Or did Peter bequeath it to him? It makes me angry that we have to read and learn such shameless, gross, and idiotic lies in the canon law, and must even hold them as Christian doctrine when they are devilish lies.

That impossible lie, the *Donation of Constantine*,[118] is the same sort of thing. It must have been some special

---

116. Cf. pp. 13-15.

117. A decree of Pope Clement V issued in 1313 and later incorporated into canon law in *Clementinarum*, lib. ii, tit. XI, C. II. *CIC* 2, cols. 1151-1153.

118. This document purported to be the testament of Emperor Constantine (306-337). It conveyed to the pope title to the city of Rome, certain lands in Italy, and "the islands of the sea." Medieval pontiffs used the document to support their claims to temporal power. Cf. *LW* 44, 166, n. 133.

plague from God that so many intelligent people have let themselves be talked into accepting such lies. They are so crude and clumsy that I should imagine any drunken peasant could lie more adroitly and skilfully. How can a man rule and at the same time preach, pray, study, and care for the poor? Yet these are the duties which most properly and peculiarly belong to the pope, and they were so earnestly imposed by Christ that he even forbade his disciples to take cloak or money with them [Matt. 10:9-10]. Christ commanded this because it is almost impossible for anybody to fulfil these duties if they have to look after one single household. Yet the pope would rule an empire and still remain pope. This is what those rogues have thought up who, under the cover of the pope's name, would like to be lords of the world and would gladly restore the Roman Empire to its former state through the pope and in the name of Christ.

10. The pope should restrain himself, take his fingers out of the pie, and claim no title to the kingdom of Naples and Sicily.[119] He has exactly as much right to that kingdom as I have, and yet he wants to be its overlord. It is property gotten by robbery and violence, like almost all his other possessions. The emperor, therefore, should not grant him this realm, and where it has been granted, he should no longer give his consent. Instead, he should draw the pope's attention to the Bible and the prayer book, that he preach and pray and leave the government of lands and people—especially those that no one has given to him—to the temporal lords.

The same goes for Bologna, Imola, Vicenza, Ravenna, and all the territories in the March of Ancona, Romagna, and other lands which the pope has seized by force and

---

119. The papal claim to sovereignty over this little kingdom goes back to the eleventh century. At the time Luther wrote this treatise, sovereignty was claimed by the royal houses of France and Spain, of which latter house Charles V was head.

possesses without right.[120] Moreover, the pope has meddled in these things against every express command of Christ and St. Paul. For as St. Paul says, "No one should be entangled in worldly affairs who should tend to being a soldier of God."[121] Now the pope should be the head and chief of these soldiers, and yet he meddles in worldly affairs more than any emperor or king. We have to pull him out of these affairs and let him tend to being a soldier. Even Christ, whose vicar the pope boasts he is, was never willing to have anything to do with temporal rule. In fact, when somebody sought a judgment from him in the matter of a brother's action, he said to that man, "Who made me a judge over you?" [Luke 12:14]. But the pope rushes in without invitation and boldly takes hold of everything as if he were a god, until he no longer knows who Christ is, whose vicar he pretends to be.

11. Further, the kissing of the pope's feet should cease. It is an un-Christian, indeed, an anti-Christian thing for a poor sinful man to let his feet be kissed by one who is a hundred times better than himself. If it is done in honor of his authority, why does the pope not do the same to others in honor of their holiness? Compare them with each other—Christ and the pope. Christ washed his disciples' feet and dried them but the disciples never washed his feet [John 13:4-16]. The pope, as though he were higher than Christ, turns that about, and allows his feet to be kissed as a great favor. Though properly, if anyone wanted to do so, the pope ought to use all his power to prevent it, as did St. Paul and Barnabas, who would not let the people of Lystra pay them divine honor, but said, "We are men like you" [Acts 14:15] But our flatterers have gone

---

120. Behind this papal claim lay a thousand years of history. When the Western half of the Roman Empire collapsed in the fifth century, the sole surviving authority was the papacy. By the end of the sixth century the Roman See held large areas of Italy and Sicily. Responsibility for these territories sometimes involved war. Cf. LW 44, 167, n. 135.

121. A free rendering of the Vulgate version of II Tim. 2:4.

so far as to make an idol [of the pope] for us, so that no one fears or honors God as much as he fears and honors the pope. They will stand for that, but not for diminishing the .pope's majesty by so much as a hairsbreadth. If they were only Christian and esteemed God's honor more than their own, the pope would never be happy to see God's honor despised and his own exalted. Nor would he let anyone honor him until he saw that God's honor was once more exalted and raised higher than his own.

Another example[122] of the same scandalous pride is that the pope is not satisfied to ride or be driven, but, although he is strong and in good health, he has himself borne by men like an idol and with unheard-of splendor. Dear readers, how does such satanic pride compare with Christ, who went on foot, as did all his disciples? Where has there ever been a worldly monarch who went about in such worldly pomp and glory as he who wants to be the head of all those who ought to despise and flee from the pomp and vanity of this world, that is, the Christians? Not that we should bother ourselves very much about him as a person, but we certainly ought to fear the wrath of God if we flatter this sort of pride and do not show our indignation. It is enough for the pope to rant and play the fool in this way. But it is more than enough for us to approve of it and let it go on.

What Christian heart can or ought to take pleasure in seeing that when the pope wishes to receive communion, he sits quietly like a gracious lord and has the sacrament brought to him on a golden rod by a bowing cardinal on bended knee? As though the holy sacrament were not worthy enough for the pope, a poor, stinking sinner, to rise and show respect to his God, when all other Christians, who are much holier than the Most Holy Father the

---

122. The rest of section eleven was not part of the first edition. Cf. *LW* **44**, 168, n. 138.

pope, receive it with all due reverence! Would it be a wonder if God sent down a plague upon us all because we tolerate such dishonor of God by our prelates and praise them for doing it, and because we share in this damnable pride by our silence or by our flattery?

It is the same when the pope carries the sacrament in procession. He must be carried, but the sacrament is set before him like a flagon of wine on a table. At Rome Christ counts for nothing, but the pope counts for everything. And yet the Romanists want to compel us—and even use threats—to approve, praise, and honor these sins of the Antichrist, even though they are against God and all Christian doctrine. Help us, O God, to get a free, general council which will teach the pope that he, too, is a man, and not more than God, as he sets himself up to be!

12. Pilgrimages to Rome should either be abolished or else no one should be allowed to make such a pilgrimage for reasons of curiosity or his own pious devotion, unless it is first acknowledged by his parish priest, his town authorities, or his overlord that he has a good and sufficient reason for doing so. I say this not because pilgrimages are bad, but because they are ill-advised at this time. At Rome men do not find a good example, but, on the contrary, pure scandal. The Romanists themselves devised the saying, "The nearer Rome, the worse Christians." After a pilgrimage to Rome men bring back with them contempt for God and his commandments. They say the first time a man goes to Rome he seeks a rascal; the second time he finds one; the third time he brings him back home with him.[123] Now, however, the Romanists have grown so clever that they can make three pilgrimages in one! The pilgrims have brought back such a pretty mess of experiences from Rome

123. Cf. Ulrich von Hutten's remark, "Three things there are which those who go to Rome usually bring back with them: a bad conscience, a ruined stomach, and an empty purse." Erasmus also criticized pilgrimages. Cf. *LW* 44, 170, n. 140.

that it would be better never to have seen Rome or known anything about it.

Even if this were not the case there is still another and a better reason: simple people[124] are led into error and misunderstanding of the divine command. Such people think that going on a pilgrimage is a precious good work. This is not true. It is a very small good work—frequently it is evil and misleading, for God has not commanded it. But God has commanded that a man should care for his wife and children, perform the duties of a husband, and serve and help his neighbor. Today a man makes a pilgrimage to Rome and spends fifty, maybe a hundred, gulden, something nobody commanded him to do. He permits his wife and child, or his neighbor at any rate, to suffer want back home. And yet the silly fellow thinks he can gloss over such disobedience and contempt of the divine commandment with his self-assigned pilgrimage, which is really nothing but impertinence or a delusion of the devil. The popes have encouraged this sort of thing with their false, feigned, foolish "golden years,"[125] by which the people are excited, torn away from God's commandments, and enticed to follow the popes' own erroneous undertakings. The popes have done the very thing they ought to have prevented. But it has brought in money and fortified their illegitimate authority. That is why it has to go on, even if it is contrary to God and the salvation of souls.

---

124. *Die einfeltigen menschen,* the simple, or those of untrained mind.

125. The "golden" or "jubilee" years were started by Boniface VIII in 1300. Originally every hundredth year was to be a jubilee, but by 1473 every twenty-fifth year was. During these years indulgences were granted to those who visited Rome. These indulgences were extended on a limited scale by Clement VI in 1350 to those who could not make the pilgrimage. Still later Boniface IX sent commissioners throughout Europe to dispense the indulgences for the cost of a journey to Rome and back. Many times these indulgences were represented as offering pardon without penitential or sacramental formality. For this representation as well as for irregularity of their financial accounts a great many commissioners were punished by the pope. Cf. *LW* 44, 171, n. 142.

To eradicate such false, seductive faith from the minds of simple Christian people and to restore a right understanding of good works, all pilgrimages should be dropped. There is no good in them: no commandment enjoins them, no obedience attaches to them. Rather do these pilgrimages give countless occasions to commit sin and to despise God's commandments. This is why there are so many beggars who commit all kinds of mischief by going on these pilgrimages. These people learn to beg when there is no need to beg, and they make a habit of begging. This accounts for vagabondage and many ills about which I shall not speak here.

If any man wants to go on a pilgrimage today or vow to make a pilgrimage, he should first show his reasons for doing so to his priest or his master. If it turns out that he wants to do it for the sake of a good work, then let the priest or master put his foot down firmly and put an end to the vow and the good work as a devilish delusion. Let priest and master show him how to use the money and effort for the pilgrimage for God's commandments and for works a thousand times better by spending it on his own family or on his poor neighbors. But if he wishes to make the pilgrimage out of curiosity, to see other lands and cities, he may be allowed to do so. But if he made the vow during an illness, then that vow must be annulled and canceled. God's commandment should be emphasized so that henceforth he will be content to keep the vow made in baptism and the commandments of God. Nevertheless, he may be allowed to perform his foolish vow just once to quiet his conscience. Nobody wants to walk in the straight path of God's commandments common to all of us. Everybody invents new ways and vows for himself as if he had already fulfilled all of God's commandments.

13. Next we come to the masses who make many vows but keep few. Do not be angry, my noble lords! I really mean it for the best. It is the bittersweet truth that the

further building of mendicant houses should not be permitted. God help us, there are already too many of them. Would to God they were all dissolved, or at least combined into two or three orders! Their running about the country has never done any good and never will do any good. My advice is to join together ten of these houses or as many as need be, and make them a single institution for which adequate provision is made so that begging will not be necessary. It is far more important to consider what the common people need for their salvation than what St. Francis, St. Dominic, and St. Augustine,[126] or anyone else has established as a rule, especially because things have not turned out as they planned.

The mendicants should also be relieved of preaching and hearing confession, unless they are called to do this by the bishops, parishes, congregations, or the civil authorities. Nothing but hatred and envy between priests and monks has come out of this kind of preaching and shriving, and this has become a source of great offense and hindrance to the common people. It ought to stop because it can well be dispensed with. It looks suspiciously as though the Holy Roman See has purposely increased this army lest the priests and bishops, unable to stand the pope's tyranny any longer, some day become too powerful for him and start a reformation. That would be unbearable to his holiness.

At the same time the manifold divisions and differences[127] within one and the same order should be abolished. These divisions have arisen from time to time for very trivial reasons; they have been maintained for even more trivial reasons, and they quarrel with each other with

---

126. Luther alludes here to the three leading mendicant orders. The Augustinian Hermits originated during the thirteenth century when several small hermit societies were united under the so-called Augustinian *Rule*. Luther was an Augustinian. Cf. also below, p. 201, n. 135.

127. Cf. p. 202, n. 138.

unspeakable hatred and envy. Nevertheless, the Christian faith, which can well exist without any of these distinctions, comes to grief because of both parties, and a good Christian life is valued and sought after only according to the standards of outward laws, works, and methods. Nothing comes of this but hypocrisy and the ruination of souls, as all can plainly see.

The pope must also be forbidden to found or endorse any more of these orders; in fact he must be ordered to abolish some and reduce the numbers of others. Inasmuch as faith in Christ,[128] which alone is the chief possession, exists without any kind of orders, there is no little danger that men will be easily led astray to live according to many and varied works and ways rather than to pay heed to faith. And unless there are wise superiors in the monasteries who preach and stress faith more than the rule of the order, it is impossible for that order not to harm and mislead the simple souls who have regard only for works.

But in our day the superiors who did have faith and who founded the orders have passed away almost everywhere. It is just as it was centuries ago among the children of Israel. When the fathers who had known the wonders and the works of God had passed on, their children, ignorant of God's works and of faith, immediately elevated idolatry and their own human works. In our day, unfortunately, these orders have no understanding of God's works or of faith, but make wretched martyrs of themselves by striving and working to keep their own rules, laws, and ways of life. Yet they never come to a right understanding of a spiritually good life. It is just as II Timothy 3 [:5, 7] declares, "They have the appearance of a spiritual life, but there is nothing behind it: they are constantly learning, but they never come to a knowledge of what true spiritual life is." If the ruling superior has no

---

128. *Der glaub Christi;* literally, "the faith of Christ."

understanding of Christian faith, it would be better to have no monastery at all; for such a superior cannot govern an order without doing hurt and harm, and the holier and better the superior appears to be in his external works, the more injury and ruin he causes.

To my way of thinking it would be a necessary measure, especially in our perilous times, to regulate convents and monasteries in the same way they were regulated in the beginning, in the days of the apostles, and for a long time afterward.[129] In those days convents and monasteries were all open to everyone to stay in them as long as he pleased. What else were the convents and monasteries but Christian schools where Scripture and the Christian life were taught, and where people were trained to rule and to preach? Thus we read that St. Agnes[130] went to school, and we still see the same practice in some of the convents, like that at Quedlinburg[131] and elsewhere. And in truth all monasteries and convents ought to be so free that God is served freely and not under compulsion. Later on, however, they became tied up with the vows and became an eternal prison. Consequently, these monastic vows are more highly regarded than the vows of baptism. We see, hear, read, and learn more and more about the fruit of all this every day.

I can well suppose that this advice of mine will be regarded as the height of foolishness, but I am not concerned about that at the moment. I advise what seems good to me, let him reject it who will. I see for myself how the vows are kept, especially the vow of chastity. This vow has become universal in these monasteries, and yet it was

---

129. Luther knew perfectly well that convents and monasteries did not exist in apostolic times. He is arguing for a monastic system based on the apostolic teaching of the New Testament. Cf. *LW* 44, 312.

130. St. Agnes, a martyr of the early fourth century, was a popular medieval saint associated with youthful chastity and innocence. Cf. *LW* 44, 174, n. 147.

131. One of the most famous German convents, founded in 936.

never commanded by Christ. On the contrary, chastity is given to very few, as he himself says [Matt. 19:11-12], as well as St. Paul [I Cor. 7:7]. It is my heartfelt wish for everybody to be helped. I do not want to let Christian souls get entangled in the self-contrived traditions and laws of men.[132]

14. We also see how the priesthood has fallen, and how many a poor priest is overburdened with wife and child, his conscience troubled. Yet no one does anything to help him, though he could easily be helped. Though pope and bishops may let things go on as they are, and allow what is heading for ruin to go to ruin, yet I will redeem my conscience and open my mouth freely, whether it vexes pope, bishop, or anybody else. And this is what I say: according to the institution of Christ and the apostles, every city should have a priest or bishop, as St. Paul clearly says in Titus 1 [:5]. And this priest should not be compelled to live without a wedded wife, but should be permitted to have one, as St. Paul writes in I Timothy 3 [:2, 4] and Titus 1 [:6-7] saying, "A bishop shall be a man who is blameless, and the husband of but one wife, whose children are obedient and well behaved," etc. According to St. Paul, and also St. Jerome,[133] a bishop and a priest are one and the same thing. But of bishops as they now are the Scriptures know nothing. Bishops have been appointed by ordinance of the Christian church, so that one of them may have authority over several priests.

So then, we clearly learn from the Apostle that it should be the custom for every town to choose from among the congregation a learned and pious citizen, enttrust to him the office of the ministry, and support him at the expense

---

132. Cf. Col. 2:20.
133. Cf. Luther's understanding of I Cor. 4:1 in *Concerning the Ministry* (*LW* 40, 35). Cf. Jerome, *Commentary on Titus*. MPL 26, 562; cf. also 22, 656.

of the congregation. He should be free to marry or not. He should have several priests or deacons, also free to marry or not as they choose, to help him minister to the congregation and the community with word and sacrament, as is still the practice in the Greek church. Because there was sometimes so much persecution and controversy with heretics after the apostolic age, there were many holy fathers who voluntarily abstained from matrimony that they might better devote themselves to study and be prepared at any moment for death or battle.

But the Roman See has interfered and out of its own wanton wickedness made a universal commandment forbidding priests to marry.[134] This was done at the bidding of the devil, as St. Paul declares in I Timothy 4 [:1, 3], "There shall come teachers who bring the devil's teaching and forbid marriage." Unfortunately so much misery has arisen from this that tongue could never tell it. Moreover, this caused the Greek church to separate,[135] and discord, sin, shame, and scandal were increased no end. But this always happens when the devil starts and carries on. What, then, shall we do about it?

My advice is, restore freedom to everybody and leave every man free to marry or not to marry. But then there would have to be a very different kind of government and administration of church property; the whole canon law would have to be demolished; and few benefices would be allowed to get into Roman hands. I fear that greed is a cause of this wretched, unchaste celibacy. As a result, everyone has wanted to become a priest and everyone wants his son to study for the priesthood, not with the idea of living in chastity, for that could be done outside

---

134. The first definitive and documented canon to prescribe and enforce clerical celibacy was that of Pope Siricius in 385. Cf. *LW* 44, 176, n. 151.

135. The controversy over celibacy was involved in the schism.

the priesthood. [Their idea is to] be supported in temporal things without work or worry, contrary to God's command in Genesis 3 [:19] that "in the sweat of your face you shall eat your bread." The Romanists have colored this to mean that their labor is to pray and say mass.

I am not referring here to popes, bishops, canons, and monks. God has not instituted these offices. They have taken these burdens upon themselves, so they will have to bear them themselves. I want to speak only of the ministry which God has instituted, the responsibility of which is to minister word and sacrament to a congregation, among whom they reside. Such ministers should be given liberty by a Christian council to marry to avoid temptation and sin. For since God has not bound them, no one else ought to bind them or can bind them, even if he were an angel from heaven, let alone a pope. Everything that canon law decrees to the contrary is mere fable and idle talk.

Furthermore, I advise anyone henceforth being ordained a priest or anything else that he in no wise vow to the bishop that he will remain celibate. On the contrary, he should tell the bishop that he has no right whatsoever to require such a vow, and that it is a devilish tyranny to make such a demand. But if anyone is compelled to say, or even wants to say, "so far as human frailty permits," as indeed many do, let him frankly interpret these same words in a negative manner to mean "I do not promise chastity." For human frailty does not permit a man to live chastely, but only the strength of angels and the power of heaven. In this way he should keep his conscience free of all vows.

I will advise neither for nor against marrying or remaining single. I leave that to common Christian order and to everyone's better judgment. I will not conceal my real opinion or withhold comfort from that pitiful band who with wives and children have fallen into disgrace and whose consciences are burdened because people call them priests' whores and their children priests' children. As the court-jester[136] I say this openly.

You will find many a pious priest against whom nobody has anything to say except that he is weak and has come to shame with a woman. From the bottom of their hearts both are of a mind to live together in lawful wedded love, if only they could do it with a clear conscience. But even though they both have to bear public shame, the two are certainly married in the sight of God. And I say that where they are so minded and live together, they should appeal anew to their conscience. Let the priest take and keep her as his lawful wedded wife, and live honestly with her as her husband, whether the pope likes it or not, whether it be against canon or human law. The salvation of your soul is more important than the observance of tyrannical, arbitrary, and wanton laws which are not necessary to salvation or commanded by God. You should do as the children of Israel did who stole from the Egyptians the wages they had earned;[137] or as a servant who steals from his wicked master the wages he has earned: steal from the pope your wedded wife and child! Let the man who has faith enough to venture this, boldly follow me. I shall not lead him astray. Though I do not have the authority of a pope, I do have the authority of a Christian to advise and help my neighbor against sins and temptations. And that not without cause or reason!

First, not every priest can do without a woman, not only on account of human frailty, but much more on account of keeping house. If he then may keep a woman, and the pope allows that, and yet may not have her in marriage, what is that but leaving a man and a woman alone together and yet forbidding them to fall? It is just like putting straw and fire together and forbidding them to smoke or burn!

---

136. Luther had cast himself in this role in the Introduction. Cf. p. 7.

137. Cf. Exod. 12:35-36.

Second, the pope has as little power to command this as he has to forbid eating, drinking, the natural movement of the bowels, or growing fat. Therefore, no one is bound to keep it, but the pope is responsible for all the sins which are committed against this ordinance, for all the souls which are lost, and for all the consciences which are confused and tortured because of this ordinance. He has strangled so many wretched souls with this devilish rope that he has long deserved to be driven out of this world. Yet it is my firm belief that God has been more gracious to many souls at their last hour than the pope was to them in their whole lifetime. No good has ever come nor will come out of the papacy and its laws.

Third, although the law of the pope is against it, nevertheless, when the estate of matrimony has been entered against the pope's law, then his law is already at an end and is no longer valid. For God's commandment, which enjoins that no man shall put husband and wife asunder [Matt. 19:6], is above the pope's law. And the commandments of God must not be broken or neglected because of the pope's commandment. Nevertheless, many foolish jurists, along with the pope, have devised impediments and thereby prevented, broken, and brought confusion to the estate of matrimony so that God's commandment concerning it has altogether disappeared.[138] Need I say more? In the entire canon law of the pope there are not even two lines which could instruct a devout Christian, and, unfortunately, there are so many mistaken and dangerous laws that nothing would be better than to make a bonfire of it.[139]

---

138. The laws governing marriage were entirely ecclesiastical and prohibited the marriage of blood relatives as far as the seventh degree of consanguinity. In 1204 the prohibition was restricted by a council to the first four degrees; lawful marriage within these degrees was possible only by dispensation, which was not difficult to secure by those willing to pay for it. The relation of godparents to godchildren was looked upon as "spiritual consanguinity."

But if you say that marriage of the clergy would give offense, and that the pope must first grant dispensation, I reply that whatever offense there is in it is the fault of the Roman See which has established such laws with no right and against God. Before God and the Holy Scriptures marriage of the clergy is no offense. Moreover, if the pope can grant dispensations from his greedy and tyrannical laws for money, then every Christian can grant dispensations from these very same laws for God's sake and for the salvation of souls. For Christ has set us free from all man-made laws, especially when they are opposed to God and the salvation of souls, as St. Paul teaches in Galatians 5 [:1] and I Corinthians 10 [:23].

15. Nor must I forget the poor monasteries. The evil spirit, who has now confused all the estates of life and made them unbearable through man-made laws, has taken possession of some abbots, abbesses, and prelates. As a result they govern their brothers and sisters in such a way that they quickly go to hell and lead a wretched existence here and now, as do the devil's martyrs. That is to say, these superiors have reserved to themselves in confession, all, or at least some, of the mortal sins which are secret, so that no brother can absolve another on pain of excommunication and under the vow of obedience. Now nobody finds angels all the time in all places; but we do find flesh and blood which would rather undergo all excommunications and threats rather than confess secret sins to prelates and appointed confessors. Thus these people go to the sacrament with such consciences that they become irregulars[140] and even worse. O blind shepherds! O mad prelates! O ravenous wolves!

---

139. This is exactly what Luther did. A copy of the canon law was burned with the papal bull of excommunication on December 10, 1520.

140. Monks who have violated the rules of their order and been deprived of the benefits enjoyed by those living within the rule. Cf. *LW* 44, 180, n. 157.

To this I say: if a sin is public or notorious, then it is proper for the prelate alone to punish it, and it is only these sins and no others that he may reserve and select for himself. He has no authority over secret sins, even if they were the worst sins that ever are or can be found. If the prelate makes exceptions of these secret sins, then he is a tyrant. He has no such right and is trespassing upon the prerogative of God's judgment.

And so I advise these children, brothers and sisters: if your superiors are unwilling to permit you to confess your secret sins to whom you choose, then take them to your brother or sister, whomever you like, and be absolved and comforted. Then go and do what you want and ought to do. Only believe firmly that you are absolved, and nothing more is needed. And do not be distressed or driven mad by threats of excommunication, becoming irregulars, or whatever else they threaten. These disciplines are valid only in the case of public or notorious sins which none will confess. They do not apply to you. What are you trying to do, you blind prelates, prevent secret sins by threats? Relinquish what you obviously cannot hold on to so that God's judgment and grace may work in the people under your care! He has not given them so entirely into your hands as to let them go entirely out of his own! In fact, you have the smaller part under you. Let your statutes be merely statutes. Do not exalt them to heaven or give them the weight of divine judgments!

16. It is also necessary to abolish all endowed masses for the dead,[141] or at least to reduce their number, since we plainly see that they have become nothing but a mock-

---

141. *Jartag, begencknis, seelmessen,* translated here as "endowed masses for the dead," were celebrated at various times: *jartag,* on the annual anniversary of the beneficiary's death; *begencknis,* on the appointed day of the year when all the benefactors of a religious order were commemorated; and *seelmessen,* the masses regularly offered in behalf of souls in purgatory. Cf. *LW* 44, 180, n. 158.

ery. God is deeply angered by these, and their only purpose is money-grubbing, gluttony, and drunkenness. What pleasure can God take in wretched vigils[142] and masses which are so miserably rattled off, not read or prayed. And if they were prayed, it would not be for God's sake and out of love, but for the sake of money and of getting a job finished. Now it is impossible for a work which is not done out of unconstrained love to please or suffice God. So it is altogether Christian to abolish, or at least diminish, everything we see which is growing into an abuse and which angers God rather than reconciles him. I would rather—in fact, it would be more pleasing to God and much better—that a chapter, church, or monastery combine all its anniversary masses and vigils and on one day, with sincerity of heart, reverence, and faith, hold one true vigil and mass on behalf of all its benefactors, than hold thousands every year for each individual benefactor without reverence and faith. O dear Christians, God does not care for much praying but for true praying. In fact, he condemns long and repetitious prayers, and says in Matthew 6 [:7; 23:14] "They will only earn the more punishment thereby." But greed, which cannot put its trust in God, brings such things to pass. Avarice is anxious lest it starve to death.

17. Certain penalties or punishments of canon law should be abolished, too, especially the interdict,[143] which without any doubt was invented by the evil spirit. Is it not a devilish work to correct one sin through many and great sins? It is actually a greater sin to silence or suppress the word and worship of God than if one had strangled twenty popes at one time, to say nothing of a priest, or had misused church holdings. This is another of the tender virtues taught in canon law. One of the reasons this law

---

142. I.e., liturgical offices connected with the festivals.
143. Cf. p. 17, n. 27.

is called "spiritual"[144] is that it comes from spirit: not from the Holy Spirit but from the evil spirit.

Excommunication must never be used except where the Scriptures prescribe its use, that is, against those who do not hold the true faith or who live in open sin, not for material advantage. But today it is the other way around. Everybody believes and lives as he pleases, especially those who use excommunication to fleece and defame other people. All the excommunications are for material advantage, for which we have nobody to thank but the holy canon law of unrighteousness. I have said more about this in an earlier discourse.[145]

The other punishments and penalties—suspension, irregularity, aggravation, reaggravation, deposition, lightning, thundering, cursings, damnings, and the rest of these devices[146]—should be buried ten fathoms deep in the earth so that their name and memory not be left on earth. The evil spirit unleashed by canon law has brought such a terrible plague and misery into the heavenly kingdom of holy Christendom, having done nothing but destroy and hinder souls by canon law, that the words of Christ in Matthew 23 [:13] may well be understood as applying to them,[147] "Woe to you scribes! You have taken upon yourselves the authority to teach, and closed up the kingdom of heaven to men. You do not go in and you stand in the way of those who enter."

18. All festivals should be abolished, and Sunday alone retained.[148] If it were desired, however, to retain the festivals of Our Lady and of the major saints, they should be

---

144. Luther's term for canon law is *geystlich recht*, i.e., "spiritual law."

145. *A Sermon on the Ban.* LW 39, 3-22.

146. Penalties imposed by the church upon priests. Aggravation is the threat of excommunication; reaggravation is excommunication itself. Deposition is a permanent expulsion from clerical office. Cf. *MA*3 2, 399.

147. I.e., those who teach and enforce canon law.

148. Luther refers here to the numerous saints' days and minor religious holidays which fell on weekdays. Cf. *Treatise on Good Works.* LW 44, 55.

transferred to Sunday, or observed only by a morning mass, after which all the rest of the day should be a working day. Here is the reason: since the feast days are abused by drinking, gambling, loafing, and all manner of sin, we anger God more on holy days than we do on other days. Things are so topsy-turvy that holy days are not holy, but working days are. Nor is any service rendered God and his saints by so many saints' days. On the contrary, they are dishonored; although some foolish prelates think that they have done a good work if each, following the promptings of his own blind devotion, celebrates a festival in honor of St. Otilie[149] or St. Barbara. But they would be doing something far better if they honored the saint by turning the saint's day into a working day.

Over and above the spiritual injury, the average man incurs two material disadvantages from this practice. First, he neglects his work and spends more money than he would otherwise spend. Second, he weakens his body and makes it less fit. We see this every day, yet nobody thinks of correcting the situation. In such cases we ought not to consider whether or not the pope has instituted the feasts, or whether we must have a dispensation or permission [to omit them]. Every town, council, or governing authority not only has the right, without the knowledge and consent of the pope or bishop, to abolish what is opposed to God and injurious to men's bodies and souls, but indeed is bound at the risk of the salvation of its souls to fight it even though popes and bishops, who ought to be the first to do so, do not consent.

Above all, we ought to abolish church anniversary celebrations[150] outright, since they have become nothing but taverns, fairs, and gambling places, and only increase the dishonoring of God and foster the soul's damnation. It

---

149. An obscure saint honored in the territory of Strassburg. Cf. *LW* **44**, 183, n. 166.

150. *Kirchweye*, the anniversary celebration of the consecration of a church.

does not help matters to boast that these festivals had a good beginning and are a good work. Did not God set aside his own law, which he had given from heaven, when it was perverted and abused? And does he not daily overturn what he has set up and destroy what he has made because of the same perversion and abuse? As it is written of him in Psalm 18 [:26], "You show yourself perverse with the perverted."

19. The grades or degrees within which marriage is forbidden, such as those affecting godparents or the third and fourth degree of kinship, should be changed. If the pope in Rome can grant dispensations and scandalously sell them for money, then every priest may give the same dispensations without price and for the salvation of souls. Would to God that every priest were able to do and remit without payment all those things we have to pay for at Rome, such as indulgences, letters of indulgence, butter letters, mass letters, and all the rest of the *confessionalia* and skullduggery[151] at Rome and free us from that golden noose the canon law, by which the poor people are deceived and cheated of their money! If the pope has the right to sell his noose of gold and his spiritual snares (I ought to say "law")[152] for money, then a priest certainly has more right to tear these nooses and snares apart, and for God's sake tread them underfoot. But if the priest does not have this right, neither has the pope the right to sell them at his disgraceful fair.

Furthermore, fasts should be left to individuals and every kind of food left optional, as the gospel makes them.[153] Even those gentlemen at Rome scoff at the fasts, and leave us commoners to eat the fat they would not

---

151. On the *confessionalia*, see p. 155, n. 103; on butter letters, see p. 155, n. 102. Mass letters were certificates entitling the holder to the benefits of masses celebrated by sodalities (Cf. p. 192, n. 94).

152. A pun on *geistliche netz*, spiritual snares, and *geystlich gesetz*, spiritual or canon law.

153. Cf. Matt. 15:11.

deign to use to grease their shoes, and then afterward they sell us the liberty to eat butter and all sorts of other things. The holy Apostle says that we already have freedom in all these things through the gospel.[154] But they have bound us with their canon law and robbed us of our rights so that we have to buy them back again with money. In so doing they have made our consciences so timid and fearful that it is no longer easy to preach about liberty of this kind because the common people take offense at it and think that eating butter is a greater sin than lying, swearing, or even living unchastely. It is still a human work decreed by men. You may do with it what you will, yet nothing good will ever come of it.

20. The chapels in forests and the churches in fields,[155] such as Wilsnack,[156] Sternberg,[157] Trier,[158] the Grimmenthal,[159] and now Regensburg[160] and a goodly number of others which recently have become the goal of pilgrimages, must be leveled. Oh, what a terrible and heavy reckoning those bishops will have to give who permit this

---

154. I Cor. 10:23; Col. 2:16.

155. Chapels built in the country for pilgrims.

156. Wilsnack, a town northwest of Berlin, was a much frequented place of pilgrimage after 1383, when three hosts, singed only about the edges, survived a fire which destroyed a church. In the middle of each host was what appeared to be a drop of blood, taken to be the blood of Christ. When these hosts were taken to a neighboring church they were said to become fiery and luminous without burning. Large numbers of pilgrims were drawn to Wilsnack, where the bishop erected a new and impressive edifice. Opposition to the pilgrimages was soon voiced by many people, including John Huss. Despite protests from several universities, the shrine continued to be popular for some years after 1548, when a Protestant pastor burned the hosts. Cf. *LW* 44, 185, n. 176.

157. A monastery which also displayed a bleeding host after 1491.

158. A garment alleged to be the seamless garment of Christ for which the executioners cast lots beneath the cross (John 19:23-24) was first exhibited in Trier in 1512.

159. Grimmenthal had attracted pilgrimages since 1499. An image of the Virgin, said to have been miraculously created, was displayed there.

160. A shrine to the "Fair Virgin of Regensburg," an image similar to that at Grimmenthal, was opened March 25, 1519, and within a month fifty thousand pilgrims are said to have worshiped there.

devilish deceit and profit by it.[161] They should be the first to prevent it and yet they regard it all as a godly and holy thing. They do not see that the devil is behind it all, to strengthen greed, to create a false and fictitious faith, to weaken the parish churches, to multiply taverns and harlotry, to lose money and working time to no purpose, and to lead ordinary people by the nose. If they had read Scripture as well as the damnable canon law, they would know how to deal with this matter!

The miracles that happen in these places prove nothing, for the evil spirit can also work miracles, as Christ has told us in Matthew 24 [:24]. If they took the matter seriously and forbade this sort of thing, the miracles would quickly come to an end. But if the thing were of God their prohibition would not hinder it.[162] And if there were no other evidence that it is not of God, the fact that men come running to them like herds of cattle, as if they had lost all reason, would be proof enough. This could not be possible if it were of God. Further, God never gave any command about all this. There is neither obedience nor merit in doing it. The thing to do is to step in boldly and protect the people. For whatever has not been commanded and is done beyond what God commands is certainly the devil's doing. To their disadvantage the parish churches are held in less respect. In short, these things are signs of great unbelief among the people, for if they really had faith they would find all they need in their own parish churches to which they are commanded to go.

But what shall I say now? Every bishop thinks only of how he can set up and maintain such a place of pilgrimage

---

161. Pilgrimages provided a large revenue from the sale of medals to be worn as amulets, fees for masses at the shrines, and free-will offerings of pilgrims. The popes did not overlook opportunities for selling indulgences at these shrines. The *Gravamina* of 1521 state that the bishops of the dioceses demanded at least 25 to 33 per cent of the offerings made at the shrines.

162. Cf. Acts 5:39.

in his diocese. He is not at all concerned that the people believe and live aright. The rulers are just like the people. The blind lead the blind [Luke 6:39]. In fact, where pilgrimages do not catch on, they set to work to canonize saints,[163] not to honor the saints, who would be honored enough without being canonized, but to draw the crowds and bring in the money. At this point pope and bishops lend their aid. There is a deluge of indulgences. There is always money enough for these. But nobody worries about what God has commanded. Nobody runs after these things; nobody has money for them. How blind we are! We not only give the devil free rein for his mischief, but we even strengthen and multiply his mischief. I would rather the dear saints were left in peace and the simple people not led astray! What spirit gave the pope authority to canonize saints? Who tells him whether they are saints or not? Are there not enough sins on earth already without tempting God, without interfering in his judgment and setting up the dear saints as decoys to get money?

My advice is to let the saints canonize themselves. Indeed, it is God alone who should canonize them. And let every man stay in his own parish; there he will find more than in all the shrines even if they were all rolled into one. In your own parish you find baptism, the sacrament, preaching, and your neighbor, and these things are greater than all the saints in heaven, for all of them were made saints by God's word and sacrament. As long as we esteem such wonderful things so little, God is just in his wrathful condemnation in allowing the devil to lead us where he likes, to conduct pilgrimages, found churches and chapels, canonize saints, and do other such fool's works so that we depart from true faith into a novel and wrong

---

63. Because of the income to be had from pilgrimages, church authorities were willing to pay large sums for the canonization of deceased clergy and dignitaries. Canonization is the definitive sentence by which the pope declares a soul to have entered into eternal glory.

kind of belief. This is what the devil did in ancient times to the people of Israel, when he led them away from the temple at Jerusalem to countless other places. Yet he did it all in the name of God and under the pretense of holiness. All the prophets preached against it, and they were martyred for doing so. But today nobody preaches against it. If somebody were to preach against it all, perhaps bishop, pope, priest, and monk would possibly martyr him, too. St. Antoninus of Florence[164] and certain others must now be made saints and canonized in this way, so that their holiness, which would otherwise have served only for the glory of God and set a good example, may be used to bring fame and money.

Although the canonization of saints may have been a good thing in former days, it is certainly never good practice now. Like many other things that were good in former times, feast days, church holdings, and ornaments now are scandalous and offensive. For it is evident that through the canonization of saints neither God's glory nor the improvement of Christians is sought, but only money and reputation. One church wants to have the advantage over the other and would not like to see another church enjoy that advantage in common. Spiritual treasures have even been misused to gain temporal goods in these last evil days so that everything, even God himself, has been forced into the service of Avarice. Such advantage only promotes schisms, sects, and pride. A church that has advantages over others looks down on them and exalts itself. Yet all divine treasures are common to all and serve all and ought to further the cause of unity. But the pope likes things as they are. He would not like it if all Christians were equal and one with each other.

---

164. Antoninus (1389-1459) had been archbishop of his native city of Florence and won renown as reformer of the Dominican Order. When Luther wrote this treatise the canonization of Antoninus was already underway.

It is fitting to say here that all church licenses, bulls, and whatever else the pope sells in that skinning house[165] of his in Rome should be abolished, disregarded, or extended to all. But if he sells or gives special licenses,[166] privileges, indulgences, graces, advantages, and faculties[167] to Wittenberg, Halle, Venice, and above all to his own city of Rome, why does he not give these things to all churches in general? Is it not his duty to do everything in his power for all Christians, freely and for God's sake, even shed his blood for them? Tell me, then, why does he give or sell to one church and not to another? Or must the accursed money make so great a difference in the eyes of His Holiness among Christians, who all have the same baptism, word, faith, Christ, God, and all else? Do the Romanists want us to be so blind to all these things, though we have eyes to see, and be such fools, though we have a perfectly good faculty of reason, that we worship such greed, skullduggery, and pretense? The pope is a shepherd, but only so long as you have money, and no longer. And still the Romanists are not ashamed of this rascality of leading us hither and thither with their bulls. They are concerned only about the accursed money and nothing else!

My advice is this: If such fool's work cannot be abolished, then every decent Christian should open his eyes and not permit himself to be led astray by the Romanist bulls and seals and all their glittering show. Let him stay at home in his own parish church and be content with the best; his baptism, the gospel, his faith, his Christ, and his God, who is the same God everywhere. Let the pope re-

---

165. *Schindleich,* i.e., a place where the carrion of skinned animals is piled.

166. *Indulta,* i.e., special papal dispensations.

167. Extraordinary powers to grant indulgences and absolution in reserved cases. They were usually held by legates or commissioners sent from Rome. Complaints were made at diets in 1521 and 1523 that the papal representatives interfered with normal ecclesiastical jurisdiction and appointment.

main a blind leader of the blind. Neither an angel nor a pope can give you as much as God gives you in your parish church. The fact is, the pope leads you away from the gifts of God, which are yours without cost, to his gifts, for which you have to pay. He gives you lead for gold, hide for meat, the string for the purse, wax for honey, words for goods, the letter for the spirit.[168] You see all this before your very eyes, but you refuse to take notice. If you intend to ride to heaven on his wax and parchment, this chariot will soon break down and you will fall into hell, and not in God's name!

Let this be your one sure guide: Whatever you have to buy from the pope is neither good nor from God. For what God gives is not only given without charge, but the whole world is punished and damned for not being willing to receive it as a free gift. I mean the gospel and God's work. We have deserved God's letting us be so led astray because we have despised his holy word and the grace of baptism. It is as St. Paul says, "God shall send a strong delusion upon all those who have not received the truth to their salvation, so that they believe and follow lies and knavery" [II Thess. 2:11]. This serves them right.

21. One of the greatest necessities is the abolition of all begging throughout Christendom. Nobody ought to go begging among Christians. It would even be a very simple matter to make a law to the effect that every city should look after its own poor, if only we had the courage and the intention to do so. No beggar from outside should be allowed into the city whether he might call himself pilgrim or mendicant monk. Every city should support its own poor, and if it was too small, the people in the surrounding villages should also be urged to contribute, since in any case they have to feed so many vagabonds and evil rogues

---

168. Luther alludes to the exchange of a papal bull for money. Lead was the lead seal attached to the bull; hide, the parchment on which it was written; the string was the cord from which the seal hung; wax, the seal which held the cord to the parchment.

who call themselves mendicants. In this way, too, it could be known who was really poor, and who was not.

There would have to be an overseer or warden who knows all the poor and informs the city council or the clergy what they need. Or some other better arrangement might be made. As I see it, there is no other business in which so much skullduggery and deceit are practiced as in begging, and yet it could all be easily abolished. Moreover, this unrestricted universal begging is harmful to the common people. I have figured out that each of the five or six mendicant orders[169] visits the same place more than six or seven times every year. In addition to these there are the usual beggars, the "ambassador" beggars,[170] and the panhandlers.[171] This adds up to sixty times a year that a town is laid under tribute! This is over and above what the secular authorities demand in the way of taxes and assessments. All this the Romanist See steals in return for its wares and consumes for no purpose. To me it is one of God's greatest miracles that we can still go on existing and find the wherewithal to support ourselves!

To be sure, some think that if these proposals were adopted the poor would not be so well provided for, that fewer great stone houses and monasteries would be built, and fewer so well furnished. I can well believe all this. But none of it is necessary. He who has chosen poverty ought not to be rich. If he wants to be rich, let him put his hand to the plow and seek his fortune from the land. It is enough if the poor are decently cared for so that they do not die of hunger or cold. It is not fitting that one man

---

169. Franciscans, Dominicans, Augustinians, Carmelites, and Servites.

170. I.e., wandering beggars who enrolled their benefactors on the list of beneficiaries of the saint they claimed to represent. This enrollment, they claimed, provided immunity from particular diseases, accidents, and misfortunes. Protests were raised against this practice at diets in 1521 and 1523. Cf. LW 44, 190, n. 191.

171. I.e., men who spent their lives wandering from one place of pilgrimage to another subsisting on the alms of the faithful.

should live in idleness on another's labor, or be rich and live comfortably at the cost of another's hardship, as it is according to the present perverted custom. St. Paul says, "Whoever will not work shall not eat" [II Thess. 3:10]. God has not decreed that any man shall live off another man's property, save only the clergy who preach and have a parish to care for, and these should, as St. Paul says in I Corinthians 9 [:14], on account of their spiritual labor. And also as Christ says to the apostles, "Every laborer is worthy of his wage" [Luke 10:7].

22. It is also to be feared that the many masses which were endowed in ecclesiastical foundations and monasteries are not only of little use, but arouse the great wrath of God. It would therefore be profitable not to endow any more of these masses, but rather to abolish many that are already endowed. It is obvious that these masses are regarded only as sacrifices and good works, even though they are sacraments just like baptism and penance, which profit only those who receive them and no one else. But now the custom of saying masses for the living and the dead has crept in, and all hopes are built upon them. This is why so many masses are endowed, and why the state of affairs we see around us has developed out of it.

My proposal is perhaps too bold and an unheard-of thing, especially for those who are concerned that they would lose their job and means of livelihood if such masses were discontinued. I must refrain from saying more about it until we arrive again at a proper understanding of what the mass is and what it is for. Unfortunately, for many years now it has been a job, a way to earn a living. Therefore, from now on I will advise a man to become a shepherd or some sort of workman rather than a priest or a monk, unless he knows well in advance what this celebrating of masses is all about.

I am not speaking, however, of the old foundations and cathedrals, which were doubtless established for the sake of the children of the nobility. According to German custom not every one of a nobleman's children can become a landowner or a ruler. It was intended that these children should be looked after in such foundations, and there be free to serve God, to study, to become educated people, and to educate others.[172] I am speaking now of the new foundations which have been established just for the saying of prayers and masses, and because of their example the older foundations are being burdened with the same sort of praying and mass celebrating so that even these old foundations serve little or no purpose. And it is by the grace of God that they finally hit the bottom, as they deserve. That is to say, they have been reduced to anthem singers, organ wheezers, and reciting decadent, indifferent masses to get and consume the income from the endowments. Pope, bishops, and university scholars ought to be looking into these things and writing about them, and yet it is precisely they who do the most to promote them. Whatever brings in money they let go on and on. The blind lead the blind [Luke 6:39]. This is what greed and canon law accomplish.

It should no longer be permissible for one person to hold more than one canonry or benefice. Each must be content with a modest position so that someone else may also have something. This would do away with the excuses of those who say that they must hold more than one such office to maintain their proper station. A proper station could be interpreted in such broad terms that an entire country would not be enough to maintain it. But greed and a

---

172. Bertram Lee Woolf notes that in this passage Luther touches upon an important matter in the history of social structure, namely, the appointment of the younger sons of the upper classes to ecclesiastical positions. These younger sons were embittered because the more substantial benefices were given to papal favorites. Luther's hope was that if these sons were given the opportunity to study the Bible and sound teaching they would infuse an evangelical spirit into priests and hierarchy. Cf. Woolf's *Reformation Writings of Martin Luther* (London: Lutterworth Press), I (1952), 175, n. 1.

secret lack of trust in God go hand in hand in this matter, so that what is alleged to be the needs of a proper station is nothing but greed and unbelief.

23. The brotherhoods,[173] and for that matter, indulgences, letters of indulgence, butter letters, mass letters, dispensations, and everything of that kind, should be snuffed out and brought to an end. There is nothing good about them. If the pope has the authority to grant you a dispensation to eat butter, to absent yourself from mass, and the like, then he ought also to be able to delegate this authority to the priests, from whom he had no right to take it in the first place. I am speaking especially of those brotherhoods in which indulgences, masses, and good works are apportioned. My dear friend, in your baptism you have entered into a brotherhood with Christ, with all the angels, with the saints, and with all Christians on earth. Hold fast to this and live up to its demands, and you have all the brotherhoods you want. Let the others glitter as they will. Compared with the true brotherhood in Christ those brotherhoods are like a penny compared with a gulden. But if there were a brotherhood which raised money to feed the poor or to help the needy, that would be a good idea. It would find its indulgences and its merits in heaven. But today nothing comes of these groups except gluttony and drunkenness.

Above all, we should drive out of German territory the papal legates with their faculties, which they sell to us for large sums of money. This traffic is nothing but skullduggery. For example, for payment of money they make un-

---

173. The brotherhoods flourished in the sixteenth century. Members were obligated to recite certain prayers and attend certain masses. Each member participated in the benefits accruing from the good works of all and usually enjoyed certain indulgences. In 1520 Wittenberg boasted of twenty such fraternities; Cologne, eighty; Hamburg, more than one hundred. In 1519 one Wittenberger was a member of eight brotherhoods in his hometown and of twenty-seven in other places. Luther had expressed his views on these groups more fully in his *The Blessed Sacrament of the Holy and True Body of Christ, and the Brotherhoods* (1519). *LW* 35, 47-73.

righteousness into righteousness, and they dissolve oaths, vows, and agreements, thereby destroying and teaching us to destroy the faith and fealty which have been pledged. They assert that the pope has authority to do this. It is the devil who tells them to say these things. They sell us doctrine so satanic, and take money for it, that they are teaching us sin and leading us to hell.

If there were no other base trickery to prove that the pope is the true Antichrist, this one would be enough to prove it. Hear this, O pope, not of all men the holiest but of all men the most sinful! O that God from heaven would soon destroy your throne and sink it in the abyss of hell! Who has given you authority to exalt yourself above your God, to break and loose his commandments, and teach Christians, especially the German nation, praised through-out history for its nobility, its constancy and fidelity, to be inconstant, perjurers, traitors, profligates, and faithless? God has commanded us to keep word and faith even with an enemy, but you have taken it upon yourself to loose his commandment and have ordained in your heretical, anti-Christian decretals that you have his power. Thus through your voice and pen the wicked Satan lies as he has never lied before. You force and twist the Scriptures to suit your fancy. O Christ, my Lord, look down; let the day of judgment break down and destroy this nest of devils at Rome. There sits the man of whom St. Paul said, "He shall exalt himself above you, sit in your church, and set himself up as God, that man of sin, the son of perdition" [II Thess. 2:3-5]. What else is papal power but simply the teaching and increasing of sin and wickedness? Papal power serves only to lead souls into damnation in your name and, to all outward appearances, with your approval!

In ancient times the children of Israel had to keep the oath which they had unwittingly been deceived into giving to their enemies, the Gibeonites [Josh. 9:3-21]. And King Zedekiah was miserably lost along with all his people because he broke his oath to the king of Babylon [II Kings 24:20—25:7]. In our own history, a hundred years ago, that fine king of Hungary and Poland, Ladislaus, was tragically slain by the Turk along with so many of his people because he allowed himself to be led astray by the papal legate and cardinal and broke the good and advantageous treaty and solemn agreement he had made with the Turk.[174] The pious Emperor Sigismund had no more success after the Council of Constance when he allowed those scoundrels to break the oath that had been given to John Huss and Jerome.[175] All the trouble between the Bohemians and ourselves stems from this. Even in our own times—God help us!—how much Christian blood has been shed because of the oath and the alliance which Pope Julius made between Emperor Maximilian and King Louis of France, and afterward broke![176] How could I tell all the trouble the popes have stirred up by their devilish presumption with which they annul oaths and vows made between powerful princes, making a mockery of these things, and taking money for it? I hope that the day of judgment is at hand. Things could not possibly be worse than the state of affairs the Romanist See is promoting. The pope suppresses God's commandment and exalts his own. If he is not the Antichrist, then somebody tell me who is! But more of this another time.

---

174. Ladislaus III, king of Poland (1424-1444), and as Uladislaus I, king of Hungary (1440-1444), forced the Sultan to sue for peace in 1443. The papal legate, Cardinal Caesarini, absolved the king from fulfilling the treaty's conditions. Ladislaus renewed the war and at the battle of Varna, 1444, the Hungarians were decisively defeated and Ladislaus and Caesarini both killed.

175. Huss had a safe-conduct granted by the emperor. Luther errs when he assumes that Jerome of Prague also had one. In 1415 the council decreed that "neither by natural, divine, nor human law was any promise to be observed to the prejudice of the catholic faith." Both Huss and Jerome of Prague were executed.

176. In 1508 Pope Julius II, Louis XII of France, Emperor Maximilian I, and Ferdinand the Catholic of Spain entered into an alliance against Venice. When Venice capitulated to the pope in 1510, he broke the alliance and waged war on France. Cf. *The Cambridge Modern History*, I, 130-131.

24. It is high time we took up the Bohemian question and dealt seriously and honestly with it. We should come to an understanding with them so that the terrible slander, hatred, and envy on both sides comes to an end. As befits my folly, I shall be the first to submit an opinion on this subject, with due deference to everyone who may understand the case better than I.

First, we must honestly confess the truth and stop justifying ourselves. We must admit to the Bohemians that John Huss and Jerome of Prague were burned at Constance against the papal, Christian, imperial oath and promise of safe-conduct. This happened contrary to God's commandment and gave the Bohemians ample cause for bitterness. And although they should have acted as perfect Christians and suffered this grave injustice and disobedience to God by these people, nevertheless they were not obliged to condone such conduct and acknowledge it as just. To this day they would rather give up life and limb than admit that it is right to break and deal contrarily with an imperial, papal, and Christian oath. So then, although it is the impatience of the Bohemians that is at fault, yet the pope and his crowd are still more to blame for all the misery, error, and the loss of souls which have followed that council.

I will not pass judgment here on the articles of John Huss, or defend his errors, although I have not yet found any errors in his writings according to my way of thinking. I firmly believe that those who violated a Christian safe-conduct and a commandment of God with their faithless betrayal gave neither a fair judgment nor an honest condemnation. Without doubt they were possessed more by the evil spirit than by the Holy Spirit. Nobody will doubt that the Holy Spirit does not act contrary to the commandment of God, and nobody is so ignorant as not to know that the violation of good faith and of a promise of safe-conduct is contrary to the commandment of God, even though they had been promised to the devil himself, to say nothing of a mere heretic. It is also quite evident that such a promise was made to John Huss and the Bohemians and was not kept, and that he was burnt at the stake as a result. I do not wish, however, to make John Huss a saint or a martyr, as some of the Bohemians do. But at the same time I do acknowledge that an injustice was done to him, and that his books and doctrines were unjustly condemned. For the judgments of God are secret and terrible, and no one save God alone should undertake to reveal or utter them.

I only want to say this. John Huss may have been as bad a heretic as it is possible to be; nevertheless he was burned unjustly and in violation of the commandment of God. Further, the Bohemians should not be forced to approve of such conduct, or else we shall never achieve any unity. Not obstinacy, but the open admission of the truth must make us one. It is useless to pretend, as was done at the time, that the oath of safe-conduct given to a heretic need not be kept. That is as much as to say that God's commandments need not be kept so that God's commandments may be kept. The devil made the Romanists mad and foolish so that they did not know what they had said and done. God has commanded that a promise of safe-conduct shall be kept. We should keep such a commandment though the whole world collapses. How much more, then, when it is only a question of freeing a heretic! We should overcome heretics with books, not with fire, as the ancient fathers did. If it were wisdom to vanquish heretics with fire, then the public hangmen would be the most learned scholars on earth. We would no longer need to study books, for he who overcomes another by force would have the right to burn him at the stake.

Second, the emperor and princes should send a few really godly and sensible bishops and scholars over to the

Bohemians. On no account should they send a cardinal or a papal legate or an inquisitor, for officials like these are most unversed in Christian things. They do not seek to save souls, but, like all the pope's henchmen, only their own power, profit, and prestige. In fact, these very people were the chief actors in this miserable business at Constance. The men sent into Bohemia should find out from the Bohemians how things stand in regard to their faith, and whether it is possible to unite all their sects.[177] In this case the pope ought to use his authority awhile for the sake of saving souls and, in accordance with the decree of the truly Christian Council of Nicaea, allow the Bohemians to choose an archbishop of Prague from among their number and let him be confirmed by the bishop of Olmütz in Moravia, or the bishop of Gran in Hungary, or the bishop of Gnesen in Poland, or the bishop of Magdeburg in Germany. It will be enough if he is confirmed by one or two of these, as was the custom in the time of St. Cyprian.[178] The pope has no right to oppose such an arrangement, and if he does oppose it, he will be acting like a wolf and a tyrant; no one ought to obey him and his ban should be met with a counterban.

If, however, in deference to the chair of Peter, it was desired to do this with the pope's consent, then let it be done that way, provided it does not cost the Bohemians anything and provided the pope does not put them under the slightest obligation or bind them with his tyrannical oaths and vows as he does all other bishops, contrary to God and right. If he is not satisfied with the honor of having his consent asked, then let them not bother any

---

177. After the death of Huss a number of movements holding in varying degrees to his teachings developed in Bohemia and caused political and ecclesiastical turmoil for well over a century. Many Hussites looked favorably upon Luther. Cf. *LW* 44, 197, n. 201.

178. Bishop of Carthage (249-258).

more about the pope or his vows and his rights, his laws and his tyrannies. Let the election suffice, and let the blood of all the souls endangered by this state of affairs cry out against him. No one ought to consent to what is wrong. It is enough to have shown courtesy to tyranny. If it cannot be otherwise, then an election and the approval of the common people can even now be quite as valid as confirmation by a tyrant, though I hope this will not be necessary. Someday some of the Romanists or some of the good bishops and scholars will take notice of the pope's tyranny and repudiate it.

I would also advise against compelling the Bohemians to abolish both kinds in the sacrament[179] since that practice is neither un-Christian nor heretical. If they want to, I would let them go on in the way they have been doing. Yet the new bishop should be careful that no discord arises because of such a practice. He should kindly instruct them that neither practice is wrong,[180] just as it ought not to cause dissension that the clergy differ from the laity in manner of life and dress. By the same token, if they were unwilling to receive Roman canon law, they should not be forced to so do, but rather the prime concern should be that they live sincerely in faith and in accordance with Holy Scripture. For Christian faith and life can well exist without the intolerable laws of the pope. In fact, faith cannot properly exist unless there are fewer of these Romanist laws or unless they are even abolished altogether. In baptism we have become free and have been made subject only to God's word. Why should we become bound by the word of any man? As St. Paul says, "You have become free; do not become a bondservant of men,"[181] that is, of those men who rule by man-made laws.

---

179. A chief point of controversy between the Roman church and the Hussites.
180. Luther had not yet reached the conviction that the administration of the cup to the laity was a necessity.
181. Cf. I Cor. 7:23; Gal. 5:1.

If I knew that the Pickards[182] held no other error regarding the sacrament of the altar except believing that the bread and wine are present in their true nature, but that the body and blood of Christ are truly present under them, then I would not condemn them but would let them come under the bishop of Prague. For it is not an article of faith that bread and wine are not present in the sacrament in their own essence and nature, but this is an opinion of St. Thomas[183] and the pope. On the other hand, it is an article of faith that the true natural body and blood of Christ are present in the natural bread and wine. So then, we should tolerate the opinions of both sides until they come to an agreement because there is no danger in believing that the bread is there or that it is not. We have to endure all sorts of practices and ordinances which are not harmful to faith. On the other hand, if they believed otherwise, I would rather think of them as outside,[184] though I would teach them the truth.

Whatever other errors and schisms are discovered in Bohemia should be tolerated until the archbishop has been restored and has gradually brought all the people together again in one common doctrine. They will certainly never be united by force, defiance, or by haste. Patience and gentleness are needed here. Did not even Christ have to tarry with his disciples and bear with their unbelief for a long time until they believed his resurrection? If only the Bohemians had a regular bishop and church administration again, without Romanist tyranny, I am sure that things would soon be better.

The restoration of the temporal goods which formerly belonged to the church should not be too strictly demanded, but since we are Christians and each is bound to help

---

182. The term Pickard, a corruption of Beghards, was a derisive name for the Bohemian Brethren, a Hussite sect.

183. Cf. below, p. 144, nn. 61, 62.

184. I.e., outside of the church.

the rest, we have full power to give them these things for the sake of unity and allow them to retain them in the sight of God and before the eyes of the world. For Christ says, "Where two are in agreement with one another on earth, there am I in the midst of them" [Matt. 18:19-20]. Would to God that on both sides we were working toward this unity, extending to each other the hand of brotherhood and humility. Love is greater and is more needed than the papacy at Rome, which is without love. Love can exist apart from the papacy.

With this counsel I shall have done what I could. If the pope or his supporters hinder it, they shall have to render an account for having sought their own advantage rather than their neighbor's, contrary to the love of God. The pope ought to give up his papacy and all his possessions and honors, if thereby he could save one soul. But today he would rather let the whole world perish than yield one hairsbreadth of his presumptuous authority. And yet he wants to be the holiest! With that my responsibility comes to an end.

25. The universities, too, need a good, thorough reformation. I must say that, no matter whom it annoys. Everything the papacy has instituted and ordered serves only to increase sin and error. What else are the universities, unless they are utterly changed from what they have been hitherto, than what the book of Maccabees calls *gymnasia epheborum et graecae gloriae?*[185] What are they but places where loose living is practiced, where little is taught of the Holy Scriptures and Christian faith, and where only the blind, heathen teacher Aristotle rules[186] far more than

---

185. I.e., places for training youth in the Greek way of life. Cf. II Macc. 4:9.

186. Aristotle taught that a man becomes good by doing good and ultimately led theologians to a belief in man's power to save himself. Luther taught that it was only when a man lost all belief in himself that he ever knew what it was to have faith in Christ. Luther objected to Aristotle's displacing Christ, who alone could save a man and give him true knowledge of natural and spiritual things. Roger Bacon and Erasmus were also against the Aristotelian domination in medieval universities.

Christ? In this regard my advice would be that Aristotle's *Physics, Metaphysics, Concerning the Soul,* and *Ethics,* which hitherto have been thought to be his best books, should be completely discarded along with all the rest of his books that boast about nature, although nothing can be learned from them either about nature or the Spirit. Moreover, nobody has yet understood him, and many souls have been burdened with fruitless labor and study, at the cost of much precious time. I dare say that any potter has more knowledge of nature than is written in these books. It grieves me to the quick that this damned, conceited, rascally heathen has deluded and made fools of so many of the best Christians with his misleading writings. God has sent him as a plague upon us on account of our sins.

Why, this wretched fellow in his best book, *Concerning the Soul,* teaches that the soul dies with the body, although many have tried without success to save his reputation. As though we did not have the Holy Scriptures, in which we are fully instructed about all things, things about which Aristotle has not the faintest clue! And yet this dead heathen has conquered, obstructed, and almost succeeded in suppressing the books of the living God. When I think of this miserable business I can only believe that the devil has introduced this study.

For the same reasons his book on ethics is the worst of all books. It flatly opposes divine grace and all Christian virtues, and yet it is considered one of his best works. Away with such books! Keep them away from Christians. No one can accuse me of overstating the case, or of condemning what I do not understand. Dear friend, I know what I am talking about. I know my Aristotle as well as you or the likes of you. I have lectured on him and been lectured on him,[187] and I understand him better than St.

---

187. Luther lectured on Aristotle's *Nicomachean Ethics* four times a week during his first year in Wittenberg (1508-1509).

Thomas or Duns Scotus[188] did. I can boast about this without pride and if necessary, I can prove it. It makes no difference to me that so many great minds have devoted their labor to him for so many centuries. Such objections do not disturb me as once they did, for it is plain as day that other errors have remained for even more centuries in the world and in the universities.

I would gladly agree to keeping Aristotle's books, *Logic, Rhetoric,* and *Poetics,* or at least keeping and using them in an abridged form, as useful in training young people to speak and to preach properly. But the commentaries and notes must be abolished, and as Cicero's *Rhetoric* is read without commentaries and notes, so Aristotle's *Logic* should be read as it is without all these commentaries. But today nobody learns how to speak or how to preach from it. The whole thing has become nothing but a matter for disputation and a weariness to the flesh.

In addition to all this there are, of course, the Latin, Greek, and Hebrew languages, as well as the mathematical disciplines and history. But all this I commend to the experts. In fact, reform would come of itself if only we gave ourselves seriously to it. Actually a great deal depends on it, for it is here in the universities that the Christian youth and our nobility, with whom the future of Christendom lies, will be educated and trained. Therefore, I believe that there is no work more worthy of pope or emperor than a thorough reform of the universities. And on the other hand, nothing could be more devilish or disastrous than unreformed universities.

I leave the medical men to reform their own faculties; I take the jurists and theologians as my own responsibility. The first thing I would say is that it would be a good thing if canon law were completely blotted out, from the first

---

188. Duns Scotus (d. 1308) was highly regarded in the fifteenth and sixteenth centuries as a rival to Thomas for first place among theologians.

letter to the last, especially the decretals.[189] More than enough is written in the Bible about how we should behave in all circumstances. The study of canon law only hinders the study of the Holy Scriptures. Moreover, the greater part smacks of nothing but greed and pride. Even if there were much in it that was good, it should still be destroyed, for the pope has the whole canon law imprisoned in the "chamber of his heart,"[190] so that henceforth any study of it is just a waste of time and a farce. These days canon law is not what is written in the books of law, but whatever the pope and his flatterers want. Your cause may be thoroughly established in canon law, but the pope always has his chamber of the heart in the matter, and all law, and with it the whole world, has to be guided by that. Now it is often a villain, and even the devil himself, who rules the *scrinium*—and they proudly boast that it is the Holy Spirit who rules it! Thus they deal with Christ's poor people. They impose many laws upon them but obey none themselves. They compel others to obey these laws, or buy their way out with money.

Since then the pope and his followers have suspended the whole canon law as far as they themselves are concerned, and since they pay it no heed, but give thought only to their own wanton will, we should do as they do and discard these volumes. Why should we waste our time studying them? We could never fathom the arbitrary will of the pope, which is all that canon law has become. Let canon law perish in God's name for it arose in the devil's

---

189. Papal decrees.

190. *Scrinium pectoris.* In the Roman Empire official documents were stored in a chest called the *scrinium.* This term was carried over into the Middle Ages and designated the chest in which the instruments of a monastery were stored. Boniface VIII (1294-1303), who added his own book to the five books of the decretals of Gregory IX, said, "The Roman pontiff has all laws in the chamber [*scrinium*] of his heart." This statement was incorporated within canon law and meant that the pope claimed authority over canon law. Cf. *Decretalium D. Gregorii Papae IX,* lib. vi, tit. II, C. I. *CIC* 2, 937. Cf. *CIC* 2, 929.

name. Let there be no more "doctors of decrees"[191] in the world, but only "doctors of the papal chamber of the heart,"[192] that is, popish hypocrites! It is said that there is no better temporal rule anywhere than among the Turks, who have neither spiritual nor temporal law, but only their Koran. But we must admit that there is no more shameful rule than ours with its spiritual and temporal law, which has resulted in nobody living according to common sense, much less according to Holy Scripture any more.

The secular law[193]—God help us—has become a wilderness! Though it is much better, wiser, and more honest than the spiritual law, which has nothing good about it except its name, nevertheless, there is far too much of it. Surely, wise rulers, side by side with Holy Scripture, would be law enough. As St. Paul says in I Corinthians 6 [:5-6], "Is there no one among you who can judge his neighbor's cause, that you must go to law before heathen courts?" It seems just to me that territorial laws and customs should take precedence over general imperial laws, and that the imperial laws be used only in case of necessity. Would to God that every land were ruled by its own brief laws suitable to its gifts and peculiar character. This is how these lands were ruled before these imperial laws were designed, and as many lands are still ruled without them! Rambling and farfetched laws are only a burden to the people, and they hinder cases more than they help them. But I hope that others have already given more thought and attention to this matter than I am able to do.

Our dear theologians have saved themselves worry and work. They just let the Bible alone and lecture on the

---

191. *Doctores decretorum.*

192. *Doctores scrinii papalis.*

193. Roman law had been introduced into Germany in the twelfth century and by the end of the fifteenth century it was the accepted legal system. There was a continual conflict between Roman law and the feudal customs and remnants of Germanic legal ideas, which justified Luther's description.

sentences.[194] I should have thought that the sentences ought to be the first study for young students of theology, and the Bible left to the doctors. But today it is the other way round. The Bible comes first and is then put aside when the bachelor's degree is received. The sentences come last, and they occupy a doctor as long as he lives. There is such a solemn obligation attached to these sentences that a man who is not a priest may well lecture on the Bible, but the sentences must be lectured on by a man who is a priest. As I see it, a married man may well be a Doctor of the Bible, but under no circumstances could he be a Doctor of the Sentences. How can we prosper when we behave so wrongly and give the Bible, the holy word of God, a back seat? To make things worse, the pope commands in the strongest language that his words are to be studied in the schools and used in the courts, but very little is thought of the gospel. Consequently, the gospel lies neglected in the schools and in the courts. It is pushed aside under the bench and gathers dust so that the scandalous laws of the pope alone may have full sway.

If we bear the name and title of teachers of Holy Scripture, then by this criterion we ought to be compelled to teach the Holy Scripture and nothing else, although we all know that this high and mighty title is much too exalted for a man to take pride in it and let himself be designated a Doctor of Holy Scripture. Yet that title might be permitted if the work justified the name. But nowadays, the sentences alone dominate the situation in such a way that we find among the theologians more heathenish and humanistic[195] darkness than we find the holy and certain doctrine of Scripture. What are we to do about it? I know

---

194. Cf. below, p. 144, n. 60.

195. "Heathenish" and "humanistic" are not abusive epithets. The first refers to the dominance of the heathen Aristotle in schools; the second, to the dominance of canon law and other humanly devised doctrines over the gospel.

of nothing else to do than to pray humbly to God to give us such real Doctors of Theology as we have in mind. Pope, emperor, and universities may make Doctors of Arts, of Medicine, of Laws, of the Sentences; but be assured that no man can make a Doctor of Holy Scripture except the Holy Spirit from heaven. As Christ says in John 6 [:45], "They must all be taught by God himself." Now the Holy Spirit does not ask for red or brown birettas[196] or other decorations. Nor does he ask whether a person is young or old, lay or cleric, monk or secular, unmarried or married. In fact, in ancient times he actually spoke through an ass against the prophet who was riding it [Num. 22:28]. Would to God that we were worthy to have such doctors given to us, regardless of whether they were lay or cleric, married or single! They now try to force the Holy Spirit into pope, bishops, and doctors, although there is not the slightest sign or indication whatever that he is in them.

The number of books on theology must be reduced and only the best ones published. It is not many books that make men learned, nor even reading. But it is a good book frequently read, no matter how small it is, that makes a man learned in the Scriptures and godly. Indeed, the writings of all the holy fathers should be read only for a time so that through them we may be led into the Scriptures. As it is, however, we only read them these days to avoid going any further and getting into the Bible. We are like men who read the sign posts and never travel the road they indicate. Our dear fathers wanted to lead us to the Scriptures by their writings, but we use their works to get away from the Scriptures. Nevertheless, the Scripture alone is our vineyard in which we must all labor and toil.

Above all, the foremost reading for everybody, both in the universities and in the schools, should be Holy Scripture—and for the younger boys, the Gospels. And would

---

196. A square cap worn by a teacher. Red is the academic color of theology; brown, of liberal arts.

to God that every town had a girls' school as well, where the girls would be taught the gospel for an hour every day either in German or in Latin. Schools indeed! Monasteries and nunneries began long ago with that end in view, and it was a praiseworthy and Christian purpose, as we learn from the story of St. Agnes[197] and of other saints. Those were the days of holy virgins and martyrs when all was well with Christendom. But today these monasteries have come to nothing but praying and singing. Is it not only right that every Christian man know the entire holy gospel by the age of nine or ten? Does he not derive his name and his life from the gospel? A spinner or a seamstress teaches her daughter her craft in her early years. But today even the great, learned prelates and the very bishops do not know the gospel.

Oh, we handle these poor young people who are committed to us for training and instruction in the wrong way! We shall have to render a solemn account of our neglect to set the word of God before them. Their lot is as described by Jeremiah in Lamentations 2 [:11-12], "My eyes are grown weary with weeping, my bowels are terrified, my heart is poured out upon the ground because of the destruction of the daughter of my people, for the youth and the children perish in all the streets of the entire city. They said to their mothers, 'Where is bread and wine?' as they fainted like wounded men in the streets of the city and gave up the ghost on their mothers' bosom." We do not see this pitiful evil, how today the young people of Christendom languish and perish miserably in our midst for want of the gospel, in which we ought to be giving them constant instruction and training.

Moreover, even if the universities were diligent in Holy Scripture, we need not send everybody there as we do now, where their only concern is numbers and where everybody wants a doctor's degree. We should send only

197. Cf. p. 63, n. 150.

the most highly qualified students who have been well trained in the lower schools. A prince or city council ought to see to this, and permit only the well qualified to be sent. I would advise no one to send his child where the Holy Scriptures are not supreme. Every institution that does not unceasingly pursue the study of God's word becomes corrupt. Because of this we can see what kind of people they become in the universities and what they are like now. Nobody is to blame for this except the pope, the bishops, and the prelates, who are all charged with training young people. The universities only ought to turn out men who are experts in the Holy Scriptures, men who can become bishops and priests, and stand in the front line against heretics, the devil, and all the world. But where do you find that? I greatly fear that the universities, unless they teach the Holy Scriptures diligently and impress them on the young students, are wide gates to hell.

26.[198] I know full well that the pope and his gang will pretend and boast about how the pope took the Holy Roman Empire from the Greek emperor and bestowed it upon the Germans, for which honor and benevolence he is said to have justly deserved and obtained submission, thanks, and all good things from the Germans.[199] For this reason they will, perhaps, undertake to throw all attempts to reform themselves to the four winds, and will not allow us to think about anything but the bestowal of the Roman Empire. For this cause they have persecuted and oppressed many a worthy emperor so wilfully and arrogantly that it is a shame even to mention it. And with the same adroitness they have made themselves overlords of every secular power and authority, contrary to the holy gospel. I must therefore speak of this, too.

There is no doubt that the true Roman Empire, which the writings of the prophets foretold in Numbers 24 [:17-

---

198. This section did not appear in the first edition. Cf. *LW* 44, 207, n. 224.
199. Cf. below, p. 131, n. 25.

19] and Daniel 2 [:44], has long since been overthrown and come to an end, as Balaam clearly prophesied in Numbers 24 [:24] when he said, "The Romans shall come and overthrow the Jews, and afterward they also shall be destroyed." That happened under the Goths,[200] but more particularly when the Muslim empire arose almost a thousand years ago. Then eventually Asia and Africa fell away, and in time France and Spain. Finally Venice arose, and nothing was left to Rome of its former power.

Now when the pope could not subdue to his arrogant will the Greeks and the emperor at Constantinople, who was the hereditary Roman emperor, he invented a little device to rob this emperor of his empire and his title and to turn it over to the Germans, who at that time were warlike and of good repute. In so doing, the Romanists brought the power of the Roman Empire under their control so they could parcel it out themselves. And this is just what happened. The empire was taken away from the emperor at Constantinople, and its very name and title given to us Germans. Through this we became servants of the pope. There is now a second Roman Empire, built by the pope upon the Germans. The former Roman Empire, the first one, has long since fallen, as I said earlier.

So, then, the Roman See now gets its own way. It has taken possession of Rome, driven out the German emperor, and bound him by oaths not to dwell at Rome. He is supposed to be Roman emperor, and yet he is not to have possession of Rome; and besides, he is to be dependent on and move within the limits of the good pleasure of the pope and his supporters. We have the title, but they have the land and the city. They have always abused our simplicity to serve their own arrogant and tyrannical designs. They call us crazy Germans for letting them make fools and monkeys of us as they please.

---

200. Rome was sacked by the Visigoths in A.D. 410.

All right! It is a small thing for God to throw empires and principalities about. He is so gentle with them that once in a while he gives a kingdom to a scoundrel and takes one from a good man, sometimes by the treachery of wicked, faithless men, and sometimes by inheritance. This is what we read about the kingdoms of Persia and Greece, and about almost all kingdoms. It says in Daniel 2 [:21] and 4 [:34-35], "He who rules over all things dwells in heaven, and it is he alone who overthrows kingdoms, tosses them to and fro, and establishes them." Since no one, particularly a Christian, can think it a very great thing to have a kingdom given him, we Germans, too, need not lose our heads because a new Roman Empire is bestowed on us. For in God's eyes it is but a trifling gift, one which he often gives to the most unworthy, as it says in Daniel 4 [:35], "All who dwell on earth are as nothing in his eyes, and he has the power in all the kingdoms of men to give them to whom he will."

But although the pope used violence and unjust means to rob the true emperor of his Roman Empire, or of the title of his Roman Empire, and gave it to us Germans, yet it is nevertheless certain that God has used the pope's wickedness to give such an empire to the German nation, and after the fall of the first Roman Empire, to set up another, the one which now exists. And although we had nothing to do with this wickedness of the popes, and although we did not understand their false aims and purposes, nevertheless, we have paid tragically and far too dearly for such an empire with incalculable bloodshed, with the suppression of our liberty, the hazarding and theft of all our possessions, especially of our churches and benefices, and with the suffering of unspeakable deception and insult. We carry the title of empire, but it is the pope who has our wealth, honor, body, life, soul, and all that we possess. This is how they deceive the Germans and cheat us with tricks.[201] What the popes have gladly sought was to be emperors, and when they could not achieve this, they at least succeeded in setting themselves over the emperors.

Since the empire has been given us by the providence of God as well as by the plotting of evil men, without any guilt on our part, I would not advise that we give it up, but rather that we rule it wisely and in the fear of God, as long as it pleases him for us to rule it. For, as has been said already, it does not matter to him where an empire comes from; his will is that it be governed. Though the popes were wrong in taking it from others, we were not wrong in receiving it. It has been given us through evil men by the will of God: it is the will of God we have regard for rather than the wicked intentions of the popes. Their intention when they gave it to us was to be emperors, indeed, more than emperors, and only to fool and mock us with the title. The king of Babylon also seized his kingdom by robbery and violence. Yet it was God's will that that kingdom be ruled by the holy princes Daniel, Hananiah, Azariah, and Michael.[202] Much more, then, is it God's will that this empire should be ruled by the Christian princes of Germany, no matter whether the pope stole it, got it by force, or established it fresh. It is all God's ordering, which came about before we knew about it.

Therefore, the pope and his followers have no right to boast that they have done the German nation a great favor by giving us the Roman Empire. In the first place, they did not mean it for our good. Rather, they took advantage of our simplicity when they did it in order to strengthen their proud designs against the real Roman emperor at Constantinople. The pope took this empire against God and right,

---

201. *Szo sol man die Deutschen teuschen und mit teuschen teuschenn,* an untranslatable pun on *Deutschen* ("German") and *teuschenn* ("to deceive").

202. Dan. 1:6-7; 2:48; 5:29.

which he had no right to do. In the second place, the pope's intention was not to give us the empire, but to get it for himself that he might bring all our power, our freedom, our wealth, our souls and bodies into subjection to himself, and through us (had God not prevented it) to subdue all the world. He clearly says so himself in his decretals, and has attempted to do so by means of many wicked wiles with a number of the German emperors. Thus have we Germans been taught our German. While we supposed we were going to be masters, we became in fact slaves of the most deceitful tyrants of all time. We have the name, the title, and the insignia of empire, but the pope has its treasures, authority, rights, and liberties. The pope gobbles the kernel while we are left playing with the husk!

Now may God, who, as we have said, tossed this empire into our lap by the wiles of tyrants and has charged us with its rule, help us to live up to the name, title, and insignia, and to retrieve our liberty. Let the Romanists see once and for all what it is that we have received from God through them! If they boast that they have bestowed an empire on us, let them! If that is true, then let the pope give us back Rome and all that he has gotten from the empire; let him free our land from his intolerable taxing and fleecing; let him give us back our liberty, our rights, our honor, our body and soul; and let the empire be what an empire should be, so that the pope's words and pretensions might be fulfilled.

If he will not do that, then what is he playing at with his false and lying words and his juggler's tricks? Has there not been enough of constantly and rudely leading this noble nation by the nose for these many centuries? It does not follow that the pope must be above the emperor because he crowns him or appoints him. The prophet St. Samuel anointed and crowned the kings Saul and David[203]

203. Cf. I Sam. 10:1; I Sam. 16:13.

at God's command, and yet he was their subject. The prophet Nathan anointed King Solomon,[204] but he was not set over the king on that account. Similarly, St. Elisha had one of his servants anoint Jehu[205] king of Israel, but they still remained obedient and subject to the king. It has never happened in all the history of the world that he who consecrated or crowned the king was over the king, except in this single instance of the pope.

If the pope lets himself be crowned by three cardinals who are beneath him, he is nonetheless their superior. Why should he then go against his own example, against universal practice, and against the teaching of Scripture by exalting himself above temporal authority or imperial majesty simply because he crowns or consecrates the emperor? It is quite enough that he is the emperor's superior in the things of God, that is, in preaching, teaching, and the administration of the sacraments. In these respects any bishop and any priest is over everybody else, just as St. Ambrose in his see was over the emperor Theodosius,[206] the prophet Nathan over David, and Samuel over Saul. Therefore, let the German emperor be really and truly emperor. Let neither his authority nor his power be suppressed by such sham pretensions of these papist deceivers as though they were to be excepted from his authority and were themselves to rule in all things.

27.[207] Enough has now been said about the failings of the clergy, though you may find more and will find more if you look in the right place. We shall now devote a section to the failings of the temporal estate.

In the first place, there is a great need for a general law and decree in the German nation against extravagant and

---

204. Cf. I Kings 1:39. Luther errs; Zadok the priest did the anointing.
205. Cf. II Kings 9:6.
206. On a possible historical allusion, cf. *LW* 44, 211, n. 233.
207. This section followed immediately after section 25 in the first edition and was numbered 26. Cf. *WA* 6, 465, n. 2.

costly dress, because of which so many nobles and rich men are impoverished.[208] God has certainly given us, as he has to other countries, enough wool, hair, flax, and everything else necessary for the seemly and honorable dress of every class. We do not need to waste fantastic sums for silk, velvet, golden ornaments, and foreign wares. I believe that even if the pope had not robbed us with his intolerable fleecing, we would still have more than enough of these domestic robbers, the silk and velvet merchants. We see that now everybody wants to be like everybody else, and pride and envy are thereby aroused and increased among us, as we deserve. All this misery and much more besides would be happily left behind if only our desire to be noticed would let us be thankful and satisfied with the good things God has already given us.

It is also necessary to restrict the spice traffic, which is another of the great ships in which money is carried out of German lands. By the grace of God more things to eat and drink grow in our own land than in any other, and they are just as nourishing and good. Perhaps my proposals seem foolish, impractical, and give the impression that I want to ruin the greatest of all trades, that of commerce. But I am doing my best, and if there is no improvement in these matters, then let him who will try his hand at improving them. I do not see that many good customs have ever come to a land through commerce, and in ancient times God made his people Israel dwell away from the sea on this account, and did not let them engage in much commerce.

But the greatest misfortune of the German nation is certainly the *zynskauf*.[209] If that did not exist many a man would have to leave his silks, velvets, golden ornaments, spices, and display of every kind unbought. This traffic has

208. Such a law was proposed to the Diet of Worms in 1521.
209. A technically nonusurious way to lend money profitably. Cf. *LW* 44, 96, n. 61.

not existed much longer than a hundred years, and it has already brought almost all princes, endowed institutions, cities, nobles, and their heirs to poverty, misery, and ruin. If it goes on for another hundred years, Germany will not have a penny left, and the chances are we shall have to eat one another. The devil invented the practice, and by confirming it[210] the pope has brought woe upon the whole world.

Therefore, I beg and pray at this point that everyone open his eyes and see the ruin of his children and heirs. Ruin is not just at the door, it is already in the house. I pray and beseech emperor, princes, lords, and city councilors to condemn this trade as speedily as possible and prevent it from now on, regardless of whether the pope with all his law—"unlaw" rather—objects or whether benefices or monasteries are based upon it. It is better for a city to have one benefice supported by honest legacies or revenue than to have a hundred benefices supported by *zynskauf*. Indeed, a benefice supported by a *zynskauf* is more grievous and oppressive than twenty supported by legacies. In fact, the *zynskauf* must be a sign and proof that the world has been sold to the devil because of its grievous sins and that at the same time we are losing both temporal and spiritual possessions. And yet we do not even notice it.

In this connection, we must put a bit in the mouth of the Fuggers and similar companies. How is it possible in the lifetime of one man to accumulate such great possessions, worthy of a king, legally and according to God's will? I don't know. But what I really cannot understand is how a man with one hundred gulden can make a profit of twenty in one year. Nor, for that matter, can I understand how a man with one gulden can make another—and all this not from tilling the soil or raising cattle, where the

---

210. The *zynskauf* was legalized by the Fifth Lateran Council in 1512.

increase of wealth depends not on human wit but on God's blessing. I leave this to men who understand the ways of the world. As a theologian I have no further reproof to make on this subject except that it has an evil and offending appearance, about which St. Paul says, "Avoid every appearance or show of evil" [I Thess. 5:22]. I know full well that it would be a far more godly thing to increase agriculture and decrease commerce. I also know that those who work on the land and seek their livelihood from it according to the Scriptures do far better. All this was said to us and to everybody else in the story of Adam, "Cursed be the ground when you work it; it shall bear you thistles and thorns, and in the sweat of your face you shall eat your bread" [Gen. 3:17-19]. There is still a lot of land lying unworked and neglected.

Next comes the abuse of eating and drinking,[211] which gives us Germans a bad reputation in foreign lands, as though it were a special vice of ours. Preaching cannot stop it, so deeply is it rooted and so firmly has it got the upper hand. The waste of money would be its least evil, were it not followed by all the vices that accompany it—murder, adultery, stealing, blasphemy, and every other form of immorality. Government can do something to prevent it; otherwise, what Christ says will come to pass, that the last day shall come like a secret snare, when they shall be eating and drinking, marrying and wooing, building and planting, buying and selling.[212] It is so much like what is now going on that I sincerely hope the day of judgment is at hand, although very few people give it any thought.

Finally, is it not lamentable that we Christians tolerate open and common brothels in our midst, when all of us are baptized unto chastity? I know perfectly well what

---

211. The diets of Augsburg (1500) and Cologne (1512) passed edicts against drunkenness. The Diet of Worms (1521) adjourned before a recommendation that these earlier edicts be reaffirmed was acted upon.

212. Cf. Luke 21:34, 12:45, and Matt. 24:36-44.

some say to this, that is, that it is not a custom peculiar to one nation, that it would be difficult to put a stop to it, and, moreover, that it is better to keep such a house than that married women, or girls, or others of still more honorable estate should be outraged. Nevertheless, should not the government, which is temporal and also Christian, realize that such evil cannot be prevented by that kind of heathenish practice? If the children of Israel could exist without such an abomination, why cannot Christians do as much? In fact, how do so many cities, country towns, market towns, and villages do without such houses? Why can't large cities do without them as well?

In this matter of brothels, and in other matters previously mentioned, I have tried to point out how many good works the temporal government could do, and what the duty of every government should be, so that everyone may learn what an awful responsibility it is to rule and sit in high places. What use would it be if an overlord were as holy in his own life as St. Peter, if he did not diligently try to help his subjects in these matters? His very authority will condemn him. It is the duty of authorities to seek the best for those they govern. But if the authorities were to give some thought to how young people might be brought together in marriage, the hope of marriage would greatly help every one of them to endure and resist temptation.

But today everybody is attracted to the priesthood or the monastic life, and among them, I am sorry to say, there is not one in a hundred who has any other reason than that he seeks a living and doubts that he will ever be able to support himself and a family. Therefore, they live wildly enough beforehand, and wish, as they say, to get it out of their system, but experience shows that it is only more deeply embedded in them. I find the proverb true, "Despair makes most monks and priests."[213] That is what happens and that is how it is, as we see.

---

213. *Desperatio facit monachum.*

I will, however, sincerely advise that to avoid the many sins which entice so shamelessly, neither youth nor maid should be bound by the vow of chastity or a vow to adopt the religious life before the age of thirty.[214] Chastity, as St. Paul says, is a special gift [I Cor. 7:7]. Therefore, I would advise those upon whom God has not conferred his special gift not to enter religious orders or take the vows. Furthermore, I say that if you trust God so little that you cannot support yourself as a married man and wish to become a religious only because of this distrust, then I beg you for your own soul's sake not to become a religious at all, but rather a farmer or anything you like. For where a single measure of faith in God is needed to earn your daily bread, there must be ten times that amount of faith to remain a religious. If you do not trust God to support you in temporal things, how will you trust him to support you in spiritual things? Alas, unbelief and distrust spoil everything and lead us into all kinds of misery, as we see in all walks of life.

Much more could be said of this pitiable state of affairs. The young people have nobody to look after them. They all do as they please, and the government is as much use to them as if it never existed. And yet the care of young people ought to be the chief concern of the pope, bishops, the ruling classes, and of the councils. They want to exercise authority far and wide, and yet they help nobody. For just this reason a lord and ruler will be a rare sight in heaven, even though he build a hundred churches for God and raise up all the dead!

That is enough for the moment. [I think I have said enough in my little book *Treatise on Good Works* about what the secular authorities and the nobility ought to do.

---

214. In *Discussion on How Confession Should Be Made* (1520) Luther sets the minimum age for men at eighteen or twenty and for women at fifteen or sixteen (*LW* 39, 44). In *The Judgment of Martin Luther on Monastic Vows* (1521) he sets the minimum age at sixty (*LW* 44, 387-388).

There is certainly room for improvement in their lives and in their rule, yet the abuses of the temporal power are not to be compared with those of the spiritual power, as I have shown in that book.][215]

I know full well that I have been very outspoken. I have made many suggestions that will be considered impractical. I have attacked many things too severely. But how else ought I to do it? I am duty-bound to speak. If I had the power, these are the things I would do. I would rather have the wrath of the world upon me than the wrath of God. The world can do no more to me than take my life. In the past I have made frequent overtures of peace to my enemies, but as I see it, God has compelled me through them to keep on opening my mouth wider and wider and to give them enough to say, bark, shout, and write because they have nothing else to do. Well, I know another little song about Rome and the Romanists.[216] If their ears are itching to hear it, I will sing that one to them, too—and pitch it in the highest key! You understand what I mean, dear Rome.

Moreover, many times have I offered my writings for investigation and hearing, but to no avail. Nevertheless, I know full well that if my cause is just, it must be condemned on earth and be justified only by Christ in heaven, for all the Scriptures show that the cause of Christians and of Christendom must be judged by God alone. Moreover, no cause has ever yet been justified on earth by men because the opposition has always been too great and too strong. It is still my greatest concern and anxiety that my cause may not be condemned, by which I would know for certain that it is not yet pleasing to God.

---

215. Cf. *LW* 44, 15-114. The bracketed material did not appear in the first edition.

216. This little song is *The Babylonian Captivity of the Church*, written shortly after the present treatise was published. Cf. below, pp. 113-260.

Therefore, just let them go hard at it, pope, bishop, priest, monk, or scholar. They are just the ones to persecute the truth, as they have always done.

God give us all a Christian mind, and grant to the Christian nobility of the German nation in particular true spiritual courage to do the best they can for the poor church. Amen.

Wittenberg, in the year 1520.

THE
BABYLONIAN CAPTIVITY
OF THE CHURCH

Translated by A. T. W. Steinhäuser
Revised by Frederick C. Ahrens and
Abdel Ross Wentz

INTRODUCTION

The primary importance of this treatise for the present-day reader of Luther lies in its courageous interpretation of the sacraments. But it is important also for its place in Luther's progressive assault upon the total position of the Romans. In *To the Christian Nobility of the German Nation,*[1] Luther demolished the three walls behind which Rome sat entrenched in her spiritual-temporal power. Now in *The Babylonian Captivity of the Church* he enters and takes her central stronghold and sanctuary—the sacramental system by which she accompanied and controlled her members from the cradle to the grave. Only then could he set forth, in language of almost lyrical rapture, *The Freedom of a Christian.*[2]

Luther was thinking of such a treatise long before it was written. In the first of the reformatory treatises of 1520, as they have been called, we read at the close: "Well, I know another little song about Rome and the Romanists. If their ears are itching to hear it, I will sing that one to them, too—and pitch it in the highest key!"[3] In this book on the "Babylonian Captivity," later that year, he fulfills his promise and the "little song" becomes a veritable "prelude."

Luther intends his book to be only an introduction to his major engagement on this theme of the sacraments. He expects that after this "Prelude" the Romans will gird themselves for battle and attack him in force, but he intends to

1. Pp. 1-112 above.
2. Pp. 261-316 below.
3. P. 111 above.

keep one step ahead of them and lead them on. In fact, he fully expects a papal bull against him threatening him with the most dire consequences if he does not recant, and in the closing paragraphs of this treatise he explains in bitter irony that he intends this document to be the beginning or prelude of his "recantation." If he is to recant or rechant or unsing what he has been singing hitherto, he will not really "change his tune," but will only "pitch it in a higher key."

This book is therefore only a skirmish preliminary to the main engagement, or, as a musician might say, a mere prelude introducing the main theme of the suite. It is a promise of more complete and more positive treatises on the sacraments in the future. And this promise was fulfilled. For that reason this "Prelude" is presented first among the treatises in this volume on the sacraments.

The theme that is presented by the Prelude Luther calls "The Babylonian Captivity of the Church." The reference is clear from the contents of the document: just as the Jews were carried away from Jerusalem into captivity under the tyranny of the Babylonian Empire, so in Europe the Christians have been carried away from the Scriptures and made subject to the tyranny of the papacy. This tyranny has been exercised by the misuse of the sacraments, chiefly the sacrament of the Lord's Supper.

After Luther had promised in his first reformatory treatise of 1520 that he would "sing another little song about Rome if their ears itch to hear it," he found that some ears were itching to hear the new song. This was brought home to him especially by two writings. One of these appeared in the summer of 1520; the other had been published the previous autumn but had not reached Wittenberg until some months later. The first came from the pen of Augustinus Alveld, that "celebrated Romanist of Leipzig," against whom Luther had fulminated in *The Papacy at Rome*, promising further disclosures if "Alveld came again."

He did come again, this time with a *Tractatus de communione sub utraque specie* [*Treatise Concerning Communion in Both Kinds*]. It was dedicated June 23, 1520. "The Leipzig ass has set up a fresh braying against me, full of blasphemies"; thus Luther describes it in a letter to Spalatin, July 22, 1520.

The other work was the anonymous tract of a "certain Italian friar of Cremona," who has only recently been identified as Isidoro Isolani, a Dominican hailing from Milan, who taught theology in various Italian cities, wrote a number of controversial works, and died in 1528. The title of the tract is *Revocatio Martini Lutheri Augustiniani ad sanctam sedem* [*The Recantation of the Augustinian Martin Luther before the Holy See*]. Its date is November 22, 1519, at Cremona. It begins and ends with a letter, and one paragraph from each of these is translated in Preserved Smith, *Luther's Correspondence* (Philadelphia, 1913), Vol. I, No. 199.

These two writings may be regarded as the immediate occasion for the writing of *The Babylonian Captivity*, but the *Captivity* is in no sense a direct reply to either of them. "I will not reply to Alveld," Luther writes on August 5 to Spalatin, "but he will be the occasion of my publishing something by which the vipers will be more irritated than ever." [4] Indeed, he had promised some such work more than half a year before, in a letter to Spalatin of December 18, 1519: "There is no reason why you or anyone else should expect from me a treatise on the sacraments [besides baptism, the Lord's Supper, and penance] until I am taught by what text I can prove that they are sacraments. I regard none of the others as a sacrament, for there is no sacrament except where there is a direct divine promise, exercising our faith. We can have no intercourse with God except by the word of Him promising, and by the faith of man receiv-

4. Smith, *op. cit.*, No. 283.

ing. At another time you shall hear more about their fables of the seven sacraments."[5]

Thus the Prelude grows under his hand and assumes the form of an elaborate examination of the whole sacramental system of the church. He makes short work of his two opponents, and after a few pages of delicious irony, of which Erasmus was suspected in some quarters of being the author, he turns his back on them and addresses himself to a positive and constructive treatment of the larger theme, lenient toward all nonessentials, but inexorable toward everything truly essential, that is, scriptural.

Luther discusses each one of the seven sacraments of the Roman church, but devotes nearly half of the book to the Lord's Supper and Baptism. The worst tyranny of the papacy he finds in the sacrament of the Lord's Supper and to this he gives his chief attention. The first captivity is the withholding of the cup from the laity; the second is found in the doctrine of transubstantiation; and the third is the sacrifice of the mass. The Sacrament of the Altar is not a magical device by which the priest brings God down from heaven but God's own revelation of himself where he is. In his discussion of Baptism Luther repudiates monasticism and insists that no vow should ever be taken beyond the baptismal vow.

The other five ceremonies he rejects as sacraments. Penance he would retain in purified form, but not as a sacrament, because it lacks a visible sign appointed by God; however, he strongly rejects priestly absolution. Everywhere he repudiates the authority of the church to institute new means of grace or new promises of mercy, and everywhere he bases upon the Holy Scriptures his general conception of a sacrament and his understanding of the individual sacraments.

---

5. *Ibid.*, No. 206.

Passage after passage, often whole pages, from the *Explanations of the Ninety-five Theses,*[6] *The Holy and Blessed Sacrament of Baptism,*[7] *A Discussion on How Confession Should Be Made,*[8] *A Treatise on the New Testament, that is, the Holy Mass*[9] and *The Blessed Sacrament of the Holy and True Body of Christ, and the Brotherhoods*[10] are transferred bodily to this new and definitive work, and find in it the goal toward which they had been unconsciously tending.

The *Captivity* was written in Latin because it is a theological treatise and was not intended for the rank and file of the Christian congregation. In this respect the treatise stands in contrast to several other treatises he wrote on the sacraments, which were written in German and were intended for laymen or theologians.

All in all, the Prelude was a deadly dagger aimed at the very heart of sacramentalism and clericalism and monasticism. It was the most devastating assault Luther had yet undertaken against Roman teaching and practice. It marked Luther's final and irrevocable break with the church of Rome. There is special significance in the fact that in the same letter to Spalatin (October 3) in which he mentions the arrival of Eck in Leipzig armed with the papal bull, he also announces the publication of his book on the captivity of the church for the following Saturday (October 6).[11]

Both sides of the controversy took the book very seriously. In ducal Saxony it was rigorously suppressed. Before the imperial council at Worms, the middle of December, 1520, and again at the imperial diet the following February, the papal nuncio Aleander bitterly assailed the *Captivity* as completely blasphemous because it questioned the authority

---

6. *LW* 31, 83-252.
7. *LW* 35, 23-43.
8. *LW* 39, 23-47.
9. *LW* 35, 75-111.
10. *LW* 35, 45-73.
11. Smith, op. cit., No. 303.

of the pope. John Glapion, the father confessor of Charles V, declared that it shocked him from head to foot. Erasmus now saw that his efforts to restore peace in the church would be futile: "The breach is irreparable." The University of Paris promptly condemned the document. One of Luther's most bitter enemies, Thomas Murner, translated it into German, confident that it would expose Luther to the rank and file of the people as a radical heretic and dangerous foe of the church. Of special significance was the action of Henry VIII of England. Not content with ordering Luther's writings to be publicly burned in London, he also turned theologian and wrote a book of 78 quarto pages dedicated to the pope, denouncing Luther and defending the Catholic positions on the sacraments. Henry's book so pleased the pope that he issued a special bull declaring that it was written with the help of the Holy Spirit, granting an indulgence of ten years to everyone who would read it, and bestowing upon Henry and his successors the title "Defender of the Faith."

On the other hand, the *Captivity* cleared the atmosphere for many thoughtful people and brought Luther not a few new friends. The most outstanding example of this was John Bugenhagen, who had previously regarded Luther as a reckless heretic, but on reading through the *Captivity* was completely converted to the cause of the Reformation and became one of Luther's ablest co-workers in the movement.

Julius Köstlin, probably the most thorough among modern analysts of Luther's theological development, says of the treatise: "The whole treatment of the subject is earnest and dignified. It is based upon biblical principles and shows thorough insight into the meaning of the Bible. At the same time it shows thorough acquaintance with the positions of the opponents and uses a dialectic that is a match for all the arts of the scholastics. Among all the scientific works of Luther this one stands at the top, but it also presents with clarity and warmth the simple religious interest of the Christian soul. It is sharp in its attitude toward the errors and tyranny of Rome but conservative toward the past and considerate toward such external practices as cannot be abrogated at once without injury to human consciences."

This is the fourth published translation of this treatise into English. The first was made by Wace and Buchheim (London, 1896). The second was by A. T. W. Steinhäuser and is included in the second volume of the Philadelphia edition of Luther's works (1915). The third came from the facile pen of Bertram Lee Woolf (*Reformation Writings of Martin Luther:* Vol. I, The Basis of the Protestant Reformation) and was published by the Lutterworth Press of London in 1952.

This revision is based on Steinhäuser's translation, but in every word there has been careful comparison with the original text and with the other English translations. The result is in some measure a new translation. The English of the Steinhäuser text has been revised in order to bring it into accord with present-day usage. Effort has been made also to conform a bit more closely to Luther's words. Some changes have been made in the interest of greater readability. We have sought to limit the use of intolerably long sentences. Also, there is more frequent paragraphing. The quotations from the Bible have been changed to the Revised Standard Version, except in the few instances where the context requires the King James Version or the Vulgate. Several paragraphs in the original that were omitted by Steinhäuser have been included here. The footnotes in Steinhäuser have, for the most part, been reproduced here, and they have been supplemented a bit.

The original Latin text of the treatise is in *WA* 6, 497-573.

THE
BABYLONIAN CAPTIVITY
OF THE CHURCH

A Prelude of Martin Luther

On the Babylonian Captivity of the Church

JESUS

Martin Luther, Augustinian, to his friend, Hermann Tulich,[1] greeting.

Whether I wish it or not, I am compelled to become more learned every day, with so many and such able masters eagerly driving me on and making me work. Some two years ago I wrote on indulgences, but in such a way that I now deeply regret having published that little book.[2] At that time I still clung with a mighty superstition to the tyranny of Rome, and so I held that indulgences should not be altogether rejected, seeing that they were approved by the common consent of so many. No wonder, for at the time I was still engaged singlehanded in this Sisyphean task.

---

1. Tulich was born at Steinheim, near Paderborn, in Westphalia; graduated from Wittenberg (A.B., 1511); was a proofreader in Melchior Lotter's printing-house at Leipzig. He returned to Wittenberg in 1519 and received the doctorate in 1520; became professor of poetry at the university; rector of the same, 1525. He was a staunch supporter of Luther; rector of the school at Lüneberg from 1532 until his death in 1540.
2. Probably the *Explanations of the Ninety-five Theses* (1518). LW 31, 83-252.

Afterwards, thanks to Sylvester,[3] and aided by those friars who so strenuously defended indulgences, I saw that they were nothing but impostures of the Roman flatterers, by which they rob men of their money and their faith in God. Would that I could prevail upon the booksellers and persuade all who have read them to burn the whole of my booklets on indulgences, and instead of all that I have written on this subject adopt this proposition: INDULGENCES ARE WICKED DEVICES OF THE FLATTERERS OF ROME.

Next, Eck and Emser[4] and their fellow-conspirators undertook to instruct me concerning the primacy of the pope. Here too, not to prove ungrateful to such learned men, I acknowedge that I have profited much from their labors. For while I denied the divine authority of the papacy, I still admitted its human authority.[5] But after hearing and reading the super-subtle subtleties of these coxcombs,[6] with which they so adroitly prop up their idol (for my mind is not altogether unteachable in these matters), I now know for certain that the papacy is the kingdom of Babylon and the power of Nimrod, the mighty hunter [Gen. 10:8-9]. Once more, therefore, that all may turn out to my friends' advantage, I beg both the booksellers and my readers that after burning what I have published on this

3. Sylvester Prierias (more properly called Mazzolini), from Prierio in Piedmont (1456-1523), was a prior of the Dominicans. He became Grand Inquisitor and Censor of Books in 1515. He and others of the order (e.g., Tetzel and Hochstraten) had written against Luther.
4. Johann Eck (properly Maier) from Eck in the Allgäu (1486-1543), had become professor at Ingolstadt in 1510. His criticism of the Ninety-five Theses in his *Obelisci*, to which Luther replied with the *Asterisci* (WA 1, 281-314; St.L. 18, 536-589), culminated in their Leipzig disputation in 1519. Jerome Emser (1477-1527) had been a humanist professor at Erfurt during Luther's student days, and was later secretary to Duke George of Saxony in Dresden. Luther is referring to the treatises both men published against him as a consequence of the disputation.
5. *Resolutio Lutheriana super propositione sua decima tertia de potestate papae (per autorem locupletata)* (1519). WA 2, 180-240.
6. *Trossulorum,* originally a designation for Roman knights who had conquered the city Trossulum, later came to have the derogatory sense of a fop, someone who pretends to rank and authority. St.L. 19, 6 n. 1.

subject they hold to this proposition: THE PAPACY IS THE
GRAND HUNTING OF THE BISHOP OF ROME. This is proved by
the arguments of Eck, Emser, and the Leipzig lecturer on
the Scriptures.[7]

Now they are making a game of schooling me concerning communion in both kinds and other weighty subjects:
here I must take pains lest I listen in vain to these "eminent
teachers"[8] of mine. A certain Italian friar of Cremona has
written a "Recantation of Martin Luther before the Holy
See,"[9] which is not that I revoke anything, as the words
declare, but that he revokes me. This is the kind of Latin
the Italians are beginning to write nowadays. Another
friar, a German of Leipzig, that same lecturer, as you know,
on the whole canon of Scripture [Alveld] has written
against me concerning the sacrament in both kinds and is
about to perform, as I understand, still greater and more
marvelous things. The Italian [Isolani] was canny enough
to conceal his name, fearing perhaps the fate of Cajetan[10]
and Sylvester. The man of Leipzig, on the other hand, as
becomes a fierce and vigorous German, boasts on his ample
title page of his name, his life, his sanctity, his learning,
his office, his fame, his honor, almost his very clogs.[11] From
him I shall doubtless learn a great deal, since he writes
his dedicatory epistle to the Son of God himself: so familiar

---

7. Augustinus Alveld, a Franciscan. This reference by Luther is his chief
claim to fame. Cf. the Introduction.

8. *Cratippos.* Cratippus, a peripatetic philosopher of Mytilene, had taught
Cicero's son at Athens and received the rights of Roman citizenship
through the orator's efforts. In addition to instructing the youth of Athens,
he wrote on divination and the interpretation of dreams.

9. *Revocatio Martini Lutheri Augustiniani ad sanctam sedem* by Isidoro Isolani.
Cf. the Introduction. Cf. *WA* 6, 486–487.

10. Thomas Cajetan (1469–1534), Italian cardinal, general of the Dominican
order and foremost authority on Thomistic theology, found himself unequal
to the task of testing and refuting Luther at Augsburg. Cf. *Proceedings at
Augsburg* (1518). *LW* 31, 253–292.

11. The title page of Alveld's treatise contained twenty-six lines. Luther's *Calo-
podia* (perhaps originally intended as *calcipodium*) may have been a reference to the wooden-soled sandals worn by Alveld's order.

are these saints with Christ who reigns in heaven! Here it seems three magpies are addressing me, the first in good Latin, the second in better Greek, the third in purest Hebrew. What do you think, my dear Hermann, I should do but prick up my ears? The matter is being dealt with at Leipzig by the "Observance" of the Holy Cross.[12]

Fool that I was, I had hitherto thought that it would be well if a general council were to decide that the sacrament should be administered to the laity in both kinds.[13] This view our more than learned friar would correct, declaring that neither Christ nor the apostles had either commanded or advised that both kinds be administered to the laity; it was therefore left to the judgment of the church what to do or not to do in this matter, and the church must be obeyed. These are his words.

You will perhaps ask, what madness has entered into the man, or against whom is he writing? For I have not condemned the use of one kind, but have left the decision about the use of both kinds to the judgment of the church. This is the very thing he attempts to assert, in order to attack me with this same argument. My answer is that this sort of argument is common to all who write against Luther: either they assert the very things they assail, or they set up a man of straw whom they may attack. This is the way of Sylvester and Eck and Emser, and of the men of Cologne and Louvain,[14] and if this friar had not been one of their kind, he would never have written against Luther.

This man turned out to be more fortunate than his fellows, however, for in his effort to prove that the use of

---

12. Concerning Alveld's lengthy title and his peculiar spelling, IHSVH, for Jesus, which he tried to justify by arguments involving an admixture of the three languages, cf. WA 6, 485. He was a member of the stricter Observantine Franciscans, at that time separate from the Conventuals.

13. Cf. *The Blessed Sacrament. LW* 35, 50.

14. The universities of Cologne and Louvain had ratified Eck's "victory" over Luther at Leipzig.

both kinds was neither commanded nor advised, but left to the judgment of the church, he brings forward the Scriptures to prove that the use of one kind for the laity was ordained by the command of Christ. So it is true, according to this new interpreter of the Scriptures, that the use of one kind was not commanded and at the same time was commanded by Christ! This novel kind of argument is, as you know, the one which these dialecticians of Leipzig are especially fond of using. Does not Emser profess to speak fairly of me in his earlier book,[15] and then, after I had convicted him of the foulest envy and shameful lies, confess, when about to confute me in his later book,[16] that both were true, and that he has written in both a friendly and an unfriendly spirit? A fine fellow, indeed, as you know!

But listen to our distinguished distinguisher of "kinds,"[17] to whom the decision of the church and the command of Christ are the same thing, and again the command of Christ and no command of Christ are the same thing. With such dexterity he proves that only one kind should be given to the laity, by the command of Christ, that is, by the decision of the church. He puts it in capital letters, thus: THE INFALLIBLE FOUNDATION. Then he treats John 6 [:35, 41] with incredible wisdom, where Christ speaks of the bread of heaven and the bread of life, which is He Himself. The most learned fellow not only refers these words to the Sacrament of the Altar, but because Christ says: "I am the living bread" [John 6:51] and not "I am the living cup," he actually concludes that we have in this passage the institution of the sacrament in only one kind

---

15. _De disputatione Lipsicensi_ (1519).

16. _Assertion of the Goat Against Luther's Hunt_ (1519). LW 39, 109.

17. _speciosum speciatorem._ In this play on words, Luther coined the second word to hint at the _species_ or elements in the sacrament, while at the same time connoting ironically someone who tries to make his case appear plausible and favorable. St.L. 19, 9 n. 1.

for the laity. But here follow the words: "For my flesh is food indeed, and my blood is drink indeed" [John 6:55] and, "Unless you eat the flesh of the Son of man and drink his blood" [John 6:53]. When it dawned upon the good friar that these words speak undeniably for both kinds and against one kind—presto! how happily and learnedly he slips out of the quandary by asserting that in these words Christ means to say only that whoever receives the sacrament in one kind receives therein both flesh and blood. This he lays down as his "infallible foundation" of a structure so worthy of the holy and heavenly "Observance."

I pray you now to learn along with me from this that in John 6 Christ commands the administration of the sacrament in one kind, yet in such a way that his commanding means leaving it to the decision of the church; and further that Christ is speaking in this same chapter only of the laity and not of the priests. For to the latter the living bread of heaven, that is the sacrament in our kind, does not belong, but perhaps the bread of death from hell! But what is to be done with deacons and subdeacons,[18] who are neither laymen nor priests? According to this distinguished writer they ought to use neither the one kind nor both kinds! You see, my dear Tulich, what a novel and "Observant" method of treating Scripture this is.

But learn this too: In John 6 Christ is speaking of the Sacrament of the Altar, although he himself teaches us that he is speaking of faith in the incarnate Word, for he says: "This is the work of God, that you believe in him whom he has sent" [John 6:29]. But we'll have to give him credit: this Leipzig professor of the Bible can prove anything he

---

18. These are the sixth and fifth of the seven grades through which clergy advanced to the priesthood. Some then-contemporary Catholic theologians (e.g., Cajetan and Durandus) doubted whether the Sacrament of Order was actually received by deacons. They were later overruled by the Council of Trent which decided that it was. *The Catholic Encyclopedia* (15 vols.), IV, 650.

pleases from any passage of Scripture he pleases. For he is an Anaxagorian,[19] or rather an Aristotelian,[20] theologian for whom nouns and verbs when interchanged mean the same thing and any thing. Throughout the whole of his book he so fits together the testimony of the Scriptures that if he set out to prove that Christ is in the sacrament he would not hesitate to begin thus: "The lesson is from the book of the Revelation of St. John the Apostle." All his quotations are as apt as this one would be, and the wiseacre imagines he is adorning his drivel with the multitude of his quotations. The rest I will pass over, lest I smother you with the filth of this vile-smelling cloaca.

In conclusion, he brings forward I Cor. 11 [:23], where Paul says that he received from the Lord and delivered to the Corinthians the use of both the bread and the cup. Here again our distinguisher of kinds, treating the Scriptures with his usual brilliance, teaches that Paul permitted, but did not deliver, the use of both kinds. Do you ask where he gets his proof? Out of his own head, as he did in the case of John 6. For it does not behoove this lecturer to give a reason for his assertions; he belongs to that order whose members prove and teach everything by their visions.[21] Accordingly we are here taught that in this passage the apostle did not write to the whole Corinthian congregation, but to the laity alone—and therefore gave no "permission" at all to the clergy, but deprived them of the sacrament altogether! Further, according to a new kind of grammar, "I have received from the Lord" means the same as "it is permitted by the Lord," and "I have delivered to you" is the same as "I have permitted to you." I pray you, mark

---

19. Anaxagoras (*circa* 500-428 B.C.), a Greek philosopher, was accused of atheism by his contemporaries because of his new interpretation of the myths of the gods.

20. For Luther's opinion of Aristotle, cf. *To the Christian Nobility of the German Nation.* Pp. 92-94 above.

21. The Franciscans. Perhaps an allusion to the seraphic vision of St. Francis.

this well. For by this method not only the church, but any worthless fellow, will be at liberty, according to this master, to turn all the universal commands, institutions, and ordinances of Christ and the apostles into mere "permission."

I perceive therefore that this man is driven by a messenger of Satan [II Cor. 12:7] and that he and his partners are seeking to make a name for themselves in the world through me, as men who are worthy to cross swords with Luther. But their hopes shall be dashed. In my contempt for them I shall never even mention their names, but content myself with this one reply to all their books. If they are worthy of it, I pray that Christ in his mercy may bring them back to a sound mind. If they are not worthy, I pray that they may never leave off writing such books, and that the enemies of truth may never deserve to read any others. There is truth and popular saying:

"This I know for certain—whenever I fight with filth,
Victor or vanquished, I am sure to be defiled."[22]

And since I see that they have an abundance of leisure and writing paper, I shall furnish them with ample matter to write about. For I shall keep ahead of them, so that while they are triumphantly celebrating a glorious victory over one of my heresies (as it seems to them), I shall meanwhile be devising a new one. I too am desirous of seeing these illustrious leaders in battle decorated with many honors. Therefore, while they murmur that I approve of communion in both kinds, and are most happily engrossed with this important and worthy subject, I shall go one step further and undertake to show that all who deny communion in both kinds to the laity are wicked men. To do this more conveniently I shall compose *a prelude on the*

---

22. The saying was also used later (1530) in the explanation to the fable about the ass and the lion in Luther's little book on Aesop's Fables, which included his translation of 14 of the fables. *Luther's Werke*, ed. Arnold E. Berger, III, 113. Cf. *MA*³ 2, 405-406.

captivity of the Roman church.[23] In due time, when the most learned papists have disposed of this book, I shall offer more.

I take this course, lest any pious reader who may chance upon this book should be offended by the filthy matter with which I deal and should justly complain that he finds nothing in it which cultivates or instructs his mind or which furnishes any food for learned reflection. For you know how impatient my friends are that I waste my time on the sordid fictions of these men. They say that the mere reading of them is ample confutation; they look for better things from me, which Satan seeks to hinder through these men. I have finally resolved to follow the advice of my friends and to leave to those hornets the business of wrangling and hurling invectives.

Of that Italian friar of Cremona [Isolani] I shall say nothing. He is an unlearned man and a simpleton, who attempts with a few rhetorical passages to recall me to the Holy See, from which I am not as yet aware of having departed, nor has anyone proved that I have. His chief argument in those silly passages[24] is that I ought to be moved by my monastic vows and by the fact that the empire has been transferred to the Germans.[25] Thus he does not seem to have wanted to write my "recantation" so much as the praise of the French people and the Roman pontiff. Let him attest his allegiance in this little book, such as it is. He does not deserve to be harshly treated, for he seems

---

23. We have retained the italics of the original for the most part where they serve the purpose of emphasis, or of pointing up the organizational structure of the treatise, or both.
24. Cf. p. 125 n. 9.
25. Cf. *To the Christian Nobility of the German Nation.* Pp. 100-105 above. Since the coronation of Charlemagne in 800, the German Empire had been regarded as the continuation of the Roman Empire, a fiction fostered by the pope, who had the right to crown an emperor. Perhaps, though, Luther is referring to the election of the half-German Charles V, despite papal agitation in favor of a French king. *Luthers Werke für das christliche Haus,* ed. Buchwald, *et al.* (Braunschweig, 1890) [hereinafter cited as Buchwald], II, 386 n. 1.

to have been prompted by no malice; nor does he deserve to be learnedly refuted, since all his chatter is sheer ignorance and inexperience.

To begin with, I must deny that there are seven sacraments, and for the present[26] maintain that there are but three: baptism, penance, and the bread.[27] All three have been subjected to a miserable captivity by the Roman curia, and the church has been robbed of all her liberty. Yet, if I were to speak according to the usage of the Scriptures, I should have only one single sacrament,[28] but with three sacramental signs, of which I shall treat more fully at the proper time.

Now concerning the sacrament of the bread first of all.[29]

I shall tell you now what progress I have made as a result of my studies on the administration of this sacrament. For at the time when I was publishing my treatise on the Eucharist,[30] I adhered to the common custom and did not concern myself at all with the question of whether the pope was right or wrong. But now that I have been challenged and attacked, nay, forcibly thrust into this arena, I shall freely speak my mind, whether all the papists laugh or weep together.

In the first place the sixth chapter of John must be entirely excluded from this discussion, since it does not refer

---

26. The "present" did not last very long as far as penance was concerned. Cf. p. 258.

27. Luther uses the commonly accepted designation for the Lord's Supper, a name derived from the fact that the wine was being withheld from the laity.

28. In I Tim. 3:16 Christ himself is called the *sacramentum* (Vulgate). Cf. *PE* 2, 177 n. 5; Julius Köstlin, *The Theology of Luther,* trans. Charles E. Hay (Philadelphia, 1897), I, 403; and below, pp. 221-22.

29. Luther inserted this sentence instead of a subtitle as in the case of the other sacraments to follow.

30. Cf. *The Blessed Sacrament. LW* 35, 45-73.

to the sacrament in a single syllable. Not only because the sacrament was not yet instituted, but even more because the passage itself and the sentences following plainly show, as I have already stated,[31] that Christ is speaking of faith in the incarnate Word. For he says: "My words are spirit and life" [John 6:63], which shows that he was speaking of a spiritual eating, by which he who eats has life; whereas the Jews understood him to mean a bodily eating and therefore disputed with him. But no eating can give life except that which is by faith, for that is truly a spiritual and living eating. As Augustine[32] also says: "Why do you make ready your teeth and your stomach? Believe, and you have eaten."[33] For the sacramental eating does not give life, since many eat unworthily. Hence Christ cannot be understood in this passage to be speaking about the sacrament.

Some persons, to be sure, have misapplied these words in their teaching concerning the sacrament, as in the decretal *Dudum*[34] and many others. But it is one thing to misapply the Scriptures and another to understand them in their proper sense. Otherwise, if in this passage Christ were enjoining a sacramental eating, when he says: "Unless you eat my flesh and drink my blood, you have no life in you" [John 6:53], he would be condemning all infants, all the sick, and all those absent or in any way hindered from the sacramental eating, however strong their faith might be. Thus Augustine in his *Contra Julianum*,[35] Book II, proves from Innocent[36] that even infants eat the flesh and

---

31. Cf. p. 128.
32. St. Augustine (354-430), bishop of Hippo in North Africa.
33. *Sermo* 112, cap. 5. Migne 38, 645.
34. Luther's reference to the Decretals is correct. His citation of *Dudum* is wrong. It should have been *Quum Marthae, Decretalium Gregorii IX*, lib. iii, tit. XLI: *de celebratione missarum, et sacramento eucharistiae et divinis officiis*, cap. 6. Cf. the text in *Corpus Iuris Canonici*, ed. Aemilius Friedberg (Graz, 1955), II, col. 638.
35. *Contra Julianum* ii, cap. 36. Migne 44, 699-700.
36. Innocent I, bishop of Rome 402-417, energetic opponent of Pelagius and other heretics.

drink the blood of Christ without the sacrament; that is, they partake of them through the faith of the church. Let this then be accepted as proved: John 6 does not belong here. For this reason I have written elsewhere[37] that the Bohemians[38] cannot properly rely on this passage in support of the sacrament in both kinds.

Now there are two passages that do bear very clearly upon this matter: the Gospel narratives of the Lord's Supper and Paul in I Cor. 11. Let us examine these. Matthew [26], Mark [14], and Luke [22] agree that Christ gave the whole sacrament to all his disciples. That Paul delivered both kinds is so certain that no one has ever had the temerity to say otherwise. Add to this that Matt. [26:27] reports that Christ did not say of the bread, "eat of it, all of you," but of the cup, "drink of it, all of you." Mark [14:23] likewise does not say, "they all ate of it," but "they all drank of it." Both attach the note of universality to the cup, not to the bread, as though the Spirit foresaw this schism, by which some would be forbidden to partake of the cup, which Christ desired should be common to all. How furiously do you suppose, would they rave against us, if they had found the word "all" attached to the bread instead of to the cup? They would certainly leave us no loophole to escape. They would cry out and brand us as heretics and damn us as schismatics. But now, when the Scripture is on our side and against them, they will not allow themselves to be bound by any force of logic. Men of the most free will[39] they are, even in the things that are God's; they change and change again, and throw everything into confusion.

37. *Verklärung etlicher Artikel in einem Sermon vom heiligen Sakrament* (1520). WA 6, 80.

38. Followers of the martyred John Huss (1369-1415); permitted by compromise agreements with Rome to administer Communion in both kinds.

39. For Luther's denial of his opponents' doctrine of the complete freedom of the will, cf. his *De servo arbitrio* (1525), WA 18, 600-787, St.L. 18, 1668-1969; *The Bondage of the Will*, trans. J. I. Packer and O. R. Johnston (Westwood, New Jersey, 1957).

But imagine me standing over against them and interrogating my lords, the papists. In the Lord's Supper, the whole sacrament, or communion in both kinds, is given either to the priests alone or else it is at the same time given to the laity. If it is given only to the priests (as they would have it), then it is not right to give it to the laity in either kind. For it must not be given rashly to any to whom Christ did not give it when he instituted the sacrament. Otherwise, if we permit one institution of Christ to be changed, we make all of his laws invalid, and any man may make bold to say that he is not bound by any other law or institution of Christ. For a single exception, especially in the Scriptures, invalidates the whole. But if it is given also to the laity, it inevitably follows that it ought not to be withheld from them in either form. And if any do withhold it from them when they ask for it they are acting impiously and contrary to the act, example, and institution of Christ.

I acknowledge that I am conquered by this argument, which to me is irrefutable. I have neither read nor heard nor found anything to say against it. For here the word and example of Christ stand unshaken when he says, not by way of permission, but of command: "Drink of it, all of you" [Matt. 26:27]. For if all are to drink of it, and the words cannot be understood as addressed to the priests alone, then it is certainly an impious act to withhold the cup from the laymen when they desire it, even though an angel from heaven [Gal. 1:8] were to do it. For when they say that the distribution of both kinds is left to the decision of the church, they make this assertion without reason and put it forth without authority. It can be ignored just as readily as it can be proved. It is of no avail against an opponent who confronts us with the word and work of Christ; he must be refuted with the word of Christ, but this we[40] do not possess.

40. Here Luther identifies himself with the erring priesthood.

If, however, either kind may be withheld from the laity, then with equal right and reason a part of baptism or penance might also be taken away from them by this same authority of the church. Therefore, just as baptism and absolution must be administered in their entirety, so the sacrament of the bread must be given in its entirety to all laymen, if they desire it. I am much amazed, however, by their assertion that the priests may never receive only one kind in the mass under pain of mortal sin; and that for no other reason except (as they unanimously say) that the two kinds constitute one complete sacrament, which may not be divided. I ask them, therefore, to tell me why it is lawful to divide it in the case of the laity, and why they are the only ones to whom the entire sacrament is not given? Do they not acknowledge, by their own testimony, either that both kinds are to be given to the laity or that the sacrament is not valid when only one kind is given to them? How can it be that the sacrament in one kind is not complete in the case of the priests, yet in the case of the laity it is complete? Why do they flaunt the authority of the church and the power of the pope in my face? These do not annul the words of God and the testimony of the truth.

It follows, further, that if the church can withhold from the laity one kind, the wine, it can also withhold from them the other, the bread. It could therefore withhold the entire Sacrament of the Altar from the laity and completely annul Christ's institution as far as they are concerned. By what authority, I ask. If the church cannot withhold the bread, or both kinds, neither can it withhold the wine. This cannot possibly be gainsaid; for the church's power must be the same over either kind as it is over both kinds, and if it has no power over both kinds, it has none over either kind. I am curious to hear what the flatterers of Rome will have to say to this.

But what carries most weight with me, however, and is quite decisive for me is that Christ says: "This is my blood, which is poured out for you and for many for the forgive-ness of sins."[41] Here you see very clearly that the blood is given to all those for whose sins it was poured out. But who will dare to say that it was not poured out for the laity? And do you not see whom he addresses when he gives the cup? Does he not give it to all? Does he not say that it is poured out for all? "For you" [Luke 22:20], he says—let this refer to the priests. "And for many" [Matt. 26:28], however, cannot possibly refer to the priests. Yet he says: "Drink of it, all of you" [Matt. 26:27]. I too could easily trifle here and with my words make a mockery of Christ's words, as my dear trifler[42] does. But those who rely on the Scriptures in opposing us must be refuted by the Scriptures.

This is what has prevented me from condemning the Bohemians,[43] who, whether they are wicked men or good, certainly have the word and act of Christ on their side, while we[44] have neither, but only that inane remark of men: "The church has so ordained." It was not the church which ordained these things, but the tyrants of the churches, without the consent of the church, which is the people of God.

But now I ask, where is the necessity, where is the religious duty, where is the practical use of denying both kinds, that is, the visible sign, to the laity, when everyone concedes to them the grace of the sacrament[45] without the sign? If they concede the grace, which is the greater, why not the sign, which is the lesser? For in every sacra-ment the sign as such is incomparably less than the thing

---

41. A harmony of Matt. 26:28 and Luke 22:20 in the Vulgate, whereby "for you" and "for many" are conjoined in the traditional manner of the canon of the mass. Cf. p. 154 n. 84.
42. Alveld, cf. p. 125 n. 7.
43. Cf. p. 134 n. 38.
44. Cf. n. 41 above.
45. The *res sacramenti*. The sacrament consisted of two parts—the *sacramentum*, or external sign, and the *res sacramenti*, or the thing signified, the sacra-mental grace.

signified. What then, I ask, is to prevent them from conceding the lesser, when they concede the greater? Unless indeed, as it seems to me, it has come about by the permission of an angry God in order to give occasion for a schism in the church, to bring home to us how, having long ago lost the grace of the sacrament, we contend for the sign, which is the lesser, against that which is the most important and the chief thing; just as some men for the sake of ceremonies contend against love. This monstrous perversion seems to date from the time when we began to rage against Christian love for the sake of the riches of this world. Thus God would show us, by this terrible sign, how we esteem signs more than the things they signify. How preposterous it would be to admit that the faith of baptism is granted to the candidate for baptism, and yet to deny him the sign of this very faith, namely, the water!

Finally, Paul stands invincible and stops the mouth of everyone when he says in I Cor. 11 [:23]: "For I received from the Lord what I also delivered to you." He does not say: "I permitted to you," as this friar of ours lyingly asserts out of his own head.[46] Nor is it true that Paul delivered both kinds on account of the contention among the Corinthians. In the first place, the text shows that their contention was not about the reception of both kinds, but about the contempt and envy between rich and poor. The text clearly states: "One is hungry and another is drunk, and you humiliate those who have nothing" [I Cor. 11:21-22]. Moreover, Paul is not speaking of the time when he first delivered the sacrament to them, for he does not say "I receive from the Lord" and "I give to you," but "I received" and "I delivered"—namely, when he first began to preach among them, a long while before this contention. This shows that he delivered both kinds to them, for "delivered" means the same as "commanded," for elsewhere he uses the

---

46. The passage from Alveld is quoted in WA 6, 505 n. 1.

word in this sense. Consequently there is nothing in the friar's fuming about permission; he has raked it together without Scripture, without reason, without sense. His opponents do not ask what he has dreamed, but what the Scriptures decree in the matter, and out of the Scriptures he cannot adduce one jot or tittle in support of his dreams, while they can produce mighty thunderbolts in support of their faith.

Rise up then, you popish flatterers, one and all! Get busy and defend yourselves against the charges of impiety, tyranny, and lèse-majesté against the gospel, and of the crime of slandering your brethren. You decry as heretics those who refuse to contravene such plain and powerful words of Scripture in order to acknowledge the mere dreams of your brains! If any are to be called heretics and schismatics, it is not the Bohemians or the Greeks,[47] for they take their stand upon the Gospels. It is you Romans who are the heretics and godless schismatics, for you presume upon your figments alone against the clear Scriptures of God. Wash yourself of that, men!

But what could be more ridiculous and more worthy of this friar's brains than his saying that the Apostle wrote these words and gave this permission, not to the church universal, but to a particular church, that is, the Corinthian? Where does he get his proof? Out of one storehouse, his own impious head. If the church universal receives, reads, and follows this epistle as written for itself in all other respects, why should it not do the same with this portion also? If we admit that any epistle, or any part of any epistle, of Paul does not apply to the church universal, then the whole authority of Paul falls to the ground. Then the Corinthians will say that what he teaches about faith in the

---

47. Greek Church is a common designation for that entire branch of Christendom known as Eastern Orthodoxy, which was split from Western or Latin Christianity in the year 1054. Its theologies and liturgies are written mostly in the Greek language.

Epistle to the Romans does not apply to them. What greater blasphemy and madness can be imagined than this! God forbid that there should be one jot or tittle in all of Paul which the whole church universal is not bound to follow and keep! The Fathers never held an opinion like this, not even down to these perilous times of which Paul was speaking [II Tim. 3:1-9] when he foretold that there would be blasphemers and blind, insensate men. This friar is one of them, perhaps even the chief.

However, suppose we grant the truth of this intolerable madness. If Paul gave his permission to a particular church, then, even from your own point of view, the Greeks and Bohemians are in the right, for they are particular churches. Hence it is sufficient that they do not act contrary to Paul, who at least gave permission. Moreover, Paul could not permit anything contrary to Christ's institution. Therefore, O Rome, I cast in your teeth, and in the teeth of all your flatterers, these sayings of Christ and Paul, on behalf of the Greeks and the Bohemians. I defy you to prove that you have been given any authority to change these things by as much as one hair, much less to accuse others of heresy because they disregard your arrogance. It is rather you who deserve to be charged with the crime of godlessness and despotism.

Concerning this point we may read Cyprian,[48] who alone is strong enough to refute all the Romanists. In the fifth book of his treatise, *On the Lapsed*, he testifies that it was the widespread custom in that church [at Carthage] to administer both kinds to the laity, even to children, indeed, to give the body of the Lord into their hands. And of this he gives many examples. Among other things, he reproves some of the people as follows: "The sacrilegious man is angered at the priests because he does not immediately

---

48. Bishop of Carthage, (249-258), who was beheaded as a martyr for the faith. The treatise was written about 251-252.

receive the body of the Lord with unclean hands, or drink the blood of the Lord with unclean lips."[49] He is speaking here, you see, of irreverent laymen who desired to receive the body and the blood from the priests. Do you find anything to snarl at here, wretched flatterer? Will you say that this holy martyr, a doctor of the church endowed with the apostolic spirit, was a heretic, and that he used this permission in a particular church?

In the same place Cyprian narrates an incident that came under his own observation. He describes at length how a deacon was administering the cup to a little[50] girl, and when she drew away from him he poured the blood of the Lord into her mouth.[51] We read the same of St. Donatus, and how trivially does this wretched flatterer dispose of his broken chalice![52] "I read of a broken chalice," he says, "but I do not read that the blood was administered."[53] No wonder! He that finds what he pleases in the Holy Scriptures will also read what he pleases in the histories. But can the authority of the church be established, or the heretics be refuted, in this way?

But enough on this subject! I did not undertake this work

49. St. Cyprian, "The Lapsed," trans. Maurice Bévenot, S. J. (Westminster, Maryland, 1957), p. 31. (Vol. 25 of *Ancient Christian Writers.*)

50. *infanti*, a child under the age of seven years. *St.L.* 19, 21 n. 2.

51. St. Cyprian, *op. cit.*, pp. 32-33.

52. Donatus, bishop of Arezzo, whither he had fled during the persecution of Diocletian (303-305); martyred under Julian the Apostate, August 7, 362. In a collection of legendary lives of the saints, compiled by Jacobus de Voragine (*circa* 1230-1298), it is related: "And one day, as Gregory relates in his *Dialogue*, the people were receiving the holy Communion in the Mass, and the deacon was distributing the Blood of Christ, when the pagans pushed him so rudely that he fell, and the holy chalice was shattered. As he and the people were sorely grieved thereat, Donatus gathered the fragments of the chalice, and having prayed, restored it to its former shape." *The Golden Legend of Jacobus de Voragine,* trans. Granger Ryan and Helmut Ripperger (New York, 1941), Part Two, 433-34.

53. Alveld quotes the story of the broken cup in order to refute the practice in administration of the sacrament which it implies. He says: "I read of the repairing of the chalice in Gregory, but do not find there the administration of the blood." Cf. *WA* 6, 506 n. 2.

141

for the purpose of answering one who is not worthy of a reply, but to bring the truth of the matter to light.

I conclude, then, that it is wicked and despotic to deny both kinds to the laity, and that this is not within the power of any angel, much less of any pope or council. Nor does the Council of Constance[54] give me pause, for if its authority is valid, why not that of the Council of Basel as well, which decreed to the contrary that the Bohemians should be permitted to receive the sacrament in both kinds? That decision was reached only after considerable discussion, as the extant records and documents of the Council show. And to this Council the ignorant flatterer refers[55] in support of his dream; with such wisdom does he handle the whole matter.

The first captivity of this sacrament, therefore, concerns its substance or completeness, which the tyranny of Rome has wrested from us. Not that those who use only one kind sin against Christ, for Christ did not command the use of either kind, but left it to the choice of each individual, when he said: "As often as you do this, do it in remembrance of me" [I Cor. 11:25]. But they are the sinners, who forbid the giving of both kinds to those who wish to exercise this choice. The fault lies not with the laity, but with the priests. The sacrament does not belong to the priests, but to all men. The priests are not lords, but servants in duty bound to administer both kinds to those who desire them, as often as they desire them. If they wrest this right from the laity and deny it to them by force, they are tyrants; but the laity

---

54. Alveld had cited the *Decretum Constantiense,* which approved the withholding of the cup from the laity. Cf. *WA* 6, 507 n. 1.
55. The Council of Constance did sanction withholding of the cup from the laity, and burned John Huss at the stake for disputing it (July 6, 1415). Alveld, however, was wrong, as Luther says, in citing also the Council of Basel. That Council concluded the *Compactata* of Prague (November 30, 1433), granting to the followers of Huss (the "Bohemians") the privilege of administering the sacrament in both kinds.

are without fault, whether they lack one kind or both kinds. In the meantime they must be preserved by their faith and by their desire for the complete sacrament. These same servants are likewise bound to administer baptism and absolution to everyone who seeks them, because he has a right to them; but if they do not administer them, the seeker has the full merit of his faith, while they will be accused before Christ as wicked servants. Thus the holy fathers of old in the desert did not receive the sacrament in any form for many years at a time.[56]

Therefore I do not urge that both kinds be seized upon by force, as if we were bound to this form by a rigorous command, but I instruct men's consciences so that they may endure the Roman tyranny, knowing well that they have been forcibly deprived of their rightful share in the sacrament because of their own sin. This only do I desire—that no one should justify the tyranny of Rome, as if it were doing right in forbidding one kind to the laity. We ought rather to abhor it, without our consent, and endure it just as we should do if we were held captive by the Turk and not permitted to use either kind. This is what I meant by saying that it would be a good thing, in my opinion, if this captivity were ended by the decree of a general council,[57] our Christian liberty restored to us out of the hands of the Roman tyrant, and every one left free to seek and receive this sacrament, just as he is free to receive baptism and penance. But now we are compelled by the same tyranny to receive the one kind year after year, so utterly lost is the liberty which Christ has given us. This is the due reward of our godless ingratitude.

The second captivity of this sacrament is less grievous as far as the conscience is concerned, yet the gravest of dan-

---

56. Cf. *A Sermon on the Ban.* LW 39, 10.
57. Cf. p. 126 n. 13.

gers threatens the man who would attack it, to say nothing of condemning it. Here I shall be called a Wycliffite[58] and a heretic by six hundred names. But what of it? Since the Roman bishop has ceased to be a bishop and has become a tyrant, I fear none of his decrees; for I know that it is not within his power, nor that of any general council, to make new articles of faith

Some time ago, when I was drinking in scholastic theology, the learned Cardinal of Cambrai[59] gave me food for thought in his comments on the fourth book of the *Sentences*.[60] He argues with great acumen that to hold that real bread and real wine, and not merely their accidents,[61] are present on the altar, would be much more probable and require fewer superfluous miracles—if only the church had not decreed otherwise. When I learned later what church it was that had decreed this, namely the Thomistic[62]—that is, the Aristotelian church—I grew bolder, and after floating in a sea of doubt,[63] I at last found rest for my conscience in the above view, namely, that it is real bread and real wine,

58. John Wycliffe (d. 1384), the most prominent English reformer before the Reformation and keenest of medieval critics of the doctrine of transubstantiation, was posthumously condemned as a heretic by the Council of Constance on May 4, 1415.
59. Pierre d'Ailly (1350-1420), a pupil of Ockham, influenced Luther greatly. He was chairman of that session of the Council of Constance which examined and condemned John Huss in 1415. Luther is referring to d'Ailly's *Questiones quarti libri sententiarum*, quest. 6. E; folio cclxiv a.
60. Famous medieval textbook of theology, compiled *circa* 1150 by Peter Lombard (d. 1160), and containing brief statements or "sentences" of the main arguments pro and con with respect to the principal themes in Christian doctrine. The fourth book treats of the sacraments in general.
61. "Accidents" were the qualities which, in medieval thought, were held to adhere to the invisible "substance" and, together with it, form the object. In transubstantiation the "substance" of the bread and wine was changed into the "substance" of Christ's body and blood, while only the "accidents" or "form" of the bread and wine (such as shape, color, and taste) remained.
62. The name refers to Thomas Aquinas (1225-1274), a Dominican, greatest of the scholastic theologians, still regarded as the foremost doctrinal authority in the Roman Catholic church. He taught transubstantiation.
63. *inter sacrum et saxum*. In his *Adagia*, Erasmus says the phrase is used of those who in their perplexity are carried to the point of grave danger. CL 1, 438 n. 29.

in which Christ's real flesh and real blood are present in no other way and to no less a degree than the others assert them to be under their accidents. I reached this conclusion because I saw that the opinions of the Thomists, whether approved by pope or by council, remain only opinions, and would not become articles of faith even if an angel from heaven were to decree otherwise [Gal. 1:8]. For what is asserted without the Scriptures or proven revelation may be held as an opinion, but need not be believed. But this opinion of Thomas hangs so completely in the air without support of Scripture or reason that it seems to me he knows neither his philosophy nor his logic. For Aristotle speaks of subject and accidents so very differently[64] from St. Thomas that it seems to me this great man is to be pitied not only for attempting to draw his opinions in matters of faith from Aristotle, but also for attempting to base them upon a man whom he did not understand, thus building an unfortunate superstructure upon an unfortunate foundation.

Therefore I permit every man to hold either of these opinions, as he chooses. My one concern at present is to remove all scruples of conscience, so that no one may fear being called a heretic if he believes that real bread and real wine are present on the altar, and that every one may feel at liberty to ponder, hold, and believe either one view or the other without endangering his salvation. However, I shall now set forth my own view.

In the first place, I do not intend to listen or attach the least importance to those who will cry out that this teaching of mine is Wycliffite, Hussite, heretical, and contrary to the decree of the church. No one will do this except those very persons whom I have convicted of manifold heresies in the matter of indulgences, freedom of the will and the grace of God, good works and sins, etc. If Wycliffe was once a

---

64. Aristotle held that a subject and its accidents are inseparable; neither can exist apart from the other. Cf *MA*³ 2, 406.

heretic, they are heretics ten times over; and it is a pleasure to be blamed and accused by heretics and perverse sophists, since to please them would be the height of impiety. Besides, the only way in which they can prove their opinions and disprove contrary ones is by saying: "That is Wycliffite, Hussite, heretical!" They carry this feeble argument always on the tip of their tongues, and they have nothing else. If you ask for scriptural proof, they say: "This is our opinion, and the church (that is, we ourselves) has decided thus." To such an extent these men, who are reprobate concerning the faith [II Tim. 3:8] and untrustworthy, have the effrontery to set their own fancies before us in the name of the church as articles of faith.

But there are good grounds for my view, and this above all—no violence is to be done to the words of God, whether by man or angel. They are to be retained in their simplest meaning as far as possible. Unless the context manifestly compels it, they are not to be understood apart from their grammatical and proper sense, lest we give our adversaries occasion to make a mockery of all the Scriptures. Thus Origen[65] was rightly repudiated long ago because, ignoring the grammatical sense, he turned the trees and everything else written concerning Paradise into allegories, from which one could have inferred that trees were not created by God. Even so here, when the Evangelists plainly write that Christ took bread [Matt. 26:26; Mark 14:22; Luke 22:19] and blessed it, and when the Book of Acts and the Apostle in turn call it bread [Acts 2:46; I Cor. 10:16; 11:23, 26-28], we have to think of real bread and real wine, just as we do of a real cup (for even they do not say that the cup was transubstantiated). Since it is not necessary, therefore, to assume a transubstantiation effected by divine power, it

---

65. Origen of Alexandria (*circa* 184-253) whose principles of allegorical exegesis were the source of many lengthy controversies, beginning as early as the fourth century.

must be regarded as a figment of the human mind, for it rests neither on the Scriptures nor on reason, as we shall see.

Therefore it is an absurd and unheard-of juggling with words to understand "bread" to mean "the form or accidents[66] of bread," and "wine" to mean "the form or accidents of wine." Why do they not also understand all other things to mean their "forms or accidents"? And even if this might be done with all other things, it would still not be right to enfeeble the words of God in this way, and by depriving them of their meaning to cause so much harm.

Moreover, the church kept the true faith for more than twelve hundred years, during which time the holy fathers never, at any time or place, mentioned this transubstantiation (a monstrous word and a monstrous idea), until the pseudo philosophy of Aristotle began to make its inroads into the church in these last three hundred years.[67] During this time many things have been wrongfully defined, as for example, that the divine essence is neither begotten nor begets; that the soul is the substantial form of the human body. These and like assertions are made without any reason or cause, as the Cardinal of Cambrai[68] himself admits.

Perhaps they will say that the danger of idolatry demands that the bread and wine should not be really present. How ridiculous! The laymen have never become familiar with their fine-spun philosophy of substance and accidents, and could not grasp it if it were taught to them. Besides, there is the same danger in the accidents which remain and which they see, as in the case of the substance which they

---

66. Cf. p. 144 n. 61.

67. Luther is referring to the official establishment of transubstantiation as a fixed dogma by the Fourth Lateran Council of 1215 under Innocent III. The concept was perhaps several centuries in developing prior to that time, though the earliest documentable use of the term in its technical sense was probably in a treatise by Stephen of Autun (d. 1139). *The New Schaff-Herzog Encyclopedia of Religious Knowledge* (12 volumes) [hereinafter cited as Schaff-Herzog], XI, 494.

68. Cf. p. 144 n. 59.

do not see. If they do not worship the accidents, but the Christ hidden under them, why should they worship the [substance of the] bread, which they do not see?

And why could not Christ include his body in the substance of the bread just as well as in the accidents? In red-hot iron, for instance, the two substances, fire and iron are so mingled that every part is both iron and fire. Why is it not even more possible that the body of Christ be contained in every part of the substance of the bread?

What will they reply? Christ is believed to have been born from the inviolate womb of his mother. Let them say here too that the flesh of the Virgin was meanwhile annihilated, or as they would more aptly say, transubstantiated, so that Christ, after being enfolded in its accidents, finally came forth through the accidents! The same thing will have to be said of the shut door [John 20:19, 26] and of the closed mouth of the sepulchre,[69] through which he went in and out without disturbing them.

Out of this has arisen that Babel of philosophy of a constant quantity distinct from the substance,[70] until it has come to such a pass that they themselves no longer know what are accidents and what is substance. For who has ever proved beyond the shadow of a doubt that heat, color, cold, light, weight, or shape are mere accidents? Finally, they have been driven to pretend that a new substance is created by God for those accidents on the altar, all on account of Aristotle, who says: "It is the nature of an accident to be in something," and endless other monstrosities. They would be rid of all these if they simply permitted real bread to be present. I rejoice greatly that the simple faith of this sacrament is still to be found, at least among the common people. For as they do not understand, neither do they dispute

69. Matt. 28:2; Mark 16:4; Luke 24:2; John 20:1.
70. According to scholastic teaching the substance of the bread ceases to exist. Its quantity, however, together with the other accidents, remains the same. Cf. p. 144 n. 61.

whether accidents are present without substance, but believe with a simple faith that Christ's body and blood are truly contained there, and leave to those who have nothing else to do the argument about what contains them.

But perhaps they will say: "Aristotle teaches that in an affirmative proposition subject and predicate must be identical," or (to quote the monster's own words in the sixth book of his *Metaphysics*)[71]: "An affirmative proposition requires the agreement of the subject and the predicate." They interpret agreement to mean identity. Hence, when I say: "This is my body," the subject cannot be identical with the bread, but must be identical with the body of Christ.

What shall we say when Aristotle and the doctrines of men are made to be the arbiters of such lofty and divine matters? Why do we not put aside such curiosity and cling simply to the words of Christ, willing to remain in ignorance of what takes place here and content that the real body of Christ is present by virtue of the words?[72] Or is it necessary to comprehend the manner of the divine working in every detail?

But what do they say when Aristotle admits that all of the categories[73] of accidents are themselves a subject—although he grants that substance is the chief subject? Hence for him "this is white," "this large," "this something," are all subjects, of which something is predicated. If that is correct, I ask: If a "transubstantiation" must be assumed in order that Christ's body may not be identified with the bread, why not also a "transaccidentation," in order that

---

71. Luther should have referred not to the *Metaphysics* but to the *Organon*, where in chapter 6 of *De interpretatione*, Aristotle indicates that for affirmative and negative propositions having the same subject and predicate to be truly contradictory, subject and predicate must be unequivocally (univocally) identical. In chapter 10 he holds that "the subject and predicate in an affirmation must each denote a single thing." Richard McKeon (ed.), *The Basic Works of Aristotle* (New York, 1941), pp. 43, 49.

72. Cf. *The Blessed Sacrament. LW* 35, 60-61.

73. Namely: substance, quantity, quality, relation, place, time, position, state, action, and affection.

the body of Christ may not be identified with the accidents? For the same danger remains if one understands the subject to be "this white or this round[74] is my body." And for the same reason that a "transubstantiation" must be assumed, a "transaccidentation" must also be assumed, because of this identity of subject and predicate.

If however, merely by an act of intellect, you can do away with the accident, so that it will not be regarded as the subject when you say, "this is my body," why not with equal ease transcend the substance of the bread, if you do not want it to be regarded either as the subject, so that "this my body" is no less in the substance than in the accident? After all, this is a divine work performed by God's almighty power, which can operate just as much and just as well in the accident as it can in the substance.

Let us not dabble too much in philosophy, however. Does not Christ appear to have anticipated this curiosity admirably by saying of the wine, not *Hoc est sanguis meus,* but *Hic est sanguis meus?* [Mark 14:24]. He speaks even more clearly when he brings in the word "cup" and says: "This cup [*Hic calix*] is the new testament in my blood" [Luke 22:20; I Cor. 11:25]. Does it not seem as though he desired to keep us in a simple faith, sufficient for us to believe that his blood was in the cup? For my part, if I cannot fathom how the bread is the body of Christ, yet I will take my reason captive to the obedience of Christ [II Cor. 10:5], and clinging simply to his words, firmly believe not only that the body of Christ is in the bread, but that the bread is the body of Christ. My warrant for this is the words which say: "He took bread, and when he had given thanks, he broke it and said, 'Take, eat, this (that is, this bread, which he had taken and broken) is my body'" [I Cor. 11:23-24]. And Paul says: "The bread which we break, is

---

74. i.e., the host, or wafer.

it not a participation in the body of Christ?" [I Cor. 10:16]. He does not say "in the bread there is," but "the bread itself is[75] the participation in the body of Christ." What does it matter if philosophy cannot fathom this? The Holy Spirit is greater than Aristotle. Does philosophy fathom their transubstantiation? Why, they themselves admit that here all philosophy breaks down. That the pronoun "this," in both Greek and Latin, is referred to "body," is due to the fact that in both of these languages the two words are of the same gender. In Hebrew, however, which has no neuter gender, "this" is referred to "bread," so that it would be proper to say *Hic* [bread] *est corpus meum*. Actually, the idiom of the language[76] and common sense both prove that the subject ["this"] obviously points to the bread and not to the body, when he says: *Hoc est corpus meum, das ist meyn leyp*, that is, "This very bread here [*iste panis*] is my body."

Thus, what is true in regard to Christ is also true in regard to the sacrament. In order for the divine nature to dwell in him bodily [Col. 2:9], it is not necessary for the human nature to be transbustantiated and the divine nature contained under the accidents of the human nature. Both natures are simply there in their entirety, and it is truly said: "This man is God; this God is man." Even though philosophy cannot grasp this, faith grasps it nonetheless. And the authority of God's Word is greater than the capacity of our intellect to grasp it. In like manner, it is not necessary in the sacrament that the bread and wine be transubstantiated and that Christ be contained under their accidents in order that the real body and real blood may be present. But both remain there at the same time, and it is truly said: "This bread is my body; this wine is my

---

75. Not *in pane est* but *ipse panis est*.
76. Luther assumes that the language Jesus spoke on that occasion was certainly not Greek, but probably Hebrew.

blood," and vice versa. Thus I will understand it for the time being to the honor of the holy words of God, to which I will allow no violence to be done by petty human arguments, nor will I allow them to be twisted into meanings which are foreign to them. At the same time, I permit other men to follow the other opinion, which is laid down in the decree, *Firmiter*,[77] only let them not press us to accept their opinions as articles of faith (as I have said above).[78]

The third captivity of this sacrament is by far the most wicked of all, in consequence of which there is no opinion more generally held or more firmly believed in the church today than this, that the mass is a good work and a sacrifice. And this abuse has brought an endless host of other abuses in its train, so that the faith of this sacrament has become utterly extinct and the holy sacrament has been turned into mere merchandise, a market, and a profit-making business. Hence participations,[79] brotherhoods,[80] intercessions, merits, anniversaries,[81] memorial days[82] and the like wares are bought and sold, traded and bartered, in the church. On these the priests and monks depend for their entire livelihood.

I am attacking a difficult matter, an abuse perhaps impossible to uproot, since through century-long custom and the common consent of men it has become so firmly entrenched that it would be necessary to abolish most of the

---

77. *Firmiter, Decretalium Gregorii IX*, lib. i, tit I: *de summa trinitate et fide catholica*, cap. 1, sec. 3, *Corpus Iuris Canonici, op. cit.*, II col. 5.
78. Cf. p. 143.
79. Though not actually present, one could obtain spiritual "participation" in masses which, for example, were read in a monastery.
80. These confraternities and sodalities paid to have masses said for them, and engaged in devotional exercises for gaining merit. Membership in such an association provided each person the benefits accruing from the "good works" (prayers and attendance at masses) of all the other members.
81. Masses said on behalf of the soul of a deceased person daily for a year or annually on the anniversary of his death.
82. Masses for the dead were read on memorial days.

books now in vogue, and to alter almost the entire external form of the churches and introduce, or rather reintroduce, a totally different kind of ceremonies. But my Christ lives, and we must be careful to give more heed to the Word of God than to all the thoughts of men and of angels. I will perform the duties of my office and bring to light the facts in the case. As I have received the truth freely [Matt. 10:8], I will impart it without malice. For the rest let every man look to his own salvation; I will do my part faithfully so that no one may be able to cast on me the blame for his lack of faith and his ignorance of the truth when we appear before the judgment seat of Christ.

In the first place, in order that we might safely and happily attain to a true and free knowledge of this sacrament, we must be particularly careful to put aside whatever has been added to its original simple institution by the zeal and devotion of men: such things as vestments, ornaments, chants, prayers, organs, candles, and the whole pageantry of outward things.[83] We must turn our eyes and hearts simply to the institution of Christ and this alone, and set nothing before us but the very word of Christ by which he instituted the sacrament, made it perfect, and committed it to us. For in that word, and in that word alone, reside the power, the nature, and the whole substance of the mass. All the rest is the work of man, added to the word of Christ, and the mass can be held and remain a mass just as well without them. Now the words of Christ, in which he instituted this sacrament, are these:

"Now as they were eating, Jesus took bread, and blessed, and broke it, and gave it to his disciples and said, 'Take, eat; this is my body, which is given for you.' And he took a cup, and when he had given thanks he gave it to them, saying, 'Drink of it, all of you; for this cup is the new testament in my blood, which is poured out for you and for

---

83. Cf. *A Treatise on the New Testament, that is, the Holy Mass.* LW 35, 81-82.

many for the forgiveness of sins. Do this in remembrance of me.' "[84]

These words the Apostle also delivers and more fully expounds in I Cor. 11 [:23-26]. On them we must rest; on them we must build as on a firm rock, if we would not be carried about with every wind of doctrine [Eph. 4:14], as we have till now been carried about by the wicked doctrines of men who reject the truth [Titus 1:14]. For in these words nothing is omitted that pertains to the completeness, the use, and the blessing of this sacrament; and nothing is included that is superfluous and not necessary for us to know. Whoever sets aside these words and meditates or teaches concerning the mass will teach monstrous and wicked doctrines, as they have done who have made of the sacrament an *opus operatum*[85] and a sacrifice.

Let this stand, therefore, as our first and infallible proposition—the mass or Sacrament of the Altar is Christ's testament, which he left behind him at his death to be distributed among his believers. For that is the meaning of his words, "This cup is the new testament in my blood" [Luke 22:20; I Cor. 11:25]. Let this truth stand, I say, as the immovable foundation on which we shall base all that we have to say. For, as you will see, we are going to overthrow all the godless opinions of men which have been imported into this most precious sacrament. Christ, who is the truth, truly says that this is the new testament in his blood, poured out for us [Luke 22:20]. Not without reason

---

84. Luther's rendering of the Words of Institution is similar to that of the canon of the mass in that it represents a harmony of the several scriptural accounts, incorporating features from all of them—Matt. 26:26-28; Mark 14:22-24; Luke 22:19-20; I Cor. 11:23-25. It differs from the canon of the mass in that it excludes all phrases not explicitly found in the scriptural accounts themselves, Vulgate version. Cf. *PE* 6, 74, 107-08, 126, 160.

85. A work accomplished or finished, which is supposed to impart grace simply by virtue of its having been properly performed, without reference to any faith or lack of faith on the part of the person for whom it is performed. Cf. *The Blessed Sacrament, LW* 35, 63-64, where Luther discusses this term.

do I dwell on this sentence; the matter is of no small moment, and must be most deeply impressed on our minds.

Thus, if we enquire what a testament is, we shall learn at the same time what the mass is, what its right use and blessing, and what its wrong use.

A testament, as everyone knows, is a promise made by one about to die, in which he designates his bequest and appoints his heirs. A testament, therefore, involves first, the death of the testator, and second, the promise of an inheritance and the naming of the heir. Thus Paul discusses at length the nature of a testament in Rom. 4, Gal. 3 and 4, and Heb. 9. We see the same thing clearly also in these words of Christ. Christ testifies concerning his death when he says: "This is my body, which is given, this is my blood, which is poured out" [Luke 22:19-20]. He names and designates the bequest when he says "for the forgiveness of sins" [Matt. 26:28]. But he appoints the heirs when he says "For you [Luke 22:19-20; I Cor. 11:24] and for many" [Matt. 26:28; Mark 14:24], that is, for those who accept and believe the promise of the testator. For here it is faith that makes men heirs, as we shall see.

You see, therefore, that what we call the mass is a promise of the forgiveness of sins made to us by God, and such a promise as has been confirmed by the death of the Son of God. For the only difference between a promise and a testament is that the testament involves the death of the one who makes it. A testator is a promiser who is about to die, while a promiser (if I may put it thus) is a testator who is not about to die. This testament of Christ is foreshadowed in all the promises of God from the beginning of the world; indeed, whatever value those ancient promises possessed was altogether derived from this new promise that was to come in Christ. Hence the words "compact," "convenant," and "testament of the Lord" occur so frequently in the Scriptures. These words signified that God would one day die. "For where there is a testament, the death of the testator must of necessity occur" (Heb. 9 [:16]). Now God made a testament; therefore, it was necessary that he should die. But God could not die unless he became man. Thus the incarnation and the death of Christ are both comprehended most concisely in this one word, "testament."

From the above it will at once be seen what is the right and what is the wrong use of the mass, and what is the worthy and what the unworthy preparation for it. If the mass is a promise, as has been said, then access to it is to be gained, not with any works, or powers, or merits of one's own, but by faith alone. For where there is the Word of the promising God, there must necessarily be the faith of the accepting man. It is plain therefore, that the beginning of our salvation is a faith which clings to the Word of the promising God, who, without any effort on our part, in free and unmerited mercy takes the initiative and offers us the word of his promise. "He sent forth his word, and thus [sic] healed them,"[86] not: "He accepted our work, and thus healed us." First of all there is God's Word. After it follows faith; after faith, love; then love does every good work, for it does no wrong, indeed, it is the fulfilling of the law [Rom. 13:10]. In no other way can man come to God or deal with him than through faith. That is to say, that the author of salvation is not man, by any works of his own, but God, through his promise; and that all things depend on, and are upheld and preserved by, the word of his power [Heb. 1:3], through which he brought us forth, to be a kind of first fruits of his creatures [Jas. 1:18].

Thus, in order to raise up Adam after the fall, God gave him this promise when he said to the serpent: "I will put enmity between you and the woman, and between your seed and her seed; he shall bruise your head, and you shall bruise his heel" [Gen. 3:15]. In this word of promise Adam, together with his descendants, was carried as it were in

_____
86. Ps. 107:20. *Sic* is Luther's own interpolation into the Vulgate text.

God's bosom, and by faith in it he was preserved, waiting patiently for the woman who should bruise the serpent's head, as God had promised. And in that faith and expectation he died, not knowing when or who she would be yet never doubting that she would come. For such a promise, being the truth of God, preserves even in hell those who believe it and wait for it. After this came another promise, made to Noah—to last until the time of Abraham—when a bow was set in the clouds as a sign of the covenant [Gen. 9:12-17], by faith in which Noah and his descendants found God gracious. After that, he promised Abraham that all the nations should be blessed in his seed [Gen. 22:18]. And this is Abraham's bosom [Luke 16:22], into which his descendants have been received. Then to Moses and the children of Israel [Deut. 18:18], especially to David [II Sam. 7:12-16], he gave the plainest promise of Christ, and thereby at last made clear what the promise to the men of old really was.

And so it finally came to the most perfect promise of all, that of the new testament, in which, with plain words, life and salvation are freely promised, and actually granted to those who believe the promise. And he distinguishes this testament from the old one by a particular mark when he calls it the "new testament" [Luke 22:20; I Cor. 11:25]. For the old testament given through Moses was not a promise of forgiveness of sins or of eternal things, but of temporal things, namely, of the land of Canaan, by which no man was renewed in spirit to lay hold on the heavenly inheritance. Wherefore also it was necessary that, as a figure of Christ, a dumb beast should be slain, in whose blood the same testament might be confirmed, as the blood corresponded to the testament and the sacrifice corresponded to the promise. But here Christ says "the new testament in my blood" [Luke 22:20; I Cor. 11:25], not somebody else's, but his own, by which grace is promised through the Spirit for the forgiveness of sins, that we may obtain the inheritance.

According to its substance, therefore, the mass is nothing but the aforesaid words of Christ: "Take and eat, etc." [Matt. 26:26], as if he were saying: "Behold, O sinful and condemned man, out of the pure and unmerited love with which I love you, and by the will of the Father of mercies [II Cor. 1:3], apart from any merit or desire of yours, I promise you in these words the forgiveness of all your sins and life everlasting. And that you may be absolutely certain of this irrevocable promise of mine, I shall give my body and pour out my blood, confirming this promise by my very death, and leaving you my body and blood as a sign and memorial of this same promise. As often as you partake of them, remember me, proclaim and praise my love and bounty toward you, and give thanks."

From this you will see that nothing else is needed for a worthy holding of mass than a faith that relies confidently on this promise, believes Christ to be true in these words of his, and does not doubt that these infinite blessings have been bestowed upon it. Hard on this faith there follows, of itself, a most sweet stirring of the heart, whereby the spirit of man is enlarged and enriched (that is love, given by the Holy Spirit through faith in Christ), so that he is drawn to Christ, that gracious and bounteous testator, and made a thoroughly new and different man. Who would not shed tears of gladness, indeed, almost faint for joy in Christ, if he believed with unshaken faith that this inestimable promise of Christ belonged to him? How could he help loving so great a benefactor, who of his own accord offers, promises, and grants such great riches and this eternal inheritance to one who is unworthy and deserving of something far different?

Therefore it is our one and only misfortune that we have many masses in the world, and yet none, or very few of us, recognize, consider, and receive these promises and riches that are offered to us. Actually, during the mass, we should do nothing with greater zeal (indeed, it demands all our

158

zeal) than to set before our eyes, meditate upon, and ponder these words, these promises of Christ—for they truly constitute the mass itself—in order to exercise, nourish, increase, and strengthen our faith in them by this daily remembrance. For this is what he commands, when he says: "Do this in remembrance of me" [Luke 22:19; I Cor. 11:24]. This should be done by the preachers of the gospel in order to impress this promise faithfully upon the people, to commend it to them, and to awaken their faith in it.

But how many are there today who know that the mass is the promise of Christ? I will say nothing of those godless preachers of fables, who teach human ordinances instead of this great promise. And even if they teach these words of Christ, they do not teach them as a promise or testament, neither therefore as a means of obtaining faith.

What we deplore in this captivity is that nowadays they take every precaution that no layman should hear these words of Christ, as if they were too sacred to be delivered to the common people. So mad are we priests[87] that we arrogate to ourselves alone the so-called words of consecration, to be said secretly,[88] yet in such a way that they do not profit even us, for we too fail to regard them as promises or as a testament for the strengthening of the faith. Instead of believing them, we reverence them with I know not what superstitious and godless fancies. What else is Satan trying to do to us through this misfortune of ours but to remove every trace of the [true] mass out of the church, though he is meanwhile at work filling every corner of the globe with [false] masses, that is, with abuses and mockeries of God's testament—burdening the world more and more heavily with most grievous sins of idolatry, to its deeper condemnation? For what more sinful idolatry can there be than to

87. Cf. p. 135 n. 40.
88. The words of consecration, indeed of the whole canon of the mass, were spoken very softly. Cf. *The Abomination of the Secret Mass* (1525) in *LW* 36, 310 and 314.

abuse God's promises with perverse opinions and to neglect or extinguish faith in them?

For God does not deal, nor has he ever dealt, with man otherwise than through a word of promise, as I have said. We in turn cannot deal with God otherwise than through faith in the Word of his promise. He does not desire works, nor has he need of them; rather we deal with men and with ourselves on the basis of works. But God has need of this: that we consider him faithful in his promises [Heb. 10:23], and patiently persist in this belief, and thus worship him with faith, hope, and love. It is in this way that he obtains his glory among us, since it is not of ourselves who run, but of him who shows mercy [Rom. 9:16], promises, and gives, that we have and hold all good things. Behold, this is that true worship and service of God which we ought to perform in the mass. But if the words of promise are not delivered, what exercise of faith can there be? And without faith, who can have hope or love? Without faith, hope, and love, what services of God can there be? There is no doubt, therefore, that in our day all priests and monks, together with their bishops and all their superiors, are idolators, living in a most perilous state by reason of this ignorance, abuse, and mockery of the mass, or sacrament, or promise of God.

For anyone can easily see that these two, promise and faith, must necessarily go together. For without the promise there is nothing to be believed; while without faith the promise is useless, since it is established and fulfilled through faith. From this everyone will readily gather that the mass, since it is nothing but promise, can be approached and observed only in faith. Without this faith, whatever else is brought to it by way of prayers, preparations, works, signs, or gestures are incitements to impiety rather than exercises of piety. It usually happens that those who are thus prepared imagine themselves legitimately entitled to approach the altar, when in reality they are less prepared

than at any other time or by any other work, by reason of
the unbelief which they bring with them. How many cele-
brants you can see everywhere, every day, who imagine
they—wretched men—have committed criminal offenses
when they make some petty mistake, such as wearing the
wrong vestment, or forgetting to wash their hands, or stumbling over their prayers! But the fact that they have no
regard for or faith in the mass itself, namely, the divine
promise, causes them not the slightest qualms of conscience.
O worthless religion of this age of ours, the most godless
and thankless of all ages!

Hence the only worthy preparation and proper observance is faith, the faith by which we believe in the mass,
that is, in the divine promise. Whoever, therefore, desires
to approach the altar or receive the sacrament, let him
beware lest he appear empty-handed [Exod. 23:15; 34:20;
Deut. 16:16] before the face of the Lord God. But he will
be empty-handed unless he has faith in the mass, or this
new testament. By what godless work could he sin more
grievously against the truth of God, than by this unbelief
of his? By it, as much as in him lies, he convicts God of
being a liar and a maker of empty promises. The safest
course, therefore, will be to go to the mass in the same
spirit in which you would go to hear any other promise of
God, that is, prepared not to do or contribute much yourself, but to believe and accept all that is promised you
there, or proclaimed as promises through the ministry of
the priest. If you do not come in this spirit, beware of attending at all, for you will surely be going to your condemnation [I Cor. 11:29].

I was right then in saying that the whole power of the
mass consists in the words of Christ, in which he testifies
that forgiveness of sins is bestowed on all those who believe
that his body is given and his blood poured out for them.
This is why nothing is more important for those who go to
hear mass than to ponder these words diligently and in full

faith. Unless they do this, all else that they do is in vain. This is surely true, that to every promise of his, God usually adds some sign as a memorial or remembrance of the promise, so that thereby we may serve him the more diligently and he may admonish us the more effectually. Thus, when he promised Noah that he would not again destroy the world by a flood, he added his bow in the clouds, to show that he would be mindful of his covenant [Gen. 9:8-17]. And after promising Abraham the inheritance in his seed, he gave him circumcision as a mark of his justification by faith [Gen. 17:3-11]. Thus he granted to Gideon the dry and the wet fleece to confirm his promise of victory over the Midianites [Judg. 6:36-40]. And through Isaiah he offered to Ahaz a sign that he would conquer the king of Syria and Samaria, to confirm in him his faith in the promise [Isa. 7:10-17]. And we read of many such signs of the promises of God in the Scriptures.

So in the mass also, the foremost promise of all, he adds as a memorial sign of such a great promise his own body and his own blood in the bread and wine, when he says: "Do this in remembrance of me" [Luke 22:19; I Cor. 11:24-25]. And so in baptism, to the words of promise he adds the sign of immersion in water. We may learn from this that in every promise of God two things are presented to us, the word and the sign, so that we are to understand the word to be the testament, but the sign to be the sacrament. Thus, in the mass, the word of Christ is the testament, and the bread and wine are the sacrament. And as there is greater power in the word than in the sign, so there is greater power in the testament than in the sacrament; for a man can have and use the word or testament apart from the sign or sacrament. "Believe," says Augustine, "and you have eaten."[89] But what does one believe, other than the word of the one who promises? Therefore I can hold mass every

89. Cf. p. 133 n. 33.

day, indeed, every hour, for I can set the words of Christ before me and with them feed and strengthen my faith as often as I choose. This is a truly spiritual eating and drinking.

Here you may see what great things our theologians of the *Sentences*[90] have produced in this matter. In the first place, not one of them treats of that which is first and foremost, namely, the testament and the word of promise. And thus they make us forget faith and the whole power of the mass. In addition, they discuss exclusively the second part of the mass, namely, the sign or sacrament; yet in such a way that here too they do not teach faith, but their preparations and *opera operata*,[91] participations[92] and fruits of the mass. They come then to the profundities, babble of transubstantiation and endless other metaphysical trivialities, destroy the proper understanding and use of both sacrament and testament together with faith as such, and cause Christ's people to forget their God—as the prophet says, days without number [Jer. 2:32]. Let the others tabulate the various benefits of hearing mass; you just apply your mind to this, that you may say and believe with the prophet that God has here prepared a table before you in the presence of your enemies [Ps. 23:5], at which your faith may feed and grow fat. But your faith is fed only with the word of divine promise, for "Man shall not live by bread alone, but by every word that proceeds from the mouth of God" [Deut. 8:3; Matt. 4:4]. Hence, in the mass you must pay closest heed above all to the word of promise, as to a most lavish banquet—your utterly green pastures and sacred still waters [Ps. 23:2], in order that you might esteem this word above everything else, trust in it supremely, and cling to it most firmly, even through death and all sins. If you do this, you will obtain not merely those

90. Commentators on Peter Lombard's textbook. Cf. p. 144 n. 60.
91. Cf. p. 154 n. 85.
92. Cf. p. 152 n. 79.

tiny drops and crumbs of "fruits of the mass" which some have superstitiously invented, but the very fountainhead of life, namely, that faith in the Word out of which every good thing flows, as is said in John 4:[93] "He who believes in me, 'Out of his heart shall flow rivers of living water.'" And again, "Whoever drinks of the water that I shall give him, it will become in him a spring of water welling up to eternal life" [John 4:14].

Now there are two things that are constantly assailing us, so that we fail to gather the fruits of the mass. The first is that we are sinners, and unworthy of such great things because of our utter worthlessness. The second is that, even if we were worthy, these things are so high that our faint-hearted nature does not dare to aspire to them or hope for them. For who would not simply stand awe-struck before the forgiveness of sins and life everlasting rather than seeking after them, once he had weighed properly the magnitude of the blessings which come through them, namely, to have God as father, to be his son and heir of all his goods! Against this twofold faintness of ours we must lay hold on the word of Christ, and fix our gaze much more steadfastly on it than on these thoughts of our own weakness. For "great are the works of the Lord, studied by all who have pleasure in them" [Ps. 111:2], who is able to give "more abundantly than all that we ask or think" [Eph. 3:20]. If they did not surpass our worthiness, our grasp, and all our thoughts, they would not be divine. Thus Christ also encourages us when he says: "Fear not, little flock, for it is your Father's good pleasure to give you the kingdom" [Luke 12:32]. For it is just this incomprehensible overflowing of God's goodness, showered upon us through Christ, that moves us above all to love him most ardently in return, to be drawn to him with fullest confidence, and

93. John 7:38. Luther apparently had his next quotation in mind when he cited John 4.

despising all else, be ready to suffer all things for him. Wherefore this sacrament is rightly called "a fountain of love."

Let us take an illustration of this from human experience.[94] If a very rich lord were to bequeath a thousand gulden to a beggar or to an unworthy and wicked servant, it is certain that he would boldly claim and accept them without regard to his unworthiness and the greatness of the bequest. And if anyone should seek to oppose him on the grounds of his unworthiness and the large amount of the legacy, what do you suppose the man would say? He would likely say: "What is that to you? What I accept, I accept not on my merits or by any right that I may personally have to it. I know that I am receiving more than a worthless one like me deserves; indeed, I have deserved the very opposite. But I claim what I claim by the right of a bequest and of another's goodness. If to him it was not an unworthy thing to bequeath so great a sum to an unworthy person, why should I refuse to accept it because of my unworthiness? Indeed, it is for this very reason that I cherish all the more his unmerited gift—because I am unworthy!" With that same thought every man ought to fortify his conscience against all qualms and scruples, so that he may lay hold on the promise of Christ with unwavering faith, and take the greatest care to approach the sacrament not trusting in confession, prayer, and preparation, but rather, despairing of all these, with firm confidence in Christ who gives the promise. For, as we have said often enough, the word of promise must reign alone here in pure faith; such faith is the one and only sufficient preparation.

Hence we see how great is God's wrath with us, in that he has permitted godless teachers to conceal the words of this testament from us, and thereby to extinguish this same

---

94. Repeated in a similar context in *A Treatise on the New Testament, that is, the Holy Mass* (1520). LW 35, 89-90.

faith, as far as they could. It is already easy to see what is the inevitable result of this extinguishing of the faith, namely, the most godless superstition of works. For where faith dies and the word of faith is silent, there works and the prescribing of works immediately crowd into their place. By them we have been carried away out of our own land, as into a Babylonian captivity, and despoiled of all our precious possessions. This has been the fate of the mass; it has been converted by the teaching of godless men into a good work. They themselves call it an *opus operatum,*[95] and by it they presume themselves to be all-powerful with God. Next they proceed to the very height of madness, and after inventing the lie that the mass is effective simply by virtue of the act having been performed, they add another one to the effect that the mass is none the less profitable to others even if it is harmful to some wicked priest who may be celebrating it. On such a foundation of sand they base their applications, participations,[96] brotherhoods,[97] anniversaries,[98] and numberless other lucrative and profitable schemes of that kind.

These fraudulent disguises are so powerful, so numerous. and so firmly entrenched that you can scarcely prevail against them unless you exercise unremitting care and bear well in mind what the mass is and what has been said above. You have seen that the mass is nothing else than the divine promise or testament of Christ, sealed with the sacrament of his body and blood. If that is true, you will understand that it cannot possibly be in any way a work; nobody can possibly do any thing in it, neither can it be dealt with in any other way than by faith alone. However, faith is not a work, but the lord and life of all works.[99]

---

95. Cf. p. 154 n. 85.
96. Cf. p. 152 n. 79.
97. Cf. p. 152 n. 80.
98. Cf. p. 152 n. 81.
99. On the relation between faith and works compare *Treatise on Good Works* (1520), where Luther says faith is the first and highest of all good works. *LW* 44, 23-24. Cf. also p. 184 below.

Who in the world is so foolish as to regard a promise received by him, or a testament given to him as a good work, which he renders to the testator by his acceptance of it? What heir will imagine that he is doing his departed father a kindness by accepting the terms of the will and the inheritance it bequeaths to him? What godless audacity is it, therefore, when we who are to receive the testament of God come as those who would perform a good work for him! This ignorance of the testament, this captivity of so great a sacrament—are they not too sad for tears? When we ought to be grateful for benefits received, we come arrogantly to give that which we ought to take. With unheard-of perversity we mock the mercy of the giver by giving as a work the thing we receive as a gift, so that the testator, instead of being a dispenser of his own goods, becomes the recipient of ours. Woe to such sacrilege!

Who has ever been so mad as to regard baptism as a good work, or what candidate for baptism has believed that he was performing a work which he might offer to God on behalf of himself and communicate to others? If, then, there is no good work that can be communicated to others in this one sacrament and testament, neither will there be any in the mass, since it too is nothing else than a testament and sacrament. Hence it is a manifest and wicked error to offer or apply the mass for sins, for satisfactions, for the dead, or for any needs whatsoever of one's own or of others. You will readily see the obvious truth of this if you firmly hold that the mass is a divine promise, which can benefit no one, be applied to no one, intercede for no one, and be communicated to no one, except only to him who believes with a faith of his own. Who can receive or apply, in behalf of another, the promise of God, which demands the personal faith of each one individually? Can I give to another the promise of God, even if he does not believe? Can I believe for another, or cause another to believe? But this is what must happen if I am able to apply and communicate the mass to others; for there are but two things in the mass, the divine promise and the human faith, the latter accepting what the former promises. But if it is true that I can do this, then I can also hear and believe the gospel for another, I can be baptized for another, I can be absolved from sins for another, I can also partake of the Sacrament of the Altar for another, and —to go through the list of their sacraments also—I can marry a wife for another, get ordained for another, be confirmed for another, and receive extreme unction for another!

In short, why did not Abraham believe for all the Jews? Why was faith in the promise made to Abraham demanded of every individual Jew?

Therefore, let this irrefutable truth stand fast: Where there is a divine promise, there every one must stand on his own feet; his own personal faith is demanded, he will give an account for himself and bear his own load [Gal. 6:5]; as it is said in the last chapter of Mark [16:16]: "He who believes and is baptized will be saved; but he who does not believe will be condemned." Even so each one can derive personal benefit from the mass only by his own personal faith. It is absolutely impossible to commune on behalf of anyone else. Just as the priest is unable to administer the sacrament to anyone on behalf of another, but administers the same sacrament to each one individually by himself. For in consecrating and administering, the priests are our servants. Through them we are not offering a good work or communicating something in an active sense. Rather, we are receiving through them the promises and the sign; we are being communicated unto in the passive sense. This is the view that has persisted with respect to the laity right up to the present day, for of them it is said not that they do something good but that they receive it. But the priests have strayed into godless ways; out of the sacrament and testament of God, which ought to be a good gift received, they have made for themselves a good deed performed, which they then give to others and offer up to God.

But you will say: What is this? Will you not overturn the practice and teaching of all the churches and monasteries, by virtue of which they have flourished all these centuries? For the mass is the foundation of their anniversaries, intercessions, applications, communications, etc., that is to say, of their fat income. I answer: This is the very thing that has constrained me to write of the captivity of the church. For it is in this manner that the sacred testament of God has been forced into the service of a most impious traffic. It has come through the opinions and ordinances of wicked men, who, passing over the Word of God, have dished up to us the thoughts of their own hearts and led the whole world astray. What do I care about the number and influence of those who are in this error? The truth is mightier than all of them. If you are able to refute Christ, who teaches that the mass is a testament and a sacrament, then I will admit that they are in the right. Or, if you can bring yourself to say that that man is doing a good work who receives the benefit of the testament, or to that end uses this sacrament of promise, then I will gladly condemn my teachings. But since you can do neither, why do you hesitate to turn your back on the multitude who go after evil? Why do you hesitate to give God the glory and to confess his truth—that all priests today are perversely mistaken who regard the mass as a work by which they may relieve their own needs and those of others, whether dead or alive? I am uttering unheard of and startling things, but if you will consider what the mass is, you will realize that I have spoken the truth. The fault lies with our false sense of security, which blinds us to the wrath of God that is raging against us.

I am ready to admit, however, that the prayers which we pour out before God when we are gathered together to partake of the mass are good works or benefits, which we impart, apply and communicate to one another, and which we offer for one another. Thus James [5:16] teaches us to pray for one another that we may be healed, and Paul in I Tim. 2[:1-2] commands "that supplications, prayers, and intercessions be made for all men, for kings and all who are in high positions." Now these are not the mass, but works of the mass—if the prayers of heart and lips may be called works—for they flow from the faith that is kindled or increased in the sacrament. For the mass, or the promise of God, is not fulfilled by praying, but only by believing. However, as believers we pray and perform every good work. But what priest offers up the sacrifice in this sense, that he believes he is offering up only the prayers? They all imagine that they are offering up Christ himself to God the Father as an all-sufficient sacrifice, and performing a good work for all those whom they intend to benefit, for they put their trust in the work which the mass accomplishes, and they do not ascribe this work to prayer. In this way the error has gradually grown, until they have come to ascribe to the sacrament what belongs to the prayers, and to offer to God what should be received as a benefit.

We must therefore sharply distinguish the testament and sacrament itself from the prayers which we offer at the same time. Not only this, but we must also bear in mind that the prayers avail utterly nothing, either to him who offers them or to those for whom they are offered, unless the testament is first received in faith, so that it will be faith that offers the prayers; for faith alone is heard, as James teaches in his first chapter [Jas. 1:6]. There is therefore a great difference between prayer and the mass. Prayer may be extended to as many persons as one desires, while the mass is received only by the person who believes for himself, and only to the extent that he believes. It cannot be given either to God or to men. Rather it is God alone who through the ministration of the priest gives it to men, and men receive it by faith alone without any works or merits. Nor would anyone dare to be so foolish as to assert that a ragged beggar does a good work when he comes to receive a gift from a rich man. But the mass (as I have said)[100] is the gift of the divine promise, proffered to all men by the hand of the priest.

It is certain, therefore, that the mass is not a work which may be communicated to others, but the object of faith (as has been said),[101] for the strengthening and nourishing of each one's own faith.

Now there is yet a second stumbling block that must be removed, and this is much greater and the most dangerous of all. It is the common belief that the mass is a sacrifice, which is offered to God. Even the words of the canon[102] seem to imply this, when they speak of "these gifts, these presents, these holy sacrifices," and further on "this offering." Prayer is also made, in so many words, "that the sacrifice may be accepted even as the sacrifice of Abel," etc. Hence Christ is termed "the sacrifice of the altar." Added to these are the sayings of the holy fathers, the great number of examples, and the widespread practice uniformly observed throughout the world.

Over against all these things, firmly entrenched as they are, we must resolutely set the words and example of Christ. For unless we firmly hold that the mass is the promise or testament of Christ, as the words clearly say, we shall lose the whole gospel and all its comfort. Let us permit nothing to prevail against these words—even though an angel from heaven should teach otherwise [Gal. 1:8]—for they contain nothing about a work or a sacrifice. Moreover, we also have the example of Christ on our side. When he instituted this

---

100. Cf. pp. 154-63.
101. *Ibid.*
102. The canon of the mass is the invariable part of the liturgy of the mass in which the consecration of the bread and wine is effected. Its text was translated by Luther from the Latin in his treatise on *The Abomination of the Secret Mass* (1525), and appears in *LW* 36, 314-327.

sacrament and established this testament at the Last Supper, Christ did not offer himself to God the Father, nor did he perform a good work on behalf of others, but, sitting at the table, he set this same testament before each one and proffered to him the sign. Now, the more closely our mass resembles that first mass of all, which Christ performed at the Last Supper, the more Christian it will be. But Christ's mass was most simple, without any display or vestments, gestures, chants, or other ceremonies, so that if it had been necessary to offer the mass as a sacrifice, then Christ's institution of it was not complete.

Not that any one should revile the church universal for embellishing and amplifying the mass with many additional rites and ceremonies. But what we contend for is this: No one should be deceived by the glamor of the ceremonies and entangled in the multitude of pompous forms, and thus lose the simplicity of the mass itself, and indeed practice a sort of transubstantiation by losing sight of the simple "substance" of the mass and clinging to the manifold "accidents" of outward pomp. For whatever has been added to the word and example of Christ is an "accident" of the mass, and ought to be regarded just as we regard the so-called monstrances and corporal cloths in which the host itself is contained. Therefore, just as disturbing a testament or accepting a promise differs diametrically from offering a sacrifice, so it is a contradiction in terms to call the mass a sacrifice, for the former is something that we receive and the latter is something that we give. The same thing cannot be received and offered at the same time, nor can it be both given and accepted by the same person, any more than our prayer can be the same thing as that which our prayer obtains, or the act of praying be the same thing as the act of receiving that for which we pray.

What shall we say then of the canon of the mass and the patristic authorities? First of all, I would answer: If there were nothing at all to be said against them, it would be safer to reject them all than admit that the mass is a work or a sacrifice, lest we deny the word of Christ and destroy faith together with the mass. Nevertheless, in order to retain them, we shall say that we are instructed by the Apostle in I Cor. 11 [:21,33] that it was customary for Christ's believers, when they came together for mass, to bring with them food and drink. These they called "collections," and they distributed them among all who were in want, after the example of the apostles in Acts 4 [:34-35]. From this store was taken the portion of bread and wine that was consecrated in the sacrament.[103] And since all this store was consecrated by the word and prayer [I Tim. 4:5], by being "lifted up" according to the Hebrew rite of which we read in Moses [Lev. 8:27], the words and the rite of this lifting up or offering have come down to us, although the custom of bringing along and collecting that which was offered or lifted up has long since fallen into disuse. Thus, in Isa. 37 [:4] Hezekiah commanded Isaiah to lift up his prayer in the sight of God for the remnant. In the Psalms we read: "Lift up your hands to the holy place" [Ps. 134:2]. And again: "To thee I will lift up my hands" [Ps. 63:4]. And in I Tim. 2 [:8] "In every place lifting holy hands." For this reason the words "sacrifice" and "offering" must be taken to refer not to the sacrament and testament, but to the collections themselves. From this source also the word "collect" has come down to us for prayers said in the mass.

The same thing happens when the priest elevates the bread and the cup immediately after consecrating them. By this he does not show that he is offering anything to God, for he does not say a single word here about a victim or an offering. But this elevation is either a survival of that Hebrew rite of lifting up what was received with thanksgiving and returned to God, or else it is an admonition to us to provoke us to faith in this testament which the priest

---

103. Cf. *A Treatise on the New Testament, that is, the Holy Mass.* LW 35, 94.

has set forth and exhibited in the words of Christ, so that now he also shows us the sign of the testament. Thus the oblation of the bread properly accompanies the demonstrative "this" in the words, "this is my body," and by the sign the priest addresses us gathered about him; and in like manner the oblation of the cup properly accompanies the demonstrative "this" in the words, "this cup is the new testament, etc." For it is faith that the priest ought to awaken in us by this act of elevation. And would to God that as he elevates the sign, or sacrament, openly before our eyes, he might also sound in our ears the word, or testament, in a loud, clear voice, and in the language of the people, whatever it may be, in order that faith may be the more effectively awakened. For why may mass be said in Greek and Latin and Hebrew, but not in German or any other language?

Therefore, let the priests who offer the sacrifice of the mass in these corrupt and most perilous times take heed, first, that they do not refer to the sacrament the words of the greater and lesser canon,[104] together with the collects, because they smack too strongly of sacrifice. They should refer them instead to the bread and the wine to be consecrated, or to their own prayers. For the bread and wine are offered beforehand for blessing in order that they may be sanctified by the word and by prayer [I Tim. 4:5], but after they have been blessed and consecrated they are no longer offered, but received as a gift from God. And in this rite let the priest bear in mind that the gospel is to be set above all canons and collects devised by men, and that the gospel does not sanction the idea that the mass is a sacrifice, as has been shown.

---

104. In printed missals prior to the Council of Trent, *canon minor* was the term used to designate collectively those offertory prayers within the canon itself which immediately preceded the consecration of the elements. These collects were of comparatively late origin, coming only gradually into use during the late middle ages. Valentin Thalhofer, *Handbuch der katholischen Liturgik* (Freiburg im Breisgau, 1890), II, 159.

Further, when a priest celebrates public mass, he should determine to do nothing else than to commune himself and others by means of the mass. At the same time, however, he may offer prayers for himself and others, but he must beware lest he presume to offer the mass. But let him that holds private masses[105] determine to commune himself. The private mass does not differ in the least from the ordinary communion which any layman receives at the hand of the priest, and has no greater effect. The difference is in the prayers, and in the fact that the priest consecrates the elements for himself and administers them to himself. As far as the blessing[106] of the mass and sacrament is concerned we are all equals, whether we are priests or laymen.

If a priest is requested by others to celebrate so-called "votive" masses,[107] let him beware of accepting a fee for the mass, or of presuming to offer any votive sacrifice. Rather, he should take pains to refer all this to the prayers which he offers for the dead or the living, saying to himself: "Lo, I will go and receive the sacrament for myself alone, and while doing so I will pray for this one and that one." Thus he will receive his fee for the prayers, not for the mass, and can buy food and clothing with it. Let him not be disturbed because all the world holds and practices the contrary. You have the utmost certainty of the gospel, and by relying on it, you may well disregard the belief and opinions of men. But if you disregard me and insist upon offering the mass and not the prayers alone, remember that I have faithfully warned you, and that I will be without blame on the day of judgment; you will have to bear your sin alone. I have said what I was bound to say to you as

---

105. The private mass does not require the presence of a congregation. Besides the celebrant there need be present only a ministrant. There is no music; the mass is only read.

106. The *res sacramenti*. Cf. p. 137 n. 45.

107. Masses celebrated on the request of congregations or individuals in connection with specific purposes or occasions, or in honor of certain mysteries (e.g., of the Holy Trinity, of the Holy Spirit, or of angels).

brother to brother for your salvation; yours will be the gain if you observe it, yours the loss if you neglect it. And if some should even condemn what I have said, I will reply in the words of Paul: "But evil men and impostors will go on from bad to worse, deceiving and being deceived" [II Tim. 3:13].

From the above every one will readily understand the often quoted saying of Gregory[108]: "A mass celebrated by a wicked priest is not to be considered of less effect than one celebrated by a good priest. Neither would a mass of St. Peter have been better than that of Judas the traitor, if they had offered the sacrifice of the mass." This saying has served many as a cloak to cover their godless doings, and because of it they have invented the distinction between the *opus operatum* and the *opus operantis*,[109] so as to be free to lead wicked lives themselves and yet benefit other men. Gregory speaks the truth, only they misunderstand his words. For it is true beyond a question that the testament or sacrament is given and received through the ministration of wicked priests no less completely than through the ministration of the most saintly. For who has any doubt that the gospel is preached by the ungodly? Now the mass is part of the gospel; indeed, it is the sum and substance of it. For what is the whole gospel but the good tidings of the forgiveness of sins? Whatever can be said about forgiveness of sins and the mercy of God in the broadest and richest sense is all briefly comprehended in the word of this testament. For this reason popular sermons ought to be nothing else than expositions of the mass, or explanations of the divine promise of this testament; this would be to teach the faith and truly to edify the church. But in our day

108. Pope Gregory I (590-604).
109. The former is the properly executed performance of the ritual of the mass —"the work wrought" (cf. p. 154 n. 85). The latter is the inner disposition, the faith, either of the recipient or of the celebrant—"the work of the doer."

the expounders of the mass make mockery and jest with allegorical explanations of human ceremonies.

Therefore, just as a wicked priest may baptize, that is, apply the word of promise and the sign of water to the candidate for baptism, so he may also set forth the promise of this sacrament and administer it to those who partake, and even partake himself, as did Judas the traitor at the supper of the Lord [Matt. 26:23-25]. It still remains the same sacrament and testament, which works its own work in the believer but an "alien work"[110] in the unbeliever. But when it comes to offering a sacrifice the case is quite different. For not the mass but the prayers are offered to God, and therefore it is as plain as day that the offerings of a wicked priest avail nothing, but, as Gregory says again: When an unworthy person is sent as the intercessor, the heart of the judge is only turned to greater disfavor. Therefore these two things—mass and prayer, sacrament and work, testament and sacrifice—must not be confused; for the one comes from God to us through the ministration of the priest and demands our faith, the other proceeds from our faith to God through the priest and demands his hearing. The former descends, the latter ascends. The former, therefore, does not necessarily require a worthy and godly minister, but the latter does indeed require such a one, for "God does not listen to sinners" [John 9:31]. He knows how to do good through evil men, but he does not accept the work of any evil man; as he showed in the case of Cain [Gen. 4:5], and as is said in Prov. 15 [:8]: "The sacrifice of the wicked is an abomination to the Lord," and in Rom. 14 [:23]: "Whatever does not proceed from faith is sin."

But let us bring this first part to an end, though I am ready to go on with the argument if an opponent should arise. From all that has been said we conclude that the mass was provided only for those who have a sad, afflicted,

---

110. Its own work is salvation. The "alien work" is condemnation. The expression derives from Isa. 28:21.

disturbed, perplexed and erring conscience, and that they alone commune worthily. For, since the word of divine promise in this sacrament sets forth the forgiveness of sins, let every one draw near fearlessly, whoever he may be, who is troubled by his sins, whether by remorse or by temptation. For this treatment of Christ is the one remedy against sins, past, present and future, if you but cling to it with unwavering faith and believe that what the words of the testament declare is freely granted to you. But if you do not believe this, you will never, anywhere, by any works or efforts of your own, be able to find peace of conscience. For faith alone means peace of conscience, while unbelief means only distress of conscience.

THE SACRAMENT OF BAPTISM

Blessed be God and the Father of our Lord Jesus Christ, who according to the riches of his mercy [Eph. 1:3, 7] has preserved in his church this sacrament at least, untouched and untainted by the ordinances of men, and has made it free to all nations and classes of mankind, and has not permitted it to be oppressed by the filthy and godless monsters of greed and superstition. For he desired that by it little children, who were incapable of greed and superstition, might be initiated and sanctified in the simple faith of his Word; even today baptism has its chief blessing for them. But if the intention had been to give this sacrament to adults and older people, I do not believe that it could possibly have retained its power and its glory against the tyranny of greed and superstition which has overthrown all things divine among us. Here too the wisdom of the flesh would doubtless have devised its preparations and dignities, its reservations, restrictions, and other like snares for catching money, until water brought as high a price as parchment[111] does now.

---

111. Leters of indulgence.

178

But Satan, though he could not quench the power of baptism in little children, nevertheless succeeded in quenching it in all adults, so that now there are scarcely any who call to mind their own baptism, and still fewer who glory in it; so many other ways have been discovered for remitting sins and getting to heaven. The source of these false opinions is that dangerous saying of St. Jerome[112] (either unhappily phrased or wrongly interpreted) in which he terms penance "the second plank after shipwreck," as if baptism were not penance. Hence, when men have fallen into sin, they despair of the "first plank," which is the ship, as if it had gone under, and begin to put all their trust and faith in the second plank, which is penance. This has given rise to those endless burdens of vows, religious orders, works, satisfactions, pilgrimages, indulgences, and monastic sects, and from them in turn has arisen that flood of books, questions, opinions, and man-made ordinances which the whole world cannot contain. Thus the church of God is incomparably worse off under this tyranny than the synagogue or any other nation under heaven ever was.

It was the duty of the pontiffs to remove all these evils, and to put forth every effort to recall Christians to the true understanding of baptism, so that they might know what manner of men they were and how Christians ought to live. But instead of this, their only work today is to lead the people as far astray as possible from their baptism, to immerse all men in the flood of their tyranny, and to cause the people of Christ (as the prophet says) to forget him days without number [Jer. 2:32]. How unhappy, are all who bear the name of pontiff today! For they neither know nor do what is becoming to pontiffs, but they are ignorant of what they ought to know and do. They fulfill what Isa.

---

112. St. Jerome (d. 420), ascetic, zealous exponent of the monastic life, prolific writer against the heretics, translator of an important Latin version of the Bible, was also the author of many letters—to one of which Luther is referring. *Epistola* 130, par. 9. Migne 22, 1115.

56 [:10, 11] says: "His watchmen are blind, they are all without knowledge the shepherds also have no understanding; they have all turned to their own way, each to his own gain, etc."

Now, the *first* thing to be considered about baptism is the divine promise, which says: "He who believes and is baptized will be saved" [Mark 16:16]. This promise must be set far above all the glitter of works, vows, religious orders, and whatever else man has introduced, for on it all our salvation depends. But we must so consider it as to exercise our faith in it, and have no doubt whatever that, once we have been baptized, we are saved. For unless faith is present or is conferred in baptism, baptism will profit us nothing; indeed, it will become a hindrance to us, not only at the moment when it is received, but throughout the rest of our lives. That kind of unbelief accuses God's promise of being a lie, and this is the greatest of all sins. If we set ourselves to this exercise of faith, we shall at once perceive how difficult it is to believe this promise of God. For our human weakness, conscious of its sins, finds nothing more difficult to believe than that it is saved; and yet, unless it does believe this, it cannot be saved, because it does not believe the truth of God that promises salvation.

This message should have been impressed upon the people untiringly, and this promise should have been dinned into their ears without ceasing. Their baptism should have been called to their minds again and again, and their faith constantly awakened and nourished. For just as the truth of this divine promise, once pronounced over us, continues until death, so our faith in it ought never to cease, but to be nourished and strengthened until death by the continual remembrance of this promise made to us in baptism. Therefore, when we rise from our sins or repent, we are merely returning to the power and the faith of baptism from which we fell, and finding our way back to the promise then made to us, which we deserted when we sinned. For the truth of the promise once made remains steadfast, always ready to receive us back with open arms when we return. And this, if I mistake not, is what they mean when they say, though obscurely, that baptism is the first sacrament and the foundation of all the others, without which none of the others can be received.

It will therefore be no small gain to a penitent to remember above all his baptism, and, confidently calling to mind the divine promise which he has forsaken, acknowledge that promise before his Lord, rejoicing that he is still within the fortress of salvation because he has been baptized, and abhorring his wicked ingratitude in falling away from its faith and truth. His heart will find wonderful comfort and will be encouraged to hope for mercy when he considers that the promise which God made to him, which cannot possibly lie, is still unbroken and unchanged, and indeed, cannot be changed by sins, as Paul says (II Tim. 2 [:13]): "If we are faithless, he remains faithful—for he cannot deny himself." This truth of God, I say, will sustain him, so that if all else should fail, this truth, if he believes in it, will not fail him. In it the penitent has a shield against all assaults of the scornful enemy, an answer to the sins that disturb his conscience, an antidote for the dread of death and judgment, and a comfort in every temptation—namely, this one truth—when he says: "God is faithful in his promises [Heb. 10:23; 11:11], and I received his sign in baptism. If God is for me, who is against me?" [Rom. 8:31].

The children of Israel, whenever they turned to repentance, remembered above all their exodus from Egypt, and remembering turned back to God who had brought them out. Moses impressed this memory and this protection upon them many times, and David afterwards did the same. How much more ought we to remember our exodus from Egypt, and by this remembrance turn back to him who led us through the washing of regeneration [Titus 3:5], remembrance of which is commended to us for this very reason!

This can be done most fittingly in the sacrament of bread and wine. Indeed, in former times these three sacraments— penance, baptism, and the bread—were all celebrated at the same service, and each one supplemented the other. We also read of a certain holy virgin[113] who in every time of temptation made baptism her sole defense, saying simply, "I am a Christian"; and immediately the enemy recognized the power of baptism and of her faith, which clung to the truth of a promising God, and fled from her.

Thus you see how rich a Christian is, that is, one who has been baptized! Even if he would, he could not lose his salvation, however much he sinned, unless he refused to believe. For no sin can condemn him save unbelief alone. All other sins, so long as the faith in God's promise made in baptism returns or remains, are immediately blotted out through that same faith, or rather through the truth of God, because he cannot deny himself if you confess him and faithfully cling to him in his promise. But as for contrition, confession of sins, and satisfaction,[114] along with all those carefully devised exercises of men: if you rely on them and neglect this truth of God, they will suddenly fail you and leave you more wretched than before. For whatever is done without faith in God's truth is vanity of vanities and vexation of spirit [Eccles. 1:2, 14].

You will likewise see how perilous, indeed, how false it is to suppose that penance is "the second plank after shipwreck,"[115] and how pernicious an error it is to believe that the power of baptism is broken, and the ship dashed to pieces, because of sin. The ship remains one, solid, and invincible; it will never be broken up into separate "planks." In it are all those who are brought to the harbor of salvation,

---

113. This may be a reference to Blandina, a young slave and Christian martyr, whose courage during the persecution under the Roman emperor, Marcus Aurelius (161-180), was extolled by Eusebius. CL 1, 462.
114. The three parts of the sacrament of penance.
115. Cf. p. 179 n. 112.

for it is the truth of God giving us its promise in the sacraments. Of course, it often happens that many rashly leap
overboard into the sea and perish; these are those who aban-
don faith in the promise and plunge into sin. But the ship
itself remains intact and holds its course unimpaired. If any
one is able somehow by grace to return to the ship, it is not
on any plank, but in the solid ship itself that he is borne to
life. Such a person is the one who returns through faith to
the abiding and enduring promise of God. Therefore Peter,
in II Pet. 1 [:9], rebukes those who sin, because they have
forgotten that they were cleansed from their old sins, and he
clearly rebukes their wicked unbelief and their ingratitude
for the baptism they had received.

What is the good, then, of writing so much about baptism
and yet not teaching this faith in the promise? All the sacraments were instituted to nourish faith. Yet these Godless men
pass over it so completely as even to assert that a man dare
not be certain of the forgiveness of sins or the grace of the
sacraments. With such wicked teaching they delude the
world, and not only take captive, but altogether destroy, the
sacrament of baptism, in which the chief glory of our conscience consists. Meanwhile they madly rage against the
miserable souls of men with their contritions, anxious confes-
sions, circumstances,[116] satisfactions, works, and endless
other such absurdities. Therefore read with great caution the
"Master of the *Sentences*"[117] in his fourth book; better yet,
despise him with all his commentators, who at their best
write only of the "matter" and "form"[118] of the sacraments;
that is, they treat of the dead and death-dealing letter [II

---

116. The penitent had to relate the conditions attendant upon his transgression
    to help the priest determine his state of heart and degree of guilt. Cf.
    Buchwald, *op. cit.*, II, 433 n. 1.
117. Cf. p. 144 n. 60.
118. These terms, derived from the philosophy of Aristotle, were introduced by
    scholastic theologians of the thirteenth century into their explanations of
    the sacraments. Matter was the sign, e.g., water in baptism. Form was the
    word, e.g., the Words of Institution.

Cor. 3:6] of the sacraments, but leave untouched the spirit, life, and use, that is, the truth of the divine promise and our faith.

Beware, therefore, that the external pomp of works and the deceits of man-made ordinances do not deceive you, lest you wrong the divine truth and your faith. If you would be saved, you must begin with the faith of the sacraments, without any works whatever. The works will follow faith, but do not think too lightly of faith, for it is the most excellent and difficult of all works.[119] Through it alone you will be saved, even if you should be compelled to do without any other works. For faith is a work of God, not of man, as Paul teaches [Eph. 2:8]. The other works he works through us and with our help, but this one alone he works in us and without our help.

From this we can clearly see the difference in baptism between man who administers the sacrament and God who is its author. For man baptizes, and yet does not baptize. He baptizes in that he performs the work of immersing the person to be baptized; he does not baptize, because in so doing he acts not on his own authority but in God's stead. Hence we ought to receive baptism at human hands just as if Christ himself, indeed, God himself, were baptizing us with his own hands. For it is not man's baptism, but Christ's and God's baptism, which we receive by the hand of a man, just as everything else that we have through the hand of somebody else is God's alone. Therefore beware of making any distinction in baptism by ascribing the outward part to man and the inward part to God. Ascribe both to God alone, and look upon the person administering it as simply the vicarious instrument of God, by which the Lord sitting in heaven thrusts you under the water with his own hands, and promises you forgiveness of your sins, speaking to you upon earth with a human voice by the mouth of his minister.

---

119. Cf. p. 166 n. 99.

This the words themselves indicate, when the priest says: "I baptize you in the name of the Father, and of the Son, and of the Holy Ghost. Amen," and not: "I baptize you in my own name." It is as though he said: "What I do, I do not by my own authority, but in the name and stead of God, so that you should regard it just as if our Lord himself had done it in a visible manner. The Doer and the minister are different persons, but the work of both is the same work, or rather, it is the work of the Doer alone, through my ministry." For I hold that "in the name of" refers to the person of the Doer, so that the name of the Lord is not only to be uttered and invoked while the work is being done; but the work itself is to be done as something not one's own—in the name and stead of Another. In this sense Christ says in Matt. 24 [:5], "Many will come in my name," and Rom. 1 [:5] says, "Through whom we have received grace and apostleship to bring about obedience for the sake of his name among all the nations."

This view I heartily endorse, for there is great comfort and a mighty aid to faith in the knowledge that one has been baptized, not by man, but by the Triune God himself, through a man acting among us in His name. This will put an end to that idle dispute about the "form" of baptism, as they term the words which are used. The Greeks say: "May the servant of Christ be baptized," while the Latins say: "I baptize."[120] Others again, adhering rigidly to their pedantry, condemn the use of the words, "I baptize you in the name of Jesus Christ,"[121] although it is certain the apostles used this formula in baptizing, as we read in the Acts of the Apostles [2:38; 10:48; 19:5]; they would allow no other form to be valid than this: "I baptize you in the name of the Father, and of the Son, and of the Holy Ghost. Amen." But their con-

---

120. Cf. p. 139 n. 47. The dispute had already been decided by the fifteenth-century popes: Eugene IV, Sixtus IV, and Alexander VI, who accepted the validity of the imperative or deprecatory formula of the Eastern church.

121. Alexander of Hales (d. 1245) denied the validity of baptism "in the name of Jesus"; Peter Lombard defended it.

tention is in vain, for they bring no proof, but merely assert their own dreams. Baptism truly saves in whatever way it is administered, if only it is administered not in the name of man, but in the name of the Lord. Indeed, I have no doubt that if anyone receives baptism in the name of the Lord, even if the wicked minister should not give it in the name of the Lord, he would yet be truly baptized in the name of the Lord. For the power of baptism depends not so much on the faith or use of the one who confers it as on the faith or use of the one who receives it. We have an example of this in the story of a certain actor who was baptized in jest.[122] These and similar perplexing disputes and questions are raised for us by those who ascribe nothing to faith and everything to works and rituals, whereas we owe everything to faith alone and nothing to rituals. Faith makes us free in spirit from all those scruples and fancies.

The *second* part of baptism is the sign, or sacrament, which is that immersion in water from which it derives its name, for the Greek *baptizo* means "I immerse," and *baptisma* means, "immersion." For, as has been said, along with the divine promises signs have also been given to picture that which the words signify, or as they now say, that which the sacrament "effectively signifies." We shall see how much truth there is in this.

A great majority have supposed that there is some hidden spiritual power in the word and water, which works the grace of God in the soul of the recipient. Others deny this and hold that there is no power in the sacraments, but that grace is given by God alone, who according to his covenant

---

122. Mentioned also in Luther's *Explanations of the Ninety-five Theses*, LW 31, 105, the incident is more fully described in a sermon on Matthew 18, *WA* 47, 302-03. The court jester of a certain Roman emperor, in mockery of the Christian sacrament, had himself liberally drenched in public. But while the spectators guffawed, the fool was converted through the appearance of an angel showing him a book in which were written the words of Eph. 4:5-6. He acknowledged the mock baptism to be valid, confessed Christ, and was martyred.

is present in the sacraments which he has instituted.[123] Yet all are agreed that the sacraments are "effective signs" of grace, and they reach this conclusion by this one argument: if the sacraments of the New Law were mere signs, there would be no apparent reason why they should surpass those of the Old Law. Hence they have been driven to attribute such great powers to the sacraments of the New Law that they think the sacraments benefit even those who are in mortal sin; neither faith nor grace are required—it is sufficient that no obstacle be set in the way, that is, no actual intention to sin again.

Such views, however, must be carefully avoided and shunned, because they are godless and infidel, contrary to faith and inconsistent with the nature of the sacraments. For it is an error to hold that the sacraments of the New Law differ from those of the Old Law in the effectiveness of their signs. For in this respect they are the same. The same God who now saves us by baptism and the bread, saved Abel by his sacrifice, Noah by the rainbow, Abraham by circumcision, and all the others by their respective signs. So far as the signs are concerned, there is no difference between a sacrament of the Old Law and one of the New, provided that by the Old Law you mean that which God did among the patriarchs and other fathers in the days of the Law. But those signs which were given to the patriarchs and fathers must be clearly distinguished from the legal symbols [*figurae*] which Moses instituted in his law, such as the priestly usages concerning vestments, vessels, foods, houses, and the like. For these are vastly different, not only from the sacraments of the New Law, but also from those signs which God occasionally gave to the fathers living under the law, such

---

123. A point at issue among the scholastics of the Middle Ages. Some held that the grace of the sacrament was contained in the sacramental sign and directly imparted through it; thus Hugo of St. Victor. Others contended that the sign was merely a symbol, but that God, according to a *pactio*, or agreement, imparted the grace of the sacrament when the sign was being used; thus Bonaventura, and especially Duns Scotus.

as the sign of Gideon's fleece [Judg. 6:36-40], Manoah's sacrifice [Judg. 13:16-23], or that which Isaiah offered to Ahaz in Isa. 7: [:10-14]. In each of these alike some promise was given which required faith in God.

The difference, then, between the legal symbols and the new and old signs is that the legal symbols do not have attached to them any word of promise requiring faith. Hence they are not signs of justification, for they are not sacraments of the faith that alone justifies, but only sacraments of works. Their whole power and nature consisted in works, not in faith. Whoever performed them fulfilled them, even if he did it without faith. But our signs or sacraments, as well as those of the fathers, have attached to them a word of promise which requires faith, and they cannot be fulfilled by any other work. Hence they are signs or sacraments of justification, for they are sacraments of justifying faith and not of works. Their whole efficacy, therefore, consists in faith itself, not in the doing of a work. Whoever believes them, fulfils them, even if he should not do a single work. This is the origin of the saying: "Not the sacrament, but the faith of the sacrament, justifies." Thus circumcision did not justify Abraham and his seed, and yet the Apostle calls it the seal of the righteousness by faith [Rom. 4:11], because faith in the promise, to which circumcision was added, justified him and fulfilled what the circumcision signified. For faith was the spiritual circumcision of the foreskin of the heart [Deut. 10:16; Jer. 4:4], which was symbolized by the literal circumcision of the flesh. In the same way it was obviously not Abel's sacrifice that justified him, but it was his faith [Heb. 11:4] by which he offered himself wholly to God, and this was symbolized by the outward sacrifice.

Thus it is not baptism that justifies or benefits anyone, but it is faith in that word of promise to which baptism is added. This faith justifies, and fulfils that which baptism signifies. For faith is the submersion of the old man and the emerging of the new [Eph. 4:22-24; Col. 3:9-10]. Therefore the new sacraments cannot differ from the old sacraments, for both alike have the divine promises and the same spirit of faith, although they do differ vastly from the old symbols—on account of the word of promise, which is the sole effective means of distinguishing them. Even so, today, the outward show of vestments, holy places, foods, and all the endless ceremonies doubtless symbolize excellent things to be fulfilled in the spirit, yet because there is now word of divine promise attached to these things, they can in no way be compared with the signs of baptism and the bread. Neither do they justify, nor benefit one in any way, since they are fulfilled in their very observance, even in their observance apart from faith. For while they are taking place, or being performed, they are being fulfilled, as the Apostle says of them in Col. 2 [:22]: "Which all perish as they are used, according to human precepts and doctrines." The sacraments, on the contrary, are not fulfilled when they are taking place, but when they are being believed.

It cannot be true, therefore, that there is contained in the sacraments a power efficacious for justification, or that they are "effective signs" of grace. All such things are said to the detriment of faith, and out of ignorance of the divine promise. Unless you should call them "effective" in the sense that they certainly and effectively impart grace where faith is unmistakably present. But it is not in this sense that efficacy is now ascribed to them; as witness the fact that they are said to benefit all men, even the wicked and unbelieving, provided they do not set an obstacle in the way—as if such unbelief were not in itself the most obstinate and hostile of all obstacles to grace. To such an extent have they exerted themselves to turn the sacrament into a command and faith into a work. For if the sacrament confers grace on me because I receive it, then indeed I receive grace by virtue of my work, and not by faith; and I gain not the promise in the sacrament but only the sign instituted and commanded by God. Thus you see clearly how completely the sacraments have been misunderstood by the theologians of the *Sentences*. In their discussions of the sacraments they have taken no account either of faith or of promise. They cling only to the sign and the use of the sign, and draw us away from faith to work, away from the word to the sign. Thus, as I have said,[124] they have not only taken the sacraments captive, but have completely destroyed them, as far as they were able.

Therefore let us open our eyes and learn to pay heed more to the word than to the sign, more to faith than to the work or use of the sign. We know that wherever there is a divine promise, there faith is required, and that these two are so necessary to each other that neither can be effective apart from the other. For it is not possible to believe unless there is a promise, and the promise is not established unless it is believed. But where these two meet, they give a real and most certain efficacy to the sacraments. Hence, to seek the efficacy of the sacrament apart from the promise and apart from the faith is to labor in vain and to find condemnation. Thus Christ says: "He who believes and is baptized will be saved; but he who does not believe will be condemned" [Mark 16:16]. He shows us in this word that faith is such a necessary part of the sacrament that it can save even without the sacrament, and for this reason he did not add: "He who does not believe, and is not baptized."

Baptism, then, signifies two things—death and resurrection, that is, full and complete justification. When the minister immerses the child in the water it signifies death, and when he draws it forth again it signifies life. Thus Paul expounds it in Rom. 6 [:4]: "We were buried therefore with Christ by baptism into death, so that as Christ was raised from the dead by the glory of the Father, we too might walk in newness of life." This death and resurrection we call the new creation, regeneration, and spiritual birth. This should not be understood only allegorically as the death of sin and the

---

124. Cf. p. 183.

life of grace, as many understand it, but as actual death and resurrection. For baptism is not a false sign. Neither does sin completely die, nor grace completely rise, until the sinful body that we carry about in this life is destroyed, as the Apostle says in the same passage [Rom. 6:6-7]. For as long as we are in the flesh, the desires of the flesh stir and are stirred. For this reason, as soon as we begin to believe, we also begin to die to this world and live to God in the life to come; so that faith is truly a death and a resurrection, that is, it is that spiritual baptism into which we are submerged and from which we rise.

It is therefore indeed correct to say that baptism is a washing away of sins, but the expression is too mild and weak to bring out the full significance of baptism, which is rather a symbol of death and resurrection. For this reason I would have those who are to be baptized completely immersed in the water, as the word says[125] and as the mystery indicates. Not because I deem this necessary, but because it would be well to give to a thing[126] so perfect and complete a sign that is also complete and perfect. And this is doubtless the way in which it was instituted by Christ. The sinner does not so much need to be washed as he needs to die, in order to be wholly renewed and made another creature, and to be conformed to the death and resurrection of Christ, with whom he dies and rises again through baptism. Although you may say that when Christ died and rose again he was washed clean of mortality, that is a less forceful way of putting it than if you said that he was completely changed and renewed. Similarly it is far more forceful to say that baptism signifies that we die in every way and rise to eternal life, than to say that it signifies merely that we are washed clean of sins.

Here again you see that the sacrament of baptism, even

---

125. Cf. p. 186 above, and *LW* 35, 29.
126. *res;* cf. p. 137 n. 45 above.

with respect to its sign, is not a matter of the moment, but something permanent. Although the ceremony itself is soon over, the thing it signifies continues until we die, yes, even until we rise on the last day. For as long as we live we are continually doing that which baptism signifies, that is, we die and rise again. We die, not only mentally and spiritually by renouncing the sins and vanities of this world, but in very truth we begin to leave this bodily life and to lay hold on the life to come, so that there is, as they say, a "real" and bodily passing out of this world unto the Father.

We must therefore beware of those who have reduced the power of baptism to such small and slender dimensions that, while they say grace is indeed inpoured by it, they maintain that afterwards it is poured out again through sin, and that then one must reach heaven by another way, as if baptism had now become entirely useless. Do not hold such a view, but understand that this is the significance of baptism, that through it you die and live again. Therefore, whether by penance or by any other way, you can only return to the power of your baptism, and do again that which you were baptized to do and which your baptism signified. Baptism never becomes useless, unless you despair and refuse to return to its salvation. You may indeed wander away from the sign for a time, but the sign is not therefore useless. Thus, you have been once baptized in the sacrament, but you need continually to be baptized by faith, continually to die and continually to live. Baptism swallowed up your whole body and gave it forth again; in the same way that which baptism signifies should swallow up your whole life, body and soul, and give it forth again at the last day, clad in the robe of glory and immortality. We are therefore never without the sign of baptism nor without the thing it signifies. Indeed, we need continually to be baptized more and more, until we fulfill the sign perfectly at the last day.

You will understand, therefore, that whatever we do in this life which mortifies the flesh or quickens the spirit has to do with our baptism. The sooner we depart this life, the more speedily we fulfil our baptism; and the more cruelly we suffer, the more successfully do we conform to our baptism. Hence the church was at its best at the time when martyrs were being put to death every day and accounted as sheep for the slaughter [Ps. 44:22; Rom. 8:36], for then the power of baptism reigned supreme in the church, whereas today we have lost sight of this power amid the multitude of works and doctrines of men. For our whole life should be baptism, and the fulfilling of the sign or sacrament of baptism, since we have been set free from all else and given over to baptism alone, that is, to death and resurrection.

This glorious liberty of ours and this understanding of baptism have been taken captive in our day, and to whom can we give the blame except the Roman pontiff with his despotism? More than all others, as chief shepherd it was his first duty to proclaim this doctrine and defend this liberty, as Paul says in I Cor. 4 [:1]: "This is how one should regard us, as servants of Christ and stewards of the mysteries, or sacraments,[127] of God." Instead he seeks only to oppress us with his decrees and laws, and to ensnare us as captives to his tyrannical power. By what right, I ask you, does the pope impose his laws upon us (to say nothing of his wicked and damnable neglect to teach us these mysteries)? Who gave him power to deprive us of this liberty of ours, granted to us in baptism? One thing only, as I have said, has been enjoined upon us to do all the days of our lives—to be baptized, that is, to be put to death and to live again through faith in Christ. This, and this alone, should have been taught, especially by the chief shepherd. But now faith is passed over in silence, and the church is smothered with endless laws concerning works and ceremonies; the power and understanding of baptism are set aside, and faith in Christ is obstructed.

Therefore I say: Neither pope nor bishop nor any other

---

127. Cf. pp. 221-24.

man has the right to impose a single syllable of law upon a Christian man without his consent; if he does, it is done in the spirit of tyranny. Therefore the prayers, fasts, donations and whatever else the pope ordains and demands in all of his decrees, as numerous as they are iniquitous, he demands and ordains without any right whatever; and he sins against the liberty of the church whenever he attempts any such thing. Hence it has come to pass that the churchmen of our day are such vigorous guardians of "ecclesiastical liberty"—that is, of wood and stone, of lands and rents (for to such an extent has "ecclesiastical" today come to mean the same as "spiritual"!). Yet with such verbal fictions they not only take captive the true liberty of the church; they utterly destroy it, even worse than the Turk, and in opposition to the word of the Apostle: "Do not become slaves of men" [I Cor. 7:23]. For to be subjected to their statutes and tyrannical laws is indeed to become slaves of men.

This impious and desperate tyranny is fostered by the pope's disciples, who here twist and pervert that saying of Christ: "He who hears you hears me" [Luke 10:16]. With puffed cheeks they inflate this saying to a great size in support of their own ordinances. Though Christ spoke this word to the apostles when they went forth to preach the gospel, and though it should apply only to the gospel, they pass over the gospel and apply it only to their fables. For he says in John 10 [:27, 5]: "My sheep hear my voice, but the voice of a stranger they do not hear." He left us the gospel so that the pontiffs might sound the voice of Christ. Instead they sound their own voices, and yet hope to be heard. Moreover, the Apostle says that he was not sent to baptize, but to preach the gospel [I Cor. 1:17]. Therefore, no one is obliged to obey the ordinances of the pope, or required to listen to him, except when he teaches the gospel and Christ. And the pope should teach nothing but faith without any restrictions. But since Christ says, "He who hears you [plural] hears me" [Luke 10:16], why does not the pope also

194

hear others? Christ does not say to Peter alone, "He who hears you" [singular]. In short, where there is true faith, there the word of faith must of necessity be also. Why then does not an unbelieving pope now and then hear a believing servant of his who has the word of faith? Blindness, sheer blindness, reigns among the pontiffs.

Others, even more shameless, arrogantly ascribe to the pope the power to make laws, on the basis of Matt. 16 [:19], "Whatever you bind, etc.," although Christ in this passage treats of binding and loosing sins, not of taking the whole church captive and oppressing it with laws. So this tyranny treats everything with its own lying words and violently twists and perverts the words of God. I admit indeed that Christians ought to bear this accursed tyranny just as they would bear any other violence of the world, according to Christ's word: "If any one strikes you on the right cheek, turn to him the other also" [Matt. 5:39]. But this is my complaint: that the godless pontiffs boastfully claim to do this by right, that they pretend to be seeking the church's welfare with this Babylon of theirs, and that they foist this fiction upon all mankind. For if they did these things and we suffered their violence, both sides being well aware that it was godlessness and tyranny, then we might easily number it among those things that contribute to the mortifying of this life and the fulfilling of our baptism, and might with a good conscience glory in the inflicted injury. But now they seek to deprive us of this consciousness of our liberty, and would have us believe that what they do is well done, and must not be censured or complained of as wrongdoing. Being wolves, they masquerade as shepherds, and being Antichrists, they wish to be honored as Christ.

I lift my voice simply on behalf of liberty and conscience, and I confidently cry: No law, whether of men or of angels, may rightfully be imposed upon Christians without their consent, for we are free of all laws. And if any laws are imposed upon us, we must bear them in such a way as to preserve that sense of freedom which knows and affirms with certainty that an injustice is being done to it, even though it glories in bearing this injustice—so taking care neither to justify the tyrant nor to murmur against his tyranny. "Now who is there to harm you," says Peter, "if you are zealous for what is right?" [I Pet. 3:13]. "All things work together for good to them that are the elect" [Rom. 8:28].

Nevertheless, since but few know this glory of baptism and the blessedness of Christian liberty, and cannot know them because of the tyranny of the pope, I for one will disengage myself, and keep my conscience free by bringing this charge against the pope and all his papists: Unless they will abolish their laws and ordinances, and restore to Christ's churches their liberty and have it taught among them, they are guilty of all the souls that perish under this miserable captivity, and the papacy is truly the kingdom of Babylon and of the very Antichrist. For who is "the man of sin" and "the son of perdition" [II Thess. 2:3] but he who with his doctrines and his laws increases the sins and perdition of souls in the church, while sitting in the church as if he were God? [II Thess. 2:4]. All this the papal tyranny has fulfilled, and more than fulfilled, these many centuries. It has extinguished faith, obscured the sacraments and oppressed the gospel; but its own laws, which are not only impious and sacrilegious, but even barbarous and foolish, it has decreed and multiplied without end.

Behold, then, our miserable captivity. "How lonely sits the city that was full of people! How like a widow has she become, she that was great among the nations! She that was a princess among the cities has become a vassal. She has none to comfort her; all her friends have dealt treacherously with her, etc." [Lam. 1:1-2]. There are so many ordinances, so many rites, so many sects,[128] so many vows, so many exertions

---

128. Luther means the divergences, rivalries, and jealousies between the various monastic orders and theological factions. E.g., cf. p. 202 n. 138.

and so many works, in which Christians are engaged today, that they lose sight of their baptism. Because of this swarm of locusts, palmerworms, and cankerworms [Joel 1:4], no one is able to remember that he is baptized, or what blessings baptism has brought him. We should be even as little children, when they are newly baptized, who engage in no efforts or works, but are free in every way, secure and saved solely through the glory of their baptism. For we are indeed little children. continually baptized anew in Christ.

In contradiction to what has been said, some might cite the *baptism of infants* who do not comprehend the promise of God and cannot have the faith of baptism; so that therefore either faith is not necessary or else infant baptism is without effect. Here I say what all[129] say: Infants are aided by the faith of others, namely, those who bring them for baptism. For the Word of God is powerful enough, when uttered, to change even a godless heart, which is no less unresponsive and helpless than any infant. So through the prayer of the believing church which presents it, a prayer to which all things are possible [Mark 9:23], the infant is changed, cleansed, and renewed by inpoured faith. Nor should I doubt that even a godless adult could be changed, in any of the sacraments, if the same church prayed for and presented him, as we read of the paralytic in the Gospel, who was healed through the faith of others [Mark 2:3-12]. I should be ready to admit that in this sense the sacraments of the New Law are efficacious in conferring grace, not only to those who do not, but even to those who do most obstinately present an obstacle.[130] What obstacle cannot be removed by the faith of the church and the prayer of faith? Do we not believe that Stephen converted Paul the Apostle by this power? [Acts 7:58—8:1]. But then the sacraments

---

129. This was the position of Thomas Aquinas, going back to Augustine; it was ratified by Clement V at the Council of Vienna, 1311-12. *PE* 2, 236 n. 1.
130. Cf. p. 187.

do what they do not by their own power, but by the power of faith, without which they do nothing at all, as I have said.[131]

The question remains whether an unborn infant, with only a hand or a foot projecting from the womb, can be baptized. Here I will confess my ignorance and make no hasty decision. I am not sure whether the reason they give is sufficient—that in any part of the body whatsoever the entire soul resides. For it is not the soul but the body that is externally baptized with water. But neither do I share the view of those who insist that he who is not yet born cannot be born again (even though it has considerable force). I leave these things to the teaching of the Spirit, and meanwhile allow everyone to enjoy his own opinion [Rom. 14:5].

One thing I will add—and I wish I could persuade everyone to do it—namely, that *all vows should be completely abolished and avoided,* whether of religious orders, or about pilgrimages or about any works whatsoever, that we may remain in that which is supremely religious and most rich in works—the freedom of baptism. It is impossible to say how much that most widespread delusion of vows detracts from baptism and obscures the knowledge of Christian liberty, to say nothing now of the unspeakable and infinite peril of souls which that mania for making vows and that ill-advised rashness daily increase. O most godless pontiffs and unregenerate pastors, who slumber on unheeding and indulge in your evil lusts, without pity for this most dreadful and perilous "ruin of Joseph"! [Amos 6:4-6].

Vows should either be abolished by a general edict, especially those taken for life, and all men recalled to the vows of baptism, or else everyone should be diligently warned not to take a vow rashly. No one should be encouraged to do so; indeed, permission should be given only with difficulty and

131. Cf. pp. 188-89.

198

reluctance. For we have vowed enough in baptism, more than we can ever fulfill; if we give ourselves to the keeping of this one vow, we shall have all we can do. But now we traverse sea and land to make many proselytes [Matt. 23:15]; we fill the world with priests, monks, and nuns, and imprison them all in lifelong vows. You will find those who argue and decree that a work done in fulfilment of a vow ranks higher than one done without a vow, and in heaven is to be rewarded above others with I know not what great rewards. Blind and godless Pharisees, who measure rightousness and holiness by the greatness, number, or other quality of the works! But God measures them by faith alone, and with him there is no difference among works, except insofar as there is a difference in faith.

With such bombast wicked men by their inventions puff up human opinion and human works in order to lure on the unthinking masses who are almost always led by the glitter of works to make shipwreck of their faith, to forget their baptism and to injure their Christian liberty. For a vow is a kind of law or requirement. When vows are multiplied, laws and works are necessarily multiplied, and when these are multiplied, faith is extinguished and the liberty of baptism is taken captive. Others, not content with these wicked allurements, assert in addition that entrance into a religious order is like a new baptism, which may afterward be repeated as often as the purpose to live the monastic life is renewed. Thus these votaries have appropriated to themselves all righteousness, salvation, and glory, and left to those who are merely baptized nothing to compare with them. Now the Roman pontiff, that fountain and source of all superstitions, confirms, approves, and adorns this mode of life with high-sounding bulls[132] and dispensations, while no one deems

---

132. *bulla.* An official mandate of the pope, which takes its name from the leaden seal with which the document was authenticated in the Middle Ages—a circular plate in form resembling an air bubble floating upon water.

baptism worthy of even a thought. And with such glittering pomp, as I have said, they drive the pliable people of Christ into a false sense of security,[133] so that in their ingratitude toward baptism they presume to achieve greater things by their works than others achieve by their faith.

Therefore, God again shows himself "perverse with the crooked" [Ps. 18:26], and to punish the makers of vows for their ingratitude and pride, he brings it about that they break their vows, or keep them only with prodigious labor, and remain sunk in them, never knowing the grace of faith and of baptism; that they continue in their hypocrisy to the end, since their spirit is not approved of God; and that at last they become a laughingstock to the whole world, ever pursuing righteousness and never attaining Righteousness, so that they fulfill the word of Isa. 2 [:8]: "Their land is filled with idols."

I am indeed far from forbidding or discouraging anyone who may desire to vow something privately and of his own free choice; for I would not altogether despise and condemn vows. But I would most strongly advise against setting up and sanctioning the making of vows as a public mode of life. It is enough that every one should have the private right to take a vow at his own peril; but to commend the vowing of vows as a public mode of life—this I hold to be most pernicious to the church and to simple souls. First, because it runs directly counter to the Christian life, for a vow is a kind of ceremonial law and a human ordinance or presumption, from which the church has been set free through baptism; for a Christian is subject to no law but the law of God. Second, because there is no instance in Scripture of such a vow, espe-

---

133. *in quascunque volent symplegadas.* Luther is alluding to the Symplegades rocks at the entrance to the Black Sea, through which, according to Greek legend, Jason had to lead his Argonauts in quest of the Golden Fleece. While they seemed to afford secure passage, the two cliffs actually moved on their bases and crushed whatever sought to pass.

cially of lifelong chastity, obedience, or poverty.[134] But whatever is without warrant of Scripture is most hazardous and
should by no means be urged upon any one, much less established as a common and public mode of life, even if it be
permitted to somebody who wishes to make the venture at
his own peril. For certain works are wrought by the Spirit in
a few men, but they must not be made an example or a mode
of life for all.

Moreover, I greatly fear that these votive modes of life of
the religious orders belong to those things which the Apostle
foretold: "They will be teaching lies in hypocrisy, forbidding
marriage and enjoining abstinence from foods which God
created to be received with thanksgiving" [I Tim. 4:2-3].
Let no one retort by pointing to SS. Bernard, Francis, Dominic,[135] and others, who founded or fostered monastic orders.
Terrible and marvelous is God in his counsels toward the
sons of men. He could keep Daniel, Hananiah, Azariah, and
Mishael [Dan. 1:6-21] holy at the court of the king of Babylon (that is, in the midst of godlessness); why could he not
sanctify those men also in their perilous mode of living or
guide them by the special operation of his Spirit, yet without
desiring it to be an example to others? Besides, it is certain
that none of them was saved through his vows and his "religious"[136] life; they were saved through faith alone, by which
all men are saved, and to which that showy subservience to
vows is more diametrically opposed than anything else.

But every one may hold his own view on this. I will return
to my argument. Speaking now in behalf of the church's

---

134. The threefold vow of the monastic orders involved a pledge of poverty,
chastity, and obedience.
135. Bernard of Clairvaux (1090-1153) founded 163 Cistercian monasteries in
different parts of Europe, which by his death had increased in number to
343. Francis of Assisi (1182-1226) founded the Franciscan Order. Dominic
(circa 1170-1221) founded the Order of Preachers, commonly known as
the Dominican Order.
136. religio. In medieval Latin this was a special designation for the particular
piety of the monastic orders.

liberty and the glory of baptism, I feel myself in duty bound to set forth publicly the counsel I have learned under the Spirit's guidance. I therefore counsel those in high places in the churches, first of all, to abolish all those vows and religious orders, or at least not to approve and extol them. If they will not do this, then I counsel all men who would be assured of their salvation to abstain from all vows, above all from the major and lifelong vows. I give this counsel especially to teen-agers and young people. This I do, first because this manner of life has no witness or warrant in the Scriptures, as I have said, but is puffed up solely by the bulls (and they truly are "bulls")[137] of human popes. Second, because it greatly tends to hypocrisy, by reason of its outward show and unusual character, which engender conceit and a contempt of the common Christian life. And if there were no other reason for abolishing these vows, this one would be reason enough, namely, that through them faith and baptism are slighted and works are exalted, which cannot be done without harmful results. For in the religious orders there is scarcely one in many thousands who is not more concerned about his works than about faith, and on the basis of this madness, they claim superiority over each other, as being "stricter" or "laxer," as they call it.[138]

Therefore I advise no one to enter any religious order or the priesthood, indeed, I advise everyone against it—unless he is forearmed with this knowledge and understands that the works of monks and priests, however holy and arduous they may be, do not differ one whit in the sight of God from the works of the rustic laborer in the field or the woman going about her household tasks, but

137. *bulla* also means "bubble." Cf. p. 199 n. 132.
138. Divisions resulting from disputes over the interpretation of their "rules" were common among and within the religious orders. In the case of the Franciscans, for example, there were the factions known as the *zelanti* and *relaxti* in earlier times, and later on the division between the "Strict Observance" and the "Conventuals." Cf. p. 126 n. 12.

that all works are measured before God by faith alone, as Jer. 5 [:3] says: "O Lord, do not thy eyes look for faith?"[139] and Ecclus. 32 [:23]: "In all thy works believe with faith in thy heart, for this is to keep the commandments of God." Indeed, the menial housework of a manservant or maidservant is often more acceptable to God than all the fastings and other works of a monk or priest, because the monk or priest lacks faith. Since, therefore, vows nowadays seem to tend only to the glorification of works and to pride, it is to be feared that there is nowhere less of faith and of the church than among the priets, monks, and bishops. These men are in truth heathen or hypocrites. They imagine themselves to be the church, or the heart of the church, the "spiritual" estate and the leaders of the church, when they are everything else but that. This is indeed "the people of the captivity," among whom all things freely given to us in baptism are held captive, while the few poor "people of the earth[140] who are left behind, such as the married folk,[141] appear vile in their eyes.

From what has been said we recognize two glaring errors of the Roman pontiff.

In the first place, he grants dispensation from vows, and does it as if he alone of all Christians possessed this authority; so great is the temerity and audacity of wicked men. If it is possible to grant a dispensation from a vow, then any brother may grant one to his neighbor, or even to himself.[142] But if one's neighbor cannot grant a dispensation, neither has the pope any right to do so. For where

---

139. Vulgate version.
140. The reference is to the Babylonian captivity of the Jews. "The people of the captivity" is an expression taken from the Latin title to Psalm 64 (65) in the Vulgate. Nebuchadnezzar carried into captivity in Babylon only the better classes of the population. The "people of the earth," *am haarez*, the common people, were left behind (II Kings 24:14-16) and became the nucleus of the hybrid Samaritan nation.
141. Persons under the vow of chastity held the estate of marriage to be beneath their own in terms of holiness.
142. Cf. *To the Christian Nobility of the German Nation.* P. 69 above.

does he get this authority? From the power of the keys? But the keys belong to all, and avail only for sins (Matt. 18 [:15-18]).[143] Now they themselves claim that vows are "of divine right." Why then does the pope deceive and destroy the poor souls of men by granting dispensations in matters of divine right, in which no dispensations can be granted? In the section, "Of vows and their redemption,"[144] he babbles indeed of having the power to change vows, just as in the law the firstborn of an ass was changed for a sheep [Exod. 13:13; 34:20] as if the firstborn of an ass, and the vow he commands to be offered everywhere and always, were one and the same thing; or as if when the Lord decrees in his law that a sheep shall be changed for an ass, the pope, a mere man, may straightway claim the same power, not in his own law, but in God's! It was not a pope, but an ass changed for a pope, that made this decretal; it is so egregiously senseless and godless.

The second error is this: The pope decrees, on the other hand, that a marriage is dissolved if one party enters a monastery without the consent of the other, provided that the marriage has not yet been consummated. Now I ask you, what devil puts such monstrous things into the pope's mind? God commands men to keep faith and not break their word to one another, and again, to do good with that which is their own, for he hates "robbery with a burnt offering," as he says by the mouth of Isaiah [61:8]. But one spouse is bound by the marriage contract to keep faith with the other, and he is not his own. He cannot break his faith by any right, and whatever he does with himself is robbery, if it is done without the other's consent. Why does not one who is burdened with debt follow this same rule and obtain admission into a religious order, so as to be released from

143. Cf. pp. 20-21 above.
144. *Magnae devotionis, Decretalium Gregorii IX*, lib iii, tit. XXXIV: *de voto et voti redemptione.* cap. 7. *Corpus Iuris Canonici, op. cit.,* II, col. 593.

his debts and be free to break his word? O blind, blind men! Which is greater, the fidelity commanded by God or a vow devised and chosen by men? Are you a shepherd of souls, O pope? And you who teach these things, are you doctors of sacred theology? Why then do you teach them? No doubt because you have decked out your vow as a better work than marriage; you do not exalt faith, which alone exalts all things, but works, which are nothing in the sight of God, or which are all alike as far as merit is concerned.

I am sure, therefore, that neither men nor angels can grant a dispensation from vows, if they are proper vows. But I am not fully clear in my own mind whether all the things that men vow nowadays come under the head of vows. For instance, it is simply foolish and stupid for parents to dedicate their children, before birth or in infancy, to the "religious life," or to perpetual chastity; indeed, it is certain that this can by no means be termed a vow. It seems to be a kind of mockery of God for them to vow things which are not at all in their power. As to the triple vow of the monastic orders,[145] the longer I consider it, the less I comprehend it, and I wonder where the custom of exacting this vow arose. Still less do I understand at what age vows may be taken in order to be legal and valid. I am pleased to find unanimous agreement that vows taken before the age of puberty are not valid. Nevertheless, they deceive many young children who are ignorant both of their age and of what they are vowing. They do not observe the age of puberty in receiving such children; but the children, after making their profession, are held captive and consumed by a troubled conscience as though they had afterward given their consent. As if a vow which was invalid could finally become valid with the passing of the years!

It seems absurd to me that the effective date of a legiti-

145. Cf. p. 201 n. 134.

mate vow should be predetermined for others by people who cannot predetermine it for themselves. Nor do I see why a vow taken at eighteen years of age should be valid, but not one taken at ten or twelve years. It will not do to say that at eighteen a man feels his carnal desires. What if he scarcely feels them at twenty or thirty, or feels them more keenly at thirty than at twenty? Why not also set a certain age limit for the vows of poverty and obedience? But what age will you set, by which a man should feel his greed and pride, when even the most spiritual persons hardly become aware of these emotions? Therefore, no vow will ever become binding and valid until we have become spiritual, and no longer have any need of vows. You see that these are uncertain and most perilous matters, and it would therefore be a wholesome counsel to keep such lofty modes of living free of vows, and leave them to the Spirit alone as they were of old, and never in any way to change them into a mode of life which is perpetually binding.

However, let this be sufficient for the present concerning baptism and its liberty. In due time I shall perhaps discuss vows at greater length,[146] and truly there is an urgent need for this.

THE SACRAMENT OF PENANCE

In the third place, we are to discuss the sacrament of penance. On this subject I have already given no little offense to many people by the treatises and disputations[147] already published, in which I have amply set forth my

---

146. This Luther did in November, 1521, during his sojourn at the Wartburg, in *The Judgment of Martin Luther on Monastic Vows.* LW 44, 243-400.

147. These include, among others, the *Ninety-five Theses* (1517), LW 31, 25-33, WA 1, 233-38; *A Sermon on Indulgence and Grace* (1517), Woolf, *op. cit.*, I, 50-55, WA 1, 239-246; *Sermo de poenitentia* (1518), WA 1, 319-24; *Eine Freiheit des Sermons papstlichen Ablass und Gnade Belangend* (1518), WA 1, 383-93; *Explanations of the Ninety-five Theses* (1518), LW 31, 83-252, WA 1, 525-628; and *A Discussion on How Confession Should Be Made* (1520), LW 39, 23-47.

views. These I must now briefly repeat in order to unmask the tyranny that is rampant here no less than in the sacrament of the bread. For, because these two sacraments furnish opportunity for gain and profit, the greed of the shepherds has raged in them with incredible zeal against the flock of Christ, although, as we have just seen in our discussion of vows, baptism too has sadly declined among adults and become the servant of greed.

The first and chief abuse of this sacrament is that they have completely abolished it. Not a vestige of the sacrament remains. For this sacrament, like the other two, consists in the word of divine promise and our faith, and they have undermined both of them. For they have adapted to their own tyranny the word of promise which Christ speaks in Matt. 16 [:19] and 18 [:18]: "Whatever you bind, etc.," and in the last chapter of John [20:23]: "If you forgive the sins of any, they are forgiven, etc." By these words the faith of penitents is aroused for obtaining the forgiveness of sins. But in all their writing, teaching, and preaching, their sole concern has been, not to teach what is promised to Christians in these words, or what they ought to believe, and what great consolation they might find in them, but only through force and violence to extend their own tyranny far, wide, and deep. It has finally come to such a pass that some of them have begun to command the very angels in heaven,[148] and to boast in incredible, mad wickedness that

---

148. In the jubilee year of 1500, as thousands of pilgrims died of the plague on their way through war-ravaged Lombardy toward Rome, a spurious bull of Pope Clement VI from the year 1350 was widely promulgated, in which were the words: "We command the angels of paradise that their souls (the souls of pilgrims who died en route) be taken directly to the bliss of paradise, as being fully redeemed from purgatory." WA 30ᴵᴵ, 282; Buchwald, *op. cit.*, II, 457 n. 1. In *Defense and Explanation of All the Articles* (1521), Luther writes: "This is what happened in the days of John Huss. In those days the pope commanded the angels in heaven to lead to heaven the souls of those pilgrims who died on the way to Rome. John Huss objected to this horrible blasphemy and more than diabolic presumption. This protest cost him his life, but he at least caused the pope to change his tune and, embarrassed by this sacrilege, to refrain from such proclamation." *LW* 32, 74-75.

in these words they have obtained the right to rule in heaven and earth, and possess the power to bind even in heaven. Thus they say nothing of faith which is the salvation of the people, but babble only of the despotic power of the pontiffs, whereas Christ says nothing at all of power, but speaks only of faith.

For Christ has not ordained authorities or powers or lordships in his church, but ministries, as we learn from the Apostle, who says: "This is how one should regard us, as ministers of Christ and stewards of the mysteries of God" [I Cor. 4:1]. Just as, when he said: "He who believes and is baptized will be saved" [Mark 16:16], he was calling forth the faith of those who were to be baptized, so that by this word of promise a man might be certain of his salvation if he was baptized in faith. There was no conferring of any power there, but only the instituting of the ministry of those who baptize. Similarly, here where he says, "Whatever you bind, etc." [Matt. 16:19; 18:18], he is calling forth the faith of the penitent, so that by this word of promise he might be certain that if he is absolved in faith, he is truly absolved in heaven. Here there is no mention at all of power, but only of the ministry of the one who absolves. One cannot but wonder what happened to these blind and overbearing men that they did not arrogate to themselves a despotic power from the promise of baptism; or, if they did not do it there, why they presumed to do it from the promise of penance? For in both there is a like ministry, a similar promise, and the same kind of sacrament. It cannot be denied: if baptism does not belong to Peter alone, then it is a wicked usurpation of power to claim the power of the keys for the pope alone.

Again, when Christ says: "Take, this is my body, which is given for you. This is the cup in my blood, etc." [I Cor. 11:24-25], he is calling forth the faith of those who eat, so that when their conscience has been strengthened by these words they might be certain through faith that they receive the forgiveness of sins when they have eaten. Here too, nothing is said of power, but only of the ministry.

So the promise of baptism remains to some extent, at least for infants; but the promise of the bread and the cup has been destroyed and made subservient to greed, faith has become a work and the testament has become a sacrifice. The promise of penance, however, has been transformed into the most oppressive despotism, being used to establish a sovereignty which is more than merely temporal.

Not content with these things, *this Babylon of ours has so completely extinguished faith* that it insolently *denies its necessity in this sacrament.* Indeed, with the wickedness of Antichrist it brands it as heresy for anyone to assert that faith is necessary. What more could this tyranny do than it has done? Truly, "by the waters of Babylon we sit down and weep, when we remember thee, O Zion. On the willows there we hang up our lyres" [Ps. 137:1-2]. May the Lord curse the barren willows of those streams! Amen.

Now that promise and faith have been thus blotted out and overthrown, let us see what they have put in their place. *They have divided penance into three parts—contrition, confession, and satisfaction;* but in such a way that they have removed whatever was good in each of them, and have established in each of them their caprice and their tyranny.

In the first place, they teach that contrition takes precedence over, and is far superior to, faith in the promise, as if contrition were not a work of faith, but a merit; indeed, they do not mention faith at all. They stick so closely to works and to those passages of Scripture where we read of many who obtained pardon by reason of their contrition and humility of heart; but they take no account of the faith which effected this contrition and sorrow of heart, as is written of the men of Nineveh in Jon. 3 [:5]: "And the people of Nineveh believed God; they proclaimed a fast, etc." Others again, more bold and wicked, have invented a so-called "attrition,"[149] which is converted into contrition by the power of the keys, of which they know nothing. This attrition they grant to the wicked and unbelieving, and thus abolish contrition altogether. O the intolerable wrath of God, that such things should be taught in the church of Christ! Thus, with both faith and its work destroyed, we go on secure in the doctrines and opinions of men, or rather we perish in them. A contrite heart is a precious thing, but it is found only where there is an ardent faith in the promises and threats of God. Such faith, intent on the immutable truth of God, makes the conscience tremble, terrifies it and bruises it; and afterwards, when it is contrite, raises it up, consoles it, and preserves it. Thus the truth of God's threat is the cause of contrition, and the truth of his promise the cause of consolation, if it is believed. By such a faith a man "merits" the forgiveness of sins. Therefore faith should be taught and aroused before all else. Once faith is obtained, contrition and consolation will follow inevitably of themselves.

Therefore, although there is some truth in their teaching that contrition is to be attained by the enumeration and contemplation (as they call it) of their sins, yet their teaching is perilous and perverse so long as they do not teach first of all the beginnings and causes of contrition—the immutable truth of God's threat and promise which calls forth faith—so that men may learn to pay more heed to the truth of God, by which they are cast down and lifted up, than to the multitude of their sins. If their sins are regarded apart from the truth of God, they will excite afresh and increase the desire for sin rather than lead to contrition. I will say nothing now of the insurmountable

---

149. Contrition involved a detestation of sin arising out of love for God and regret at having offended him. Attrition involved a hatred of sin arising out of lesser motives, such as loss of heaven, fear of hell, or the heinousness of guilt. Attrition, though imperfect, was held to be sufficient, since it predisposed the sinner to receive through the sacrament of penance that grace which transformed it into perfect contrition. Cf. LW 31, 21.

task which they have imposed upon us, namely, that we are to frame a contrition for every sin. That is impossible. We can know only the smaller part of our sins; and even our good works are found to be sins, according to Ps. 143 [:2]¹⁵⁰: "Enter not into judgment with thy servant; for no man living is righteous before thee." It is enough if we lament the sins which distress our conscience at the present moment, as well as those which we can readily call to mind. Whoever is in this frame of mind is without doubt ready to grieve and fear for all his sins, and will grieve and fear whenever they are brought to his knowledge in the future.

Beware then, of putting your trust in your own contrition and of ascribing the forgiveness of sins to your own remorse. God does not look on you with favor because of that, but because of the faith by which you have believed his threats and promises, and which has effected such sorrow within you. Thus we owe whatever good there may be in our penance, not to our scrupulous enumeration of sins, but to the truth of God and to our faith. All other things are the works and fruits which follow of their own accord. They do not make a man good, but are done by the man who is already made good through faith in the truth of God. Even so, "smoke goes up in his wrath; because he is angry he shakes the mountains and sets them on fire," as it is said in Ps. 18 [:8, 7]). First comes the terror of this threatening, which sets the wicked on fire; then faith, accepting this, sends up smoke-clouds of contrition, etc.

But the trouble is not so much that contrition has been exposed to tyranny and avarice, as that it has been given over completely to wickedness and pestilent teaching. It is confession and satisfaction that have become the chief workshops of greed and power.

---

150. Where Luther cites correctly the Vulgate version, in which Psalms 10-146 are numbered differently from the numbering used in the RSV, we have given the corresponding RSV Psalm reference.

Let us first take up *confession.*

There is no doubt that confession of sins is necessary and commanded of God, in Matt. 3 [:6]: "They were baptized by John in the river Jordan, confessing their sins," and in I John 1 [:9-10]: "If we confess our sins, he is faithful and just, and will forgive our sins. If we say we have not sinned, we make him a liar, and his word is not in us." If the saints may not deny their sin, how much more ought those who are guilty of great and public sins to make confession! But the institution of confession is proved most effectively of all by Matt. 18 [:15-17], where Christ teaches that a sinning brother should be told of his fault, brought before the church, accused, and if he will not hear, be excommunicated. He "hears" if he needs the rebuke and acknowledges and confesses his sin.

As to the current practice of private confession, I am heartily in favor of it, even though it cannot be proved from the Scriptures. It is useful, even necessary, and I would not have it abolished. Indeed, I rejoice that it exists in the church of Christ, for it is a cure without equal for distressed consciences. For when we have laid bare our conscience to our brother and privately made known to him the evil that lurked within, we receive from our brother's lips the word of comfort spoken by God himself. And, if we accept this in faith, we find peace in the mercy of God speaking to us through our brother. There is just one thing about it that I abominate, and that is the fact that this kind of confession has been subjected to the despotism and extortion of the pontiffs. They reserve[151] to themselves even the secret sins, and command that they be made known to confessors named by them, only to trouble the consciences of men. They merely play the pontiff, while they utterly despise the

---

151. In "reserved cases," *casus episcopales* or *casus papales,* only the bishop or pope, or one appointed by them, could absolve. Cf. *To the Christian Nobility of the German Nation.* P. 51 above.

true duties of pontiffs, which are to preach the gospel and to care for the poor. Indeed, the godless despots leave the great sins to the common priests, and reserve to themselves only those sins which are of less consequence, such as those ridiculous and fictitious things in the bull *Coena domini*.[152] To make the wickedness of their error even more apparent, they not only fail to reserve, but actually teach and approve things which are against the service of God, against faith and the chief commandments—such as their running about on pilgrimages, the perverse worship of the saints, the lying saints' legends, the various ways of trusting in works and ceremonies and practicing them. Yet in all of these faith in God is extinguished and idolatry fostered, as we see in our day. As a result we have the same kind of priests today as Jeroboam ordained of old in Dan and Beersheba, ministers of the golden calves [I Kings 12:26-32], men who are ignorant of the law of God, of faith, and of whatever pertains to the feeding of Christ's sheep. They inculcate in the people nothing but their own inventions with fear and violence.

Although I urge that this outrage of reserved cases should be borne patiently, even as Christ bids us bear all the tyranny of men, and teaches us that we should obey these extortioners; nevertheless, I deny that they have the right to make such reservations, and I do not believe that they can bring one jot or tittle of proof that they have it. But I am going to prove the contrary. In the first place, Christ speaks in Matt. 18 [:15-17] of public sins and says that if our brother hears us, when we tell him his fault, we have

---

152. *Coena domini* was a papal bull published annually against heretics since 1364 in the Lateran Church at Rome on Holy Thursday. But to the condemnation of their heresies were added those offenses, absolvable only by the pope or by his authorization, which might conceivably endanger or impair the papal state. Luther was named in the bull for the first time on March 28, 1521, along with Wycliffe and Huss. In 1522 Luther translated this bull into German as a New Year's present for the pope. WA 8, 691; cf. pp. 50-51 above.

saved the soul of our brother, and that he is to be brought before the church only if he refuses to hear us, so that his sin can be corrected among brethren. How much more will it be true of secret sins, that they are forgiven if one brother freely makes confession to another? So it is not necessary to tell it to the church, that is, as these babblers interpret it, to the prelate or priest. On this matter we have further authority from Christ, where he says in the same chapter: "Whatever you bind on earth shall be bound in heaven, and whatever you loose on earth shall be loosed in heaven" [Matt. 18:18]. For this is said to each and every Christian. Again, he says in the same place: "Again I say to you, if two of you agree on earth about anything they ask, it will be done for them by my father in heaven" [Matt. 18:19]. Now, the brother who lays his secret sins before his brother and craves pardon, certainly agrees with his brother on earth, in the truth which is Christ. Of this Christ says even more clearly, confirming his preceding words: "For truly, I say to you, where two or three are gathered in my name, there am I in the midst of them" [Matt. 18:20].

Hence, I have no doubt but that every one is absolved from his secret sins when he has made confession, privately before any brother, either of his own accord or after being rebuked, and has sought pardon and amended his ways, no matter how much the violence of the pontiffs may rage against it. For Christ has given to every one of his believers the power to absolve even open sins. Add yet this little point: If any reservation of secret sins were valid, so that one could not be saved unless they were forgiven, then a man's salvation would be prevented most of all by those aforementioned good works and idolatries which are taught by the popes nowadays. But if these most grievous sins do not prevent one's salvation, how foolish it is to reserve those lighter sins! In truth, it is the foolishness and blindness of the shepherds that produce these monstrous things in the church. Therefore I would admonish those princes of Babylon and bishops of Beth-aven[153] to refrain from reserving any cases whatsoever. Let them, moreover, permit all brothers and sisters most freely to hear the confession of secret sins, so that the sinner may make his sins known to whomever he will and seek pardon and comfort, that is, the word of Christ, by the mouth of his neighbor. For with these presumptions of theirs they only ensnare the consciences of the weak without necessity, establish their wicked despotism, and fatten their avarice on the sins and ruin of their brethren. Thus they stain their hands with the blood of souls; sons are devoured by their parents. Ephraim devours Judah, and Syria Israel, with an open mouth, as Isaiah [9:20-21] says.

To these evils they have added the "circumstances,"[154] and also the mothers, daughters, sisters, sisters-in-law, branches and fruits of sins; since these most astute and idle men have worked out, if you please, a kind of family tree of relationships and affinities even among sins—so prolific is wickedness coupled with ignorance. For this conception, whatever rogue may be its author, has become a public law, like many others. Thus do the shepherds keep watch over the church of Christ: whatever new work or superstition those most stupid devotees may have dreamed of, they immediately drag to the light of day, deck out with indulgences, and fortify with bulls. So far are they from suppressing such things and preserving for God's people true faith and liberty. For what has our liberty to do with the tyranny of Babylon?

My advice would be to ignore all "circumstances" whatsoever. With Christians there is only one circumstance—that a brother has sinned. For there is no person to be compared with a Christian brother. And the observance of

---

153. Hos. 4:15, 10:5. The prophet altered the name Bethel (house of God) to Beth-aven (house of nothingness or idolatry) because of the images which had been erected there.
154. Cf. p. 183 n. 116.

places, times, days, persons,[155] and all other rank superstition, only magnifies the things that are nothing, to the injury of the things which are everything; as if anything could be of greater weight or importance than the glory of Christian brotherhood! Thus they bind us to places, days, and persons, so that the name of "brother" loses its value, and we serve in bondage instead of being free—we, to whom all days, places, persons, and all external things are one and the same.

How unworthily they have dealt with *satisfaction*, I have abundantly shown in the controversies concerning indulgences.[156] They have grossly abused it, to the ruin of Christians in body and soul. To begin with, they have taught it in such a manner that the people have never had the slightest understanding what satisfaction really is, namely, the renewal of a man's life. Then, they so continually harp on it and emphasize its necessity that they leave no room for faith in Christ. With these scruples they torture poor consciences to death; and one runs to Rome, one to this place, another to that; this one to Chartreuse,[157] that one to some other place; one scourges himself with rods, another mortifies his body with fasts and vigils; and all cry with the same mad zeal: "Lo, here is Christ! Lo, there!" believing that the kingdom of Christ, which is within us, will come with observation.[158]

For these monstrous things we are indebted to you, O

---

155. Sins were assessed differently according to whether they were committed at a holy place or not, on holy days or on ordinary days. Murder of a priest was a more grievous sin than murder of a layman. Buchwald, *op cit.*, II, 465.
156. Cf. p. 206 n. 147; especially in the *Explanations of the Ninety-five Theses*, *LW* 31, 85, 94-96, 152-53.
157. This was the mother cloister and headquarters of the rigidly ascetic Carthusian order.
158. Luke 17:20-21. A play on *observantia*, which also means "observance," a fling at the Observants. Cf. p. 202 n. 138.

Roman See, and to your murderous laws and ceremonies, with which you have corrupted all mankind, so that they believe they can with works make satisfaction for sin to God, when he can be satisfied only by the faith of a contrite heart! Not only do you keep this faith silent with this uproar of yours, but you even oppress it, only so that your insatiable bloodsucker may have those to whom it may say, "Give, give!" [Prov. 30:15] and may traffic in sins.

Some have gone even farther and have constructed those instruments for driving souls to despair, their decrees that the penitent must rehearse all sins anew for which he neglected to make the imposed satisfaction. What would they not venture to do, these men who were born for the sole purpose of carrying all things into a tenfold captivity? Moreover, how many, I ask, are possessed with the notion that they are in a saved state and are making satisfaction for their sins, if they only mumble over, word for word, the prayers imposed by the priest, even though meanwhile they never give a thought to the amending of their way of life! They believe that their life is changed in the one moment of contrition and confession, and there remains only to make satisfaction for their past sins. How should they know better if they have not been taught otherwise? No thought is given here to the mortifying of the flesh, no value is attached to the example of Christ, who, when he absolved the woman caught in adultery, said: "Go, and do not sin again" [John 8:11], thereby laying upon her the cross, that is, the mortifying of her flesh. This perverse error is greatly encouraged by the fact that we absolve sinners before the satisfaction has been completed, so that they are more concerned about completing the satisfaction, which is a lasting thing, than they are about contrition, which they suppose to be over and done with when they have made confession. Absolution ought rather to follow on the completion of satisfaction, as it did in the early church, with the result that, after completing the work, penitents gave themselves with much greater diligence to faith and the living of a new life.

But this must suffice in repetition of what I have said more fully in connection with indulgences, and *in general this must suffice for the present concerning the three sacraments,* which have been treated, and yet not treated, in so many harmful books on the *Sentences* and on the laws. It remains to attempt some discussion of the other "sacraments" [159] also, lest I seem to have rejected them without cause.

CONFIRMATION

It is amazing that it should have entered the minds of these men to make a sacrament of confirmation out of the laying on of hands. We read that Christ touched the little children in that way [Mark 10:16], and that by it the apostles imparted the Holy Spirit [Acts 8:17; 19:6], ordained presbyters [Acts 6:6], and cured the sick [Mark 16:18]; as the Apostle writes to Timothy: "Do not be hasty in the laying on of hands" [I Tim. 5:22]. Why have they not also made a "confirmation" out of the sacrament of the bread? For it is written in Acts 9 [:19]: "And he took food and was strengthened," [160] and in Ps. 104 [:15]: "And bread to strengthen man's heart." Confirmation would thus include three sacraments—the bread, ordination, and confirmation itself. But if everything the apostles did is a sacrament, why have they not rather made preaching a sacrament?

I do not say this because I condemn the seven sacraments, but because I deny that they can be proved from the Scriptures. Would that there were in the church such a laying on of hands as there was in apostolic times, whether we chose to call it confirmation or healing! But there is nothing left of it now but what we ourselves have invented

---

159. Cf. pp. 132 and 240.
160. Luther correctly quotes *confortatus,* but thinks *confirmatus.*

to adorn the office of bishops, that they may not be entirely without work in the church. For after they relinquished to their inferiors those arduous sacraments together with the Word as being beneath their attention (since whatever the divine majesty has instituted must needs be despised of men!) it was no more than right that we should discover something easy and not too burdensome for such delicate and great heroes to do, and should by no means entrust it to the lower clergy as something common, for whatever human wisdom has decreed must be held in honor among men! Therefore, as the priests are, so let their ministry and duty be. For a bishop who does not preach the gospel or practice the cure of souls—what is he but an idol in the world [I Cor. 8:4], who has nothing but the name and appearance of a bishop?

But *instead of this we seek sacraments that have been divinely instituted, and among these we see no reason for numbering confirmation.* For to constitute a sacrament there must be above all things else a word of divine promise, by which faith may be exercised. But we read nowhere that Christ ever gave a promise concerning confirmation, although he laid hands on many and included the laying on of hands among the signs in the last chapter of Mark [16:18]: "They will lay their hands on the sick; and they will recover." Yet no one has applied this to a sacrament, for that is not possible.

For this reason it is sufficient to regard confirmation as a certain churchly rite or sacramental ceremony, similar to other ceremonies, such as the blessing of water and the like. For if every other creature is sanctified by the Word and by prayer [I Tim. 4:4-5], why should not man much rather be sanctified by the same means? Still, these things cannot be called sacraments of faith, because they have no divine promise connected with them, neither do they save; but the sacraments do save those who believe the divine promise.

Not only is marriage regarded as a sacrament without the least warrant of Scripture, but the very ordinances which extol it as a sacrament have turned it into a farce. Let us look into this a little.

We have said that in every sacrament there is a word of divine promise, to be believed by whoever receives the sign, and that the sign alone cannot be a sacrament. Nowhere do we read that the man who marries a wife receives any grace of God. There is not even a divinely instituted sign in marriage, nor do we read anywhere that marriage was instituted by God to be a sign of anything. To be sure, whatever takes place in a visible manner can be understood as a figure or allegory of something invisible. But figures or allegories are not sacraments, in the sense in which we use the term.

Furthermore, since marriage has existed from the beginning of the world and is still found among unbelievers, there is no reason why it should be called a sacrament of the New Law and of the church alone. The marriages of the ancients were no less sacred than are ours, nor are those of unbelievers less true marriages than those of believers, and yet they are not regarded as sacraments. Besides, even among believers there are married folk who are wicked and worse than any heathen; why should marriage be called a sacrament in their case and not among the heathen? Or are we going to talk the same sort of nonsense about baptism and the church and say that marriage is a sacrament only in the church, just as some make the mad claim that temporal power exists only in the church? That is childish and foolish talk, by which we expose our ignorance and foolhardiness to the ridicule of unbelievers.

But they will say, "The Apostle says in Eph. 5 [:31-32],

'The two shall become one. This is a great sacrament.' [161] Surely you are not going to contradict so plain a statement of the Apostle!" I reply: This argument like the others betrays great shallowness and a careless and thoughtless reading of Scripture. Nowhere in all of the Holy Scriptures is this word *sacramentum* employed in the sense in which we use the term; it has an entirely different meaning. For wherever it occurs it denotes not the sign of a sacred thing, but the sacred, secret, hidden thing itself. Thus Paul writes in I Cor. 4 [:1]: "This is how one should regard us, as servants of Christ and stewards of the 'mysteries' of God," that is, the sacraments. For where we have [in the Vulgate] the word *sacramentum* the Greek original has *mysterion*, which the translator sometimes translates and sometimes retains in its Greek form. Thus our verse in the Greek reads: "They two shall become one. This is a great mystery." This explains how they came to understand a sacrament of the New Law here, a thing they would never have done if they had read *mysterium*, as it is in the Greek.[162]

Thus Christ himself is called a "sacrament" in I Tim. 3 [:16]: "Great indeed, is the sacrament (that is the mystery): He was manifested in the flesh, vindicated in the Spirit, seen by angels, preached among the nations, believed on in the world, taken up in glory." Why have they not drawn out of this passage an eighth sacrament [163] of the New Law, since they have the clear authority of Paul? But if they restrained themselves here, where they had a most excellent opportunity to invent new sacraments, why are they so

---

161. The quotation is from the Vulgate. Luther points to its divergence from the Greek original, which the English versions have more literally rendered with the word "mystery."

162. Erasmus edited the first published Greek New Testament in March, 1516. Luther used Erasmus' work as soon as it came out, as may be seen in his lectures on Romans, 1515-16. In an interesting letter to Luther of February 14, 1519, Froben announces the second edition of Erasmus' New Testament, which Luther used in making his translation, 1521-22. PE 2, 258 n. 2.

163. Cf. pp. 132 and 240.

unrestrained in the other passage? Plainly, it was their ignorance of both words and things that betrayed them. They clung to the mere sound of the words, indeed, to their own fancies. For, having once arbitrarily taken the word *sacramentum* to mean a sign, they immediately, without thought or scruple, made a "sign" of it every time they came upon it in the Holy Scriptures. Such new meanings of words, human customs, and other things they have dragged into the Holy Scriptures. They have transformed the Scriptures according to their own dreams, making anything out of any passage whatsoever. Thus they continually chatter nonsense about the terms: good work, evil work, sin, grace, righteousness, virtue, and almost all the fundamental words and things. For they employ them all after their own arbitrary judgment, learned from the writings of men, to the detriment of both the truth of God and of our salvation.

Therefore, sacrament, or mystery, in Paul is that wisdom of the Spirit, hidden in a mystery, as he says in I Cor. 2 [:7], which is Christ, who for this very reason is not known to the rulers of this world, wherefore they also crucified him, and for them he remains to this day folly [I Cor. 1:23], an offense, a stumbling stone [Rom. 9:32-33], and a sign that is spoken against [Luke 2:34]. The preachers he calls stewards [I Cor. 4:1] of these mysteries because they preach Christ, the power and the wisdom of God [I Cor. 1:24], yet in such a way that, unless you believe, you cannot understand it. Therefore, a sacrament is a mystery, or secret thing, which is set forth in words, but received by the faith of the heart. Such a sacrament is spoken of in the passage before us: "The two shall become one. This is a great sacrament" [Eph. 5:31-32], which they understand as spoken of marriage, whereas Paul himself wrote these words as applying to Christ and the church, and clearly explained them himself by saying: "I take it to mean Christ and the church" [Eph. 5:32]. See how well Paul and these men agree! Paul says he is proclaiming a great sacrament in Christ and the church, but they proclaim it in terms of man and a woman! If such liberty in the interpretation of the sacred Scriptures is permitted, it is small wonder that one finds here anything he pleases, even a hundred sacraments.

Christ and the church are, therefore, a mystery, that is, a great and secret thing which can and ought to be represented in terms of marriage as a kind of outward allegory. But marriage ought not for that reason to be called a sacrament. The heavens are a type of the apostles, as Ps. 19 declares; the sun is a type of Christ; the waters, of the peoples; but that does not make those things sacraments, for in every case there are lacking both the divine institution and the divine promise, which constitute a sacrament. Hence Paul, in Eph. 5 [:29-32], following his own mind, applies to Christ these words of Gen. 2 [:24] about marriage; or else, following the general view,[164] he teaches that the spiritual marriage of Christ is also contained therein, when he says: "As Christ cherishes the church, because we are members of his body, of his flesh and his bones. 'For this reason a man shall leave his father and mother and be joined to his wife, and the two shall become one.' This is a great sacrament, and I take it to mean Christ and the church." You see, he would have the whole passage apply to Christ, and is at pains to admonish the reader to understand that the sacrament is in Christ and the church, not in marriage.[165]

---

164. The precise meaning is not clear.
165. The following paragraph, because it clearly breaks into the context and belongs elsewhere, is here relegated to a footnote:

I admit, of course, that the sacrament of penance existed in the Old Law, and even from the beginning of the world. But the new promise of penance and the gift of the keys are peculiar to the New Law. Just as we now have baptism instead of circumcision, so we have the keys instead of sacrifices and other signs of penance. We said above that the same God at various times gave different promises and diverse signs for the remission of sins and the salvation of men; nevertheless, all received the same grace. Thus it is said in II Cor. 4 [:13]: "Since we have the same spirit of

Granted that marriage is a figure of Christ and the church; yet it is not a divinely instituted sacrament, but invented by men in the church who are carried away by their ignorance of both the word and the thing. This ignorance, when it does not conflict with the faith, is to be borne in charity, just as many other human practices due to weakness and ignorance are borne in the church, so long as they do not conflict with the faith and the Holy Scriptures. But we are now arguing for the certainty and purity of faith and the Scriptures. We expose our faith to ridicule if we affirm that a certain thing is contained in the sacred Scriptures and in the articles of our faith, only to be refuted and shown that it is not contained in them; being found ignorant of our own affairs, we become a stumbling block to our opponents and to the weak. But most of all we should guard against impairing the authority of the Holy Scriptures. For those things which have been delivered to us by God in the sacred Scriptures must be sharply distinguished from those that have been invented by men in the church, no matter how eminent they may be for saintliness and scholarship.

So far concerning marriage itself.

But what shall we say *concerning the wicked laws of men by which this divinely ordained way of life has been ensnared* and tossed to and fro? Good God! It is dreadful to contemplate the audacity of the Roman despots, who

---

faith, we too believe, and so we speak." And in I Cor. 10 [:1-4]: "Our fathers all ate the same supernatural food and drank the same supernatural drink. For they drank from the supernatural Rock which followed them, and the Rock was Christ." Thus also in Heb. 11 [:13, 40]: "These all died, not having received what was promised, since God had foreseen something better for us, that apart from us they should not be made perfect." For Christ himself is, yesterday and today and forever [Heb. 13:8], the head of his church, from the beginning even to the end of the world. Therefore there are diverse signs, but the faith of all is the same. Indeed, without faith it is impossible to please God, yet by it Abel did please him (Heb. 11 [:4]).

both dissolve and compel marriages as they please. I ask you, has mankind been handed over to the caprice of these men for them to mock them and in every way abuse them and make of them whatever they please, for the sake of filthy lucre?

There is circulating far and wide and enjoying a great reputation a book whose contents have been confusedly poured together out of all the dregs and filth of man-made ordinances. Its title is "The Angelic *Summa*,"[166] although it ought rather to be "The More than Devilish *Summa*." Among endless other monstrosities, which are supposed to instruct the confessors, whereas they most mischievously confuse them, there are enumerated in this book eighteen impediments to marriage.[167] If you will examine these with the just and unprejudiced eye of faith, you will see that they belong to those things which the Apostle foretold: "There shall be those that give heed to the spirits of demons, speaking lies in hypocrisy, forbidding to marry" [I Tim. 4:1-3]. What is "forbidding to marry" if it is not this—to invent all those hindrances and set those snares in order to prevent people from marrying, or, if they are married, to annul their marriage? Who gave this power to men? Granted that they were holy men and impelled by godly zeal, why should another's holiness disturb my liberty? Why should another's zeal take me captive? Let whoever will be a saint and a zealot, and to his heart's content, only let him not bring harm upon another, and let him not rob me of my liberty!

166. The *Summa de casibus conscientiae*, popularly named after its author, Angelo Carletti di Chivasso (1411-1495); a favorite handbook on casuistry treating alphabetically all possible cases of conscience, for the guidance of priests hearing confession. Under the heading of "Matrimony" it listed 18 impediments to marriage. The book went through 31 editions between 1476 and 1520, and was among the papal books burned by Luther, together with the bull, December 10, 1520. (Cf. Luther's letter to Spalatin on the same day, *LW* 48, 186-187.)

167. For fuller discussion of the impediments see Luther's *The Estate of Marriage* (1522), *LW* 45, 23-30; see also the article on "Marriage" by E. Sehling, in Schaff-Herzog, *op. cit.*, VII, 200-03.

Yet I am glad that those shameful laws have at last reached their full measure of glory, which is this: that the Romanists of our day have through them become merchants. What is it that they sell? Vulvas and genitals— merchandise indeed most worthy of such merchants, grown altogether filthy and obscene through greed and godlessness. For there is no impediment nowadays that may not be legalized through the intercession of mammon. These laws of men seem to have sprung into existence for the sole purpose of serving those greedy men and rapacious Nimrods [Gen. 10:8-9] [168] as snares for taking money and as nets for catching souls, and in order that "abomination" might stand in "the holy place" [Matt. 24:15], the church of God, and openly sell to men the pudenda of both sexes, or (as the Scriptures say) "shame and nakedness" [Lev. 18:6-18], of which they had previously robbed them by means of their laws. O worthy trade for our pontiffs to ply, instead of the ministry of the gospel, which in their greed and pride they despise, being given up to a reprobate mind [Rom. 1.28] with utter shame and infamy.

But what shall I say or do? If I enter into details, the treatise will grow beyond all bounds. Everything is in such dire confusion that one does not know where to begin, how far to go, and where to leave off. This I do know, that no state is governed successfully by means of laws. If the ruler is wise, he will govern better by a natural sense of justice than by laws. If he is not wise, he will foster nothing but evil through legislation, since he will not know what use to make of the laws nor how to adapt them to the case at hand. Therefore, in civil affairs more stress should be laid on putting good and wise men in office than on making laws; for such men will themselves be the very best of laws, and will judge every variety of case with a lively sense of equity. And if there is knowledge of the divine

168. Cf. p. 124.

law combined with natural wisdom, then written laws will be entirely superfluous and harmful. Above all, love needs no laws whatever.

Nevertheless, I will say and do what I can. I ask and urge all priests and friars[169] when they encounter any impediment to marriage from which the pope can grant dispensation but which is not stated in the Scriptures, by all means to confirm[170] all marriages that may have been contracted[171] in any way contrary to the ecclesiastical or pontifical laws. But let them arm themselves with the divine law which says: "What God has joined together, let no man put asunder" [Matt. 19:6]. For the joining together of a man and a woman is of divine law and is binding, however much it may conflict with the laws of men; the laws of men must give way before it without any hesitation. For if a man leaves father and mother and cleaves to his wife [Matt. 19:5], how much more will he tread underfoot the silly and wicked laws of men, in order to cleave to his wife! And if pope, bishop, or official[172] should annul any marriage because it was contracted contrary to the laws of men, he is Antichrist, he does violence to nature, and is guilty of treason against the Divine Majesty, because this word stands: "What God has joined together, let no man put asunder" [Matt. 19:6].

Besides this, no man had the right to frame such laws, and Christ has granted to Christians a liberty which is above all the laws of men, especially where a law of God conflicts with them. Thus it is said in Mark 2 [:28]: "The Son of man is lord even of the sabbath," and "Man was not made for the sabbath, but the sabbath for man" [Mark

---

169. It is to be borne in mind that all that follows is in the nature of advice to confessors in dealing with difficult cases of conscience, and is parallel to the closing paragraphs of the section on the Sacrament of the Bread.
170. Namely, by officiating at the marriage ceremony.
171. Namely, by betrothal.
172. Judge of the bishop's court.

2:27]. Moreover, such laws were condemned beforehand by Paul when he foretold that there would be men forbidding to marry [I Tim. 4:3]. Here, therefore, those inflexible impediments derived from affinity, by spiritual or legal relationship,[173] and from blood relationship must give way, so far as the Scriptures permit, in which the second degree of consanguinity alone is prohibited. Thus it is written in Lev. 18 [:6-18], where there are twelve persons a man is prohibited from marrying: his mother, stepmother, full sister, half-sister by either parent, granddaughter, father's or mother's sister, daughter-in-law, brother's wife, wife's sister, stepdaughter, and his uncle's wife. Here only the first degree of affinity and the second degree of consanguinity are forbidden; yet not without exception, as will appear on closer examination, for the brother's or sister's daughter—the niece—is not included in the prohibition, although she is in the second degree. Therefore, if a marriage has been contracted outside of these degrees, which are the only ones which have been prohibited by God's appointment, it should by no means be annulled on account of the laws of men. For marriage itself, being a divine institution, is incomparably superior to any laws, so that marriage should not be annulled for the sake of the law, rather the laws should be broken for the sake of marriage.

In the same way that nonsense about compaternities, commaternities, confraternities, consororities, and conflieties must be completely abolished in the contracting of marriage. What was it but the superstition of men that invented this "spiritual affinity"? If one who baptized is not permitted to marry her whom he has baptized or stood sponsor for, what right has any Christian man to marry a Christian woman? Is the relationship that grows out of the external rite or sign of the sacrament more inimate than

---

173. Relationships arising from godparents or legal adoption. Cf. *To the Christian Nobility of the German Nation.* Above, p. 68, n. 138, p. 74.

that which grows out of the blessing of the sacrament[174] itself? Is not a Christian man the brother of a Christian woman, and is she not his sister? Is not a baptized man the spiritual brother of a baptized woman? How foolish we are! If a man instructs his wife in the gospel and in faith in Christ, does he not truly become her father in Christ? And is it not lawful for her to remain his wife? Would not Paul have had the right to marry a girl from among the Corinthians, of whom he boasts that he became their father in Christ? [I Cor. 4:15]. See then, how Christian liberty has been suppressed through the blindness of human superstition.

There is even less in the "legal affinity," and yet they have set it above the divine right of marriage. Nor would I agree to that impediment which they call "disparity of religion," which forbids one to marry an unbaptized person, either simply, or on condition that she be converted to the faith. Who made this prohibition? God or man? Who gave to men the power to prohibit such a marriage? Indeed, the spirits that speak lies in hypocrisy, as Paul says [I Tim. 4:2]. Of them it must be said: "Godless men have told me fables which do not conform to thy law" [Ps. 119:85].[175] The heathen Patricius married the Christian Monica, mother of St. Augustine; why should that not be permitted today? The same stupid, or rather, wicked severity is seen in the "impediment of crime," as when a man has married a woman with whom he previously had committed adultery, or when he plotted to bring about the death of a woman's husband in order to be able to wed the widow. I ask you, whence comes this cruelty of man toward man, which even God never demanded? Do they pretend not to know that Bathsheba, the wife of Uriah, was wed by David, a most saintly man, after the double crime of adultery and mur-

---

174. *res sacramenti*, cf. p. 137 n. 45.
175. Vulgate version.

der? [II Sam. 11:1-27]. If the divine law did this, what are these despotic men doing to their fellow servants?

They also recognize what they call "the impediment of a tie," that is, when a man is bound to another woman by betrothal. Here they conclude that, if he has had sexual relations with a second woman, his engagement to the first becomes null and void. This I do not understand at all. I hold that he who has betrothed himself to one woman no longer belongs to himself. Because of this fact, by the prohibition of the divine law, he belongs to the first with whom he has not had intercourse, even though he has had intercourse with the second. For it was not in his power to give the latter what was no longer his own; he has deceived her and actually committed adultery. But they regard the matter differently because they pay more heed to the carnal union than to the divine command, according to which the man, having plighted his troth to the first, is bound to keep it forever. For whoever would give anything must give of that which is his own. And God forbids a man to transgress and wrong his brother in any matter [I Thess. 4:6]. This must be observed over and above all the ordinances of all men. Therefore I believe that such a man cannot with a good conscience live in marriage with a second woman, and this impediment should be completely reversed. For if a monastic vow makes a man no longer his own, why does not a pledge of mutual faithfulness[176] do the same? After all, faithfulness is one of the precepts and fruits of the Spirit, in Gal. 5: [22], while a monastic vow is of human invention. And if a wife may claim her husband back, despite the fact that he has taken a monastic vow, why may not an engaged woman claim back her betrothed, even though he has intercourse with another?

---

176. *fides data et accepta.* Luther here regards the *fides* of Gal. 5:22 as *Treue* or "faithfulness." In his New Testament he later translates it as *Glaube* or "faith."

But we have said above[177] that he who has plighted his troth to a girl may not take a monastic vow, but is in duty bound to marry her because he is in duty bound to keep faith with her; and this faith he may not break for any ordinance of men, because it is commanded by God. Much more should the man here keep faith with his first betrothed, since he could not plight his troth to a second except with a lying heart; and therefore did not really plight it, but deceived her, his neighbor, against God's command. Therefore, the "impediment of error"[178] enters in here, by which his marriage to the second woman is rendered null and void.

The "impediment of ordination" is also the mere invention of men, especially since they prate that it annuls even a marriage already contracted. They constantly exalt their own ordinances above the commands of God. I do not indeed sit in judgment on the present state of the priestly order, but I observe that Paul charges a bishop to be the husband of one wife [I Tim. 3.2]. Hence, no marriage of deacon, priest, bishop or any other order can be annulled, although it is true that Paul knew nothing of this species of priests and of the orders we have today. Perish then those cursed man-made ordinances which have crept into the church only to multiply perils, sins, and evils! There exists, therefore, between a priest and his wife a true and indissoluble marriage, approved by the divine commandment. But what if wicked men in sheer despotism prohibit or annul it? So be it! Let it be wrong among men; it is nevertheless right before God, whose command must take precedence if it conflicts with the commands of men [Acts 5:29].

An equally lying invention is that "impediment of public

177. Cf. p. 204.
178. With fine sarcasm Luther here plays off one impediment against another. "Error" generally meant cases of mistaken identity or false information concerning prior marital status. Cf. WA 10^{II}, 285.

decency," by which contracted marriages are annulled. I am incensed at that barefaced wickedness which is so ready to put asunder what God has joined together that one may well recognize Antichrist in it, for it opposes all that Christ has done and taught. What earthly reason is there for holding that no relative of a deceased fiancé, even to the fourth degree of consanguinity, may marry his fiancée? That is not a judgment of public decency, but ignorance[179] of public decency. Why was not this judgment of public decency found among the people of Israel, who were endowed with the best laws, the laws of God? On the contrary, the next of kin was even compelled by the law of God to marry the widow of his relative [Deut. 25:5]. Must the people of Christian liberty be burdened with more severe laws than the people of legal bondage?

But, to make an end of these—figments rather than impediments—I will say that so far there seem to me to be no impediments that may justly annul a contracted marriage except these: sexual impotence, ignorance of a previously contracted marriage, and a vow of chastity. Still, concerning this latter vow, I am to this day so far from certain that I do not know at what age such a vow is to be regarded as binding, as I also said above in discussing the sacrament of baptism.[180] Thus you may learn, from this one question of marriage, how wretchedly and desperately all the activities of the church have been confused, hindered, ensnared and subjected to danger through the pestilent, ignorant, and wicked ordinances of men, so that there is no hope of betterment unless we abolish at one stroke all the laws of all men, and having restored the gospel of liberty we follow it in judging and regulating all things. Amen.

We must therefore speak of sexual impotence, in order

---

179. An untranslatable pun: *non iustitia sed inscitia*.
180. Cf. pp. 205-06.

that we may the more readily advise the souls that are laboring in peril.[181] But first I wish to state that what I have said about impediments is intended to apply after a marriage has been contracted. I mean to say that no marriage should be annulled by any such impediment. But as to marriages which are yet to be contracted, I would briefly repeat what I have said above.[182] If there is the stress of youthful passion or some other necessity for which the pope grants dispensation, then any brother may also grant a dispensation to another or even to himself, and following that counsel snatch his wife out of the power of tyrannical laws as best he can. For with what right am I deprived of my liberty by somebody else's superstition and ignorance? If the pope grants a dispensation for money, why should not I, for my soul's salvation, grant a dispensation to myself or to my brother? Does the pope set up laws? Let him set them up for himself, and keep hands off my liberty, or I will take it by stealth!

Now let us discuss the matter of *impotence.*

Consider the following case: A woman, wed to an impotent man, is unable to prove her husband's impotence in court, or perhaps she is unwilling to do so with the mass of evidence and all the notoriety which the law demands; yet she is desirous of having children or is unable to remain continent. Now suppose I had counseled her to procure a divorce from her husband in order to marry another, satisfied that her own and her husband's conscience and their experience were ample testimony of his impotence; but the husband refused his consent to this. Then I would further counsel her, with the consent of the man (who is not really her husband, but only a dweller under the same roof with her), to have intercourse with another, say her husband's brother, but to keep this marriage secret and to ascribe the

181. Cf. p. 227 n. 169
182. Cf. pp. 224-25.

children to the so-called putative father. The question is: Is such a woman saved and in a saved state? I answer: Certainly, because in this case an error,[183] ignorance of the man's impotence, impedes the marriage; and the tyranny of the laws permits no divorce. But the woman is free through the divine law, and cannot be compelled to remain continent. Therefore the man ought to concede her right, and give up to somebody else the wife who is his only in outward appearance.

Moreover, if the man will not give his consent, or agree to this separation—rather than allow the woman to burn [I Cor. 7:9] or to commit adultery—I would counsel her to contract a marriage with another and flee to a distant unknown place. What other counsel can be given to one constantly struggling with the dangers of natural emotions? Now I know that some are troubled by the fact that the children of this secret marriage are not the rightful heirs of their putative father. But if it was done with the consent of the husband, then the children will be the rightful heirs. If, however, it was done without his knowledge or against his will, then let unbiased Christian reason, or better, charity, decide which one of the two has done the greater injury to the other. The wife alienates the inheritance, but the husband has deceived his wife and is defrauding her completely of her body and her life. Is not the sin of a man who wastes his wife's body and life a greater sin than that of the woman who merely alienates the temporal goods of her husband? Let him, therefore, agree to a divorce, or else be satisfied with heirs not his own, for by his own fault he deceived an innocent girl and defrauded her both of life and of the full use of her body, besides giving her an almost irresistible cause for committing adultery. Let both be weighed in the same scales. Certainly, by every right, fraud should recoil on the fraudulent, and

183. Cf. p. 231 n. 178.

whoever has done an injury must make it good. What is the difference between such a husband and the man who holds another man's wife captive together with her husband? Is not such a tyrant compelled to support wife and children and husband, or else to set them free? Why should not the same hold true here? Therefore I maintain that the man should be compelled either to submit to a divorce or to support the other man's child as his heir. Doubtless this would be the judgment of charity. In that case, the impotent man, who is not really the husband, should support the heir of his wife in the same spirit in which he would at great expense wait on his wife if she fell sick or suffered some other ill; for it is by his fault and not by his wife's that she suffers this ill. This I have set forth to the best of my ability, for the strengthening of anxious consciences, because my desire is to bring my afflicted brethren in this captivity what little comfort I can.[184]

As to divorce, it is still a question for debate whether it is allowable. For my part I so greatly detest divorce that I

---

184. Several factors ought to be considered in evaluating the two preceding paragraphs, a much criticized section which Wace and Buchheim have omitted altogether from their translation: (1) Couched in the language of the scholars only, the Latin treatise was not intended for popular consumption but rather as a guide for bewildered and confused priests, who were called upon in the confessional to give practical advice and spiritual comfort to troubled souls (cf. p. 227 n. 169). (2) The impediment of impotency was, even according to Roman church law, sufficient ground for declaring a marriage null and void. (3) But the legal process of securing an annulment demanded such an involved procedure for establishing proof that it was equally unpleasant for both parties. (4) Then, as now, divorce under any circumstances was absolutely forbidden by Roman church law. (5) As an alternate to an impossible legal solution, Luther's suggestion of a secret marriage was not without precedent; common law in parts of Westphalia and Lower Saxony, for example, prescribed that a man who could not perform his conjugal duty was required to seek satisfaction for his wife through a neighbor (Jacob Grimm, *Weisthümer* [Göttingen, 1842], III, 42, 48, 70, 311). (6) That Luther's position did not involve any unconditional license for frustrated wives to engage in extra-marital liaisons, as his malicious interpreters promptly inferred, is underscored in his *The Estate of Marriage* of 1522, where he scores the offending husband even more severely than he does now ("when I was still shy"). *LW* 45, 20-21. Cf. Buchwald, *op. cit.*, II, 482 n. 4, and Woolf, *op. cit.*, p. 303 n. 2.

should prefer bigamy to it[185]; but whether it is allowable, I do not venture to decide. Christ himself, the Chief Shepherd, says in Matt. 5 [:32]: "Every one who divorces his wife, except on the ground of unchastity, makes her an adulteress; and whoever marries a divorced woman commits adultery." Christ, then, permits divorce, but only on the ground of unchastity. The pope must, therefore, be in error whenever he grants a divorce for any other cause; and no one should feel safe who has obtained a dispensation by this temerity (not authority) of the pope. Yet it is still a greater wonder to me why they compel a man to remain unmarried after being separated from his wife by divorce, and why they will not permit him to remarry. For if Christ permits divorce on the ground of unchastity and compels no one to remain unmarried, and if Paul would rather have us marry than burn [I Cor. 7:9], then he certainly seems to permit a man to marry another woman in the place of the one who has been put away. I wish that this subject were fully discussed and made clear and decided, so that counsel might be given in the infinite perils of those who, without any fault of their own, are nowadays compelled to remain unmarried; that is, those whose wives or husbands have run away and deserted them, to come back perhaps after ten years, perhaps never! This matter troubles and distresses me, for there are daily cases, whether by the special malice of Satan or because of our neglect of the Word of God.

I, indeed, who alone against all cannot establish any rule in this matter would yet greatly desire at least the passage in I Cor. 7 [:15] to be applied here: "But if the unbelieving partner desires to separate, let it be so; in such a case the brother or sister is not bound." Here the Apostle gives permission to put away the unbeliever who departs and to

---

185. As he actually did later in the case of Henry VIII and Philip of Hesse, considering it to be the lesser of two evils insofar as it was not without divinely sanctioned precedent in the Old Testament.

set the believing spouse free to marry again. Why should not the same hold true when a believer—that is, a believer in name, but in truth as much an unbeliever as the one Paul speaks of—deserts his wife, especially if he intends never to return. I certainly can see no difference between the two. But I believe that if in the Apostle's day an unbelieving deserter had returned and had become a believer or had promised to live again with his believing wife, it would not have been permitted, but he too would have been given the right to marry again. Nevertheless, in these matters I decide nothing (as I have said), although there is nothing that I would rather see decided, since nothing at present more grievously perplexes me, and many others with me. I would have nothing decided here on the mere authority of the pope and the bishops; but if two learned and good men agreed [Matt. 18:19-20] in the name of Christ and published their opinion in the spirit of Christ, I should prefer their judgment even to such councils as are assembled nowadays, famous only for numbers and authority, not for scholarship and saintliness. Therefore I hang up my lyre[186] on this matter until a better man confers with me about it.

ORDINATION

Of this sacrament the church of Christ knows nothing; it is an invention of the church of the pope. Not only is there nowhere any promise of grace attached to it, but there is not a single word said about it in the whole New Testament. Now it is ridiculous to put forth as a sacrament of God something that cannot be proved to have been instituted by God. I do not hold that this rite, which has been observed for so many centuries, should be condemned; but in sacred things I am opposed to the invention of human fictions. And it is not right to give out as divinely instituted

---

186. This is an allusion to the fact that he is writing a "prelude." Cf. Ps. 137:2.

what was not divinely instituted, lest we become a laugh-ingstock to our opponents. We ought to see that every article of faith of which we boast is certain, pure, and based on clear passages of Scripture. But we are utterly unable to do that in the case of the sacrament under consideration.

The church has no power to make new divine promises of grace, as some prate who hold what is decreed by the church is of no less authority than what is decreed by God, since the church is under the guidance of the Holy Spirit. For the church was born by the word of promise through faith, and by this same word is nourished and preserved. That is to say, it is the promises of God that make the church, and not the church that makes the promise of God. For the Word of God is incomparably superior to the church, and in this Word the church, being a creature, has nothing to decree, ordain, or make, but only to be decreed, ordained, and made. For who begets his own parent? Who first brings forth his own maker?

This one thing indeed the church can do: It can dis-tinguish the Word of God from the words of men; as Augustine confesses that he believed the gospel because he was moved by the authority of the church which pro-claimed that this is the gospel.[187] Not that the church is therefore above the gospel; if that were true, she would also be above God, in whom we believe because the church proclaims that he is God. But, as Augustine says else-where,[188] the truth itself lays hold on the soul and thus renders it able to judge most certainly of all things; how-ever, the soul is not able to judge the truth, but is compelled to say with unerring certainty that this is the truth. For

---

187. "Against the Epistle of Manichaeus Called Fundamental" in *The Nicene and Post-Nicene Fathers of the Christian Church*, ed. Philip Schaff (Buffalo, 1887), Series I, IV, 131. Migne 42, 176. Luther gives a fuller interpreta-tion of the meaning of Augustine's statement in *A Reply to the Texts Cited in Defense of the Doctrines of Men* (1522). *LW* 35, 150-153.

188. "The Trinity," 9, 6, 10, ed. John Baillie, *et al.*, *The Library of Christian Classics*, VIII (Philadelphia, 1955). 64. Migne 42, 966.

example, our mind declares with unerring certainty that three and seven are ten; and yet it cannot give a reason why this is true, although it cannot deny that it is true. It is clearly taken captive by the truth; and, rather than judging the truth, it is itself judged by it. There is such a mind also in the church, when under the enlightenment of the Spirit she judges and approves doctrines; she is unable to prove it, and yet is most certain of having it. For as among philosophers no one judges the general concepts, but all are judged by them, so it is among us with the mind of the Spirit, Who judges all things and is judged by no one, as the Apostle says [Cor. 2:16]. But of this another time.

Let this then stand fast: The church can give no promise of grace; that is the work of God alone. Therefore she cannot institute a sacrament. But even if she could, it still would not necessarily follow that ordination is a sacrament. For who knows which is the church that has the Spirit? For when such decisions are made there are usually only a few bishops or scholars present; and it is possible that these may not be really of the church. All may err, as councils have repeatedly erred, particularly the Council of Constance,[189] which erred most wickedly of all. Only that which has the approval of the church universal, and not of the Roman church alone, rests on a trustworthy foundation. I therefore admit that ordination is a certain churchly rite, on a par with many others introduced by the church fathers, such as the consecration of vessels, houses, vestments, water, salt,[190] candles,[191] herbs,[192] wine,[193] and the like. No one calls any of these a sacrament, nor is there in them any

---

189. Cf. p. 142 n. 55 and p. 144 n. 18.
190. Used in connection with baptism.
191. Used on Candlemas, Feast of the Purification of Mary, February 2.
192. Used on the Feasts of the Assumption of Mary, August 15; and of St. Peter's Chains, August 1.
193. Not the sacramental element, but the wine consecrated on the Feast of St. John, December 27, and drunk as a remembrance of John at the time of weddings, dying, and departing on a journey. Cf. Buchwald, *op. cit.*, II, 489 n. 2.

promise. In the same manner, to anoint a man's hands with oil, or to shave his head and the like is not to administer a sacrament, since no promise is attached to them; they are simply being prepared for a certain office, like a vessel or an instrument.

But you will say: "What do you do with Dionysius,[194] who in his *Ecclesiastical Hierachy* enumerates six sacraments, among which he also includes ordination?" I answer: I am well aware that this is the one writer of antiquity who is cited in support of the seven sacraments, although he omits marriage and so has only six.[195] But we read nothing at all about these "sacraments" in the rest of the fathers; nor do they ever regard them as sacraments when they speak of these things. For the invention of sacraments is of recent date.[196] Indeed, to speak more boldly, it greatly displeases me to assign such importance to this Dionysius, whoever he may have been, for he shows hardly any signs of solid learning. I would ask, by what authority and with what arguments does he prove his hodge-podge about the angels in his *Celestial Hierachy*—a book over which many curious superstitious spirits have cudgeled their brains? If one were to read and judge without prejudice, is not everything in it his own fancy and very much like a dream? But in his *Theology*, which is rightly called *Mystical*, of which certain very ignorant theologians make so much, he is downright dangerous, for he is more of a Platonist than a Chris-

---

194. Dionysius, the Areopagite, was the pseudonym of the unknown author (*circa* 500, in Syria?) of the neoplantonic writings. Of *the Celestial Hierarchy, Of the Ecclesiastical Hierarchy,* and *Of Mystical Theology.* J. P. Migne (ed.), *Patrologiae, Series Graeca,* vol. 3. Luther was among the first to question the high repute and ancient origin which tradition has assigned to these writings when it identified their author with Paul's convert of Acts 17.34.

195. Omitting marriage, confirmation, and penance, Dionysius mentions six sacraments: baptism, eucharist, unction, ordination of priests, ordination of monks, and burial rites. Schaff-Herzog, *op. cit.,* X, 142.

196. The system of seven sacraments was first generally accepted on the authority of Peter Lombard, and was first made official doctrine by the Council of Florence, 1439. Buchwald, *op. cit.,* II, 490 n. 2.

tian. So if I had my way, no believing soul would give the least attention to these books. So far, indeed, from learning Christ in them, you will lose even what you already know of him. I speak from experience. Let us rather hear Paul, that we may learn Jesus Christ and him crucified [I Cor. 2:2]. He is the way, the life, and the truth; he is the ladder [Gen. 28:12] by which we come to the Father, as he says: "No one comes to the Father, but by me" [John 14:6].

Similarly, in the *Ecclesiastical Hierarchy,* what does this Dionysius do but describe certain churchly rites, and amuse himself with allegories without proving anything? Just as has been done in our time by the author of the book entitled *Rationale divinorum.*[197] Such allegorical studies are for idle men. Do you think I should find it difficult to amuse myself with allegories about anything in creation? Did not Bonaventura by allegory draw the liberal arts into theology?[198] And Gerson even converted the smaller Donatus into a mystical theologian.[199] It would not be difficult for me to compose a better hierarchy than that of Dionysius; for he knew nothing of pope, cardinals and archbishops, and put the bishop at the top. Who has so weak a mind as not to be able to launch into allegories? I would not have a theologian devote himself to allegories until he has exhausted the legitimate and simple meaning of the Scripture; other-

---

197. William Durandus (1237-96), bishop of Mende. His book, written in 1296, is the standard authority for the laws, ceremonies, customs, and symbolism of thirteenth-century Roman rites and vestments. *Catholic Encyclopedia, op. cit.,* V, 207.

198. In his *De reductione artium ad theologiam,* the Franciscan Bonaventura (1221-1274) sought to relate all human knowledge to theology. All the arts and sciences were found to have points of contact in Scripture; and their several activities were regarded as parables of heavenly processes. Buchwald, *op. cit.,* II, 491 n. 4.

199. Donatus (*circa* 350 A.D.), famous Latin grammarian, whose, *Ars Minor* was the favorite medieval textbook. The chancellor of the University of Paris, John Gerson (1363-1429), published a *Donatus moralisatus seu per allegoriam traductus,* a mystical grammar, in which the noun was compared to man, the pronoun to man's sinful state, the verb to the divine command to love, the adverb to the fulfilment of the divine law, etc.

wise his theology will bring him into danger, as Origen[200] discovered.

Therefore a thing does not need to be a sacrament simply because Dionysius so describes it. Otherwise, why not also make a sacrament of the [funeral] processions, which he describes in his book, and which continue to this day? There will then be as many sacraments as there have been rites and ceremonies multiplied in the church. Standing on so unsteady a foundation, they have nevertheless invented "characters" [201] which they attribute to this sacrament of theirs and which are indelibly impressed on those who are ordained. Whence do such ideas come, I ask? By what authority, with what arguments, are they established? We do not object to their being free to invent, say, and assert whatever they please; but we also insist on our liberty, that they shall not arrogate to themselves the right to turn their opinions into articles of faith, as they have hitherto presumed to do. It is enough that we accommodate ourselves to their rites and ceremonies for the sake of peace; but we refuse to be bound by such things as if they were necessary to salvation, which they are not. Let them lay aside their despotic demand, and we shall yield free obedience to their wishes, in order that we may live in peace with one another.

200. Cf. p. 146 n. 65. Woolf regards Luther's anti-allegorical insistence on the plain sense of Scripture as his greatest single contribution to modern biblical scholarship, and sees a most excellent example of his exegetical method in LW 36, 117-23, where he is discussing extreme unction. Cf. Woolf, op. cit., 312 n. 1.

201. The so-called *character indelibilis*, peculiar gift of ordination, meant that "once a priest, always a priest." This "indelible mark" received authoritative statement in the bull Exultate Deo (1439). Eugene IV, summing up the decrees of the Council of Florence, says: "Among these sacraments there are three—baptism, confirmation, and orders—which indelibly impress upon the soul a character, i.e., a certain spiritual mark which distinguishes them from the rest." The Council of Trent (1563) further defined the correct Roman teachings as follows: "The Holy Synod justly condemns the opinion of those who assert that the priests of the New Testament have only temporary power, and that those once rightly ordained can again be made laymen, if they do not exercise the ministry of the Word of God." PE 2, 68 n. 5.

It is a shameful and wicked slavery for a Christian man, who is free, to be subject to any but heavenly and divine ordinances.

We come now to their strongest argument. It is this: Christ said at the Last Supper: "Do this in remembrance of me" [Luke 22:19; I Cor. 11:24-25]. "Look," they say, "here Christ ordained the apostles to the priesthood." From this passage they also concluded, among other things, that both kinds are to be administered to the priest alone.[202] In fact, they have drawn out of this passage whatever they pleased, as men who would arrogate to themselves the liberty to prove anything whatever from any words of Christ. But is that interpreting the words of God? I ask you: is it? Christ gives us no promise here, but only commands that this be done in remembrance of him. Why do they not conclude that he also ordained priests when he laid upon them the office of the Word and baptism, and said: "Go into all the world and preach the gospel to the whole creation, baptizing them in the name, etc." [Mark 16:15; Matt. 28:19]. For it is the proper duty of priests to preach and to baptize. Or, since it is nowadays the chief, and (as they say) indispensable duty of priests to read the canonical hours,[203] why have they not discovered the sacrament of ordination in those passages in which Christ commanded them to pray, as he did in many places—particularly in the garden, that they might not enter into temptation? [Matt. 26:41]. But perhaps they will evade this argument by saying that it is not commanded to pray; it is enough to read the canonical hours. Then it follows that this priestly work can be proved nowhere in the Scriptures, and thus their praying priesthood is not of God; as, indeed, it is not.

But which of the ancient Fathers claimed that in this

---

202. Cf. pp. 134-42.
203. The stated daily prayers, fixed by canon, and contained in the breviary. The seven hours are respectively: matins (including nocturns and lauds), prime, tierce, sext, nones, vespers, and compline.

passage priests were ordained? Where does this new interpretation come from? I will tell you. They have sought by
this means to set up a seed bed of implacable discord, by
which clergy and laymen should be separated from each
other farther than heaven from earth, to the incredible
injury of the grace of baptism and to the confusion of our
fellowship in the gospel. Here, indeed, are the roots of
that detestable tyranny of the clergy over the laity. Trusting in the external anointing by which their hands are
consecrated, in the tonsure and in vestments, they not only
exalt themselves above the rest of the lay Christians, who
are only anointed with the Holy Spirit, but regard them
almost as dogs and unworthy to be included with themselves in the church. Hence they are bold to demand, to
exact, to threaten, to urge, to oppress, as much as they
please. In short, the sacrament of ordination has been and
still is an admirable device for establishing all the horrible
things that have been done hitherto in the church, and are
yet to be done. Here Christian brotherhood has perished,
here shepherds have been turned into wolves, servants into
tyrants, churchmen into worse than worldlings.

If they were forced to grant that all of us that have been
baptized are equally priests, as indeed we are, and that
only the ministry was committed to them, yet with our
common consent, they would then know that they have no
right to rule over us except insofar as we freely concede it.
For thus it is written in I Pet. 2 [:9]: "You are a chosen
race, a royal priesthood, and a priestly royalty." Therefore
we are all priests, as many of us as are Christians.[204] But the
priests, as we call them, are ministers chosen from among
us. All that they do is done in our name; the priesthood is

---

204. Cf. *To the Christian Nobility of the German Nation.* Pp. 12-16 above.
    The fullest development of Luther's doctrine of the spiritual priesthood of
    believers is to be found in his writings against Emser (cf. p. 124 n. 4),
    especially his *Answer to the Hyperchristian, Hyperspiritual, and Hyper-
    learned Book by Goat Emser in Leipzig* (1521). *LW* 39, 137-224. Cf.
    also *The Misuse of the Mass* in *LW* 36, 127-230.

nothing but a ministry. This we learn from I Cor. 4 [:1]: "This is how one should regard us, as servants of Christ and stewards of the mysteries of God."

From this it follows that whoever does not preach the Word, though he was called by the church to do this very thing, is no priest at all, and that the sacrament of ordination can be nothing else than a certain rite by which the church chooses its preachers. For this is the way a priest is defined in Mal. 2 [:7]: "The lips of a priest should guard knowledge, and men should seek instruction from his mouth, for he is the messenger of the Lord of hosts." You may be certain, then, whoever is not a messenger of the Lord of hosts, or whoever is called to do anything else than such messenger service—if I may so term it—is in no sense a priest; as Hos. 4 [:6] says: "Because you have rejected knowledge, I reject you from being a priest to me." They are also called pastors because they are to pasture, that is, to teach. Therefore, those who are ordained only to read the canonical hours and to offer masses are indeed papal priests, but not Christian priests, because they not only do not preach, but they are not even called to preach. Indeed, it comes to this, that a priesthood of that sort is a different estate altogether from the office of preaching. Thus they are hour-reading and mass-saying priests—sort of living idols called priests—really such priests as Jeroboam ordained, in Beth-aven,[205] taken from the lowest dregs of the people, and not of Levi's tribe [I Kings 12:31].

See how far the glory of the church has departed! The whole earth is filled with priests, bishops, cardinals, and clergy; yet not one of them preaches so far as his official duty is concerned, unless he is called to do so by a different call over and above his sacramental ordination. Every one thinks he is doing full justice to his ordination by mumbling the vain repetitions of his prescribed prayers and by cele-

205. Cf. p. 215 n. 153.

brating masses. Moreover, he never really prays when **he** **repeats** those hours; or if he does pray, he prays them for himself. And he offers his mass as if it were a sacrifice, which is the height of perversity because the mass consists in the use made of the sacrament. It is clear, therefore, that the ordination, which, as a sacrament, makes clergymen of this sort of men, is in truth nothing but a mere fiction, devised by men who understand nothing about the church, the priesthood, the ministry of the Word, or the sacraments. Thus, as the "sacrament" is, so are the priests it makes. To such errors and such blindness has been added a still worse captivity: in order to separate themselves still farther from other Christians whom they deem profane, they have unmanned themselves, like the Galli, who were the priests of Cybele,[206] and they have taken upon themselves the burden of a spurious celibacy.

To satisfy this hypocrisy and the working of this error it was not enough that bigamy should be prohibited, that is, the having of two wives at one time, as it was forbidden in the law (and as is the accepted meaning of the term); but they have called it bigamy if a man marries two virgins, one after the other, or if he marries one widow. Indeed, so holy is the holiness of this most holy sacrament that no man can become a priest if he has married a virgin and his wife is still living. And—here we reach the very summit of sanctity—a man is even prevented from entering the priesthood if he has married a woman who was not a virgin, though he did so in ignorance or by unfortunate mischance. But if one has defiled six hundred harlots, or violated countless matrons and virgins, or even kept many Ganymedes, that would be no impediment to his becoming bishop or cardinal or pope. Moreover, the Apostle's word "husband of one wife" [I Tim. 3-2] must now be interpreted to mean

---

206. The eunuch priests of Cybele, "the Great Mother," ancient Phrygian nature goddess, were known as Galli. They ran about with dreadful cries, beating cymbals and cutting their flesh with knives.

"the prelate of one church," and this has given rise to the "incompatible benefices."[207] At the same time the pope, that munificent dispenser, may join to one man three, twenty or a hundred wives, that is, churches, if he is bribed with money or power, that is, "moved by godly charity and constrained by the care of the churches" [II Cor. 11:28].

O pontiffs worthy of this venerable sacrament of ordination! O princes, not of the catholic churches, but of the synagogues of Satan [Rev. 2:9] and of darkness itself! I would cry out with Isaiah [Isa. 28:14], "You scoffers, who rule this people in Jerusalem"; and with Amos 6 [:1], "Woe to those who are at ease in Zion, and to those who feel secure on the mountain of Samaria, the notable men of the first of the nations, that go in with state into the house of Israel, etc!" O the disgrace that these monstrous priests bring upon the church of God! Where are there any bishops or priests who even know the gospel, not to speak of preaching it? Why then do they boast of being priests? Why do they desire to be regarded as holier and better and mightier than other Christians, who are merely laymen? To read the hours—what unlearned men, or (as the Apostle says) men speaking with tongues [I Cor. 14:23] cannot do that? But to pray the hours—that belongs to monks, hermits, and men in private life, even though they are laymen. The duty of a priest is to preach, and if he does not preach he is as much a priest as a picture of a man is a man. Does ordaining such babbling priests make one a bishop? Or blessing churches and bells? Or confirming children? Certainly not. Any deacon or layman could do as much. It is the ministry of the Word that makes the priest and the bishop.

Therefore my advice is: Begone, all of you that would

---

207. The Fourth Lateran Council of 1215 had decreed that no one could simultaneously hold two offices involving pastoral care. The clever and lucrative ways in which the popes legally circumvented this statute Luther describes in *To the Christian Nobility of the German Nation*. Pp. 38-39 above.

live in safety; flee, young men, and do not enter upon this holy estate, unless you are determined to preach the gospel, and can believe that you are made not one whit better than the laity through this "sacrament" of ordination! For to read the hours is nothing, and to offer mass is to receive the sacrament. What then is there left to you that every layman does not have? Tonsure and vestments? A sorry priest, indeed, who consists of tonsure and vestments! Or the oil poured on your fingers? But every Christian is anointed and sanctified both in body and soul with the oil of the Holy Spirit. In ancient times every Christian handled the sacrament with his hands as often as the priests do now.[208] But today our superstition counts it a great crime if the laity touch either the bare chalice or the corporal; not even a nun who is a pure virgin would be permitted to wash the palls[209] and the sacred linens of the altar. O God! See how far the sacrosanct sanctity of this "sacrament" of ordination has gone! I expect the time will come when the laity will not be permitted to touch the altar—except when they offer their money. I almost burst with indignation when I contemplate the wicked tyrannies of these brazen men, who with their farcical and childish fancies mock and overthrow the liberty and glory of the Christian religion.

Let everyone, therefore, who knows himself to be a Christian, be assured of this, that we are all equally priests, that is to say, we have the same power in respect to the Word and the sacraments. However, no one may make use of this power except by the consent of the community or by the call of a superior. (For what is the common property of all, no individual may arrogate to himself, unless he is called.) And therefore this "sacrament" of ordination, if it is anything at all, is nothing else than a certain rite whereby one is called to the ministry of the church. Furthermore, the

---

208. Cf. pp. 140-41.
209. Covers for the chalice.

priesthood is properly nothing but the ministry of the Word —the Word, I say; not the law, but the gospel. And the diaconate is the ministry, not of reading the Gospel or the Epistle, as is the present practice, but of distributing the church's aid to the poor, so that the priests may be relieved of the burden of temporal matters and may give themselves more freely to prayer and the Word. For this was the purpose of the institution of the diaconate, as we read in Acts 5 [6:1-6]. Whoever, therefore, does not know or preach the gospel is not only no priest or bishop, but he is a kind of pest to the church, who under the false title of priest or bishop, or dressed in sheep's clothing, actually does violence to the gospel and plays the wolf [Matt. 7:15] in the church.

Therefore, unless these priests and bishops, with whom the church abounds today, work out their salvation [Phil. 2:12] in some other way; unless they realize that they are not priests or bishops, and bemoan the fact that they bear the name of an office whose duties they either do not know or cannot fulfil, and thus with prayers and tears lament their wretched hypocritical life—unless they do this, they are truly the people of eternal perdition, and the words of Isa. 5 [:13f.] are fulfilled in them: "Therefore my people go into exile for want of knowledge; their honored men are dying of hunger, and their multitude is parched with thirst. Therefore Hell has enlarged its appetite and opened its mouth beyond measure, and the nobility of Jerusalem and her multitude go down, her throng and he who exults in her." What a dreadful word for our age, in which Christians are swallowed up in so deep an abyss!

According to what the Scriptures teach us, what we call the priesthood is a ministry. So I cannot understand at all why one who has once been made a priest cannot again become a layman; for the sole difference between him and a layman is his ministry. But to depose a man from the priesthood is by no means impossible, because even now it is the usual penalty imposed upon guilty priests. They are either suspended temporarily, or permanently deprived of their office. For that fiction of an "indelible character" [210] has long since become a laughingstock. I admit that the pope imparts this "character," but Christ knows nothing of it; and a priest who is consecrated with it becomes the life-long servant and captive, not of Christ, but of the pope, as is the case nowadays. Moreover, unless I am greatly mistaken, if this sacrament and this fiction ever fall to the ground, the papacy with its "characters" will scarcely survive. Then our joyous liberty will be restored to us; we shall realize that we are all equal by every right. Having cast off the yoke of tyranny, we shall know that he who is a Christian has Christ; and that he who has Christ has all things that are Christ's, and can do all things [Phil. 4:13]. Of this I will write more,[211] and more vigorously, as soon as I perceive that the above has displeased my friends the papists.

THE SACRAMENT OF EXTREME UNCTION

To this rite of anointing the sick the theologians of our day have made two additions which are worthy of them: first, they call it a sacrament, and second, they make it the last sacrament. So it is now the sacrament of extreme unction, which is to be administered only to those who are at the point of death. Since they are such subtle dialecticians, perhaps they have done this in order to relate it to the first unction of baptism[212] and the two subsequent ones of confirmation and ordination. But here they are able to cast in my teeth that, in the case of this sacrament, there are on the authority of the apostle James both promise and sign, which, as I have maintained all along, do constitute

---

210. Cf. p. 242 n. 201.
211. These basic ideas received expanded treatment about six weeks later in *The Freedom of a Christian*, pp. 277-316.
212. In the order for baptism, just after the Creed, the child was anointed with oil on chest and shoulders. Buchwald, *op. cit.*, II 501 n. 1.

a sacrament. For the apostle says [Jas. 5:14-15]: "Is any among you sick? Let him call for the elders of the church, and let them pray over him, anointing him with oil in the name of the Lord; and the prayer of faith will save the sick man, and the Lord will raise him up; and if he has committed sins, he will be forgiven." There, they say, you have the promise of the forgiveness of sins and the sign of the oil.

But I say: If ever folly has been uttered, it has been uttered especially on this subject: I will say nothing of the fact than many[213] assert with much probability that this epistle is not by James the apostle, and that it is not worthy of an apostolic spirit; although, whoever was its author, it has come to be regarded as authoritative. But even if the apostle James did write it, I still would say, that no apostle has the right on his own authority to institute a sacrament, that is, to give a divine promise with a sign attached. For this belongs to Christ alone. Thus Paul says that he received from the Lord [I Cor. 11:23] the sacrament of the Eucharist, and that he was not sent to baptize, but to preach the gospel [I Cor. 1:17]. And nowhere do we read in the gospel of the sacrament of extreme unction. But let us also pass over this point. Let us examine the words of the apostle, or whoever was the author of the epistle, and we shall see at once how little heed these multipliers of sacraments have given to them.

In the first place, if they believe the apostle's words to be true and binding, by what right do they change and contradict them? Why do they make an extreme and a special kind of unction out of that which the apostle wished to be general? For the apostle did not desire it to be an extreme unction or administered only to the dying, but he

---

213. Eusebius (*circa* 275-340) classed it among the *antilegomena* or contested writings. Jerome (*circa* 340-420) says it was regarded as pseudonymous in the Latin church. Luther's contemporaries, the humanist Erasmus and the Catholic Cajetan, both contested its authenticity.

says expressly: "Is any one sick?" He does not say: "Is any one dying?" I do not care what learned discussions Dionysius has on this point in his *Ecclesiastical Hierarchy*.[214] The apostle's words are clear enough, on which he has well as they rely; but they do not follow them. It is evident, therefore, that they have arbitrarily and without any authority made a sacrament and an extreme unction out of the words of the apostle which they have wrongly interpreted. And this works to the detriment of all other sick persons, whom they have deprived on their own authority of the benefit of the unction which the apostle enjoined.

But this is even a finer point: The apostle's promise expressly declares: "The prayer of faith will save the sick man, and the Lord will raise him up, etc." [Jas. 5:15]. See, the apostle in this passage commands us to anoint and to pray, in order that the sick man may be healed and raised up; that is, that he may not die, and that it may not be an extreme unction. This is proved also by the prayers which are used even to this day during the anointing, because the prayers are for the recovery of the sick man. But they say, on the contrary, that the unction must be administered to none but the dying;[215] that is, that they may not be healed and raised up. If it were not so serious a matter, who could help laughing at this beautiful, apt, and sensible exposition of the apostle's words? Is not the folly of the sophists here shown in its true colors? Because here, as in so many other places, it affirms what the Scriptures deny, and denies what the Scriptures affirm. Why should we not give thanks to these excellent masters of ours?[216] Surely I spoke the truth when I said that they never uttered greater folly than on this subject.

Furthermore, if this unction is a sacrament, it must neces-

---

214. Cf. p. 240 n. 194.
215. All editions have *discessuris,* "departing," but WA 6, 568 n. 35, suggests *decessuris,* "dying.'
216. Cf. pp. 123-24

sarily be (as they say) an "effective sign" [217] of that which it signifies and promises. Now it promises health and recovery to the sick, as the words plainly say: "The prayer of faith will save the sick man, and the Lord will raise him up" [Jas. 5:15]. But who does not see that this promise is seldom, if ever, fulfilled? Scarcely one in a thousand is restored to health, and when one is restored nobody believes that it came about through the sacrament, but through the working of nature or of medicine. Indeed to the sacrament they ascribe the opposite effect. What shall we say then? Either the apostle lies in making this promise or else this unction is no sacrament. For the sacramental promise is certain; but this promise fails in the majority of cases. Indeed—and here again we recognize the shrewdness and foresight of these theologians—for this very reason they would have it to be extreme unction, that the promise should not stand; in other words, that the sacrament should be no sacrament. For if it is extreme unction, it does not heal, but gives way to the disease; but if it heals, it cannot be extereme unction. Thus, by the interpretation of these masters, James is shown to have contradicted himself, and to have instituted a sacrament in order not to institute one; for they must have an extreme unction just to make untrue what the apostle intends, namely, the healing of the sick by it. If this is not madness, I ask you what is?

The word of the apostle in I Tim. 1 [:7] describes these people: "Desiring to be teachers of the law, without understanding either what they are saying or the things about which they make assertions." Thus they read and follow everything uncritically. With the same carelessness they have also found auricular confession in the apostle's words: "Confess your sins to one another" [Jas. 5:16]. But they do not observe the command of the apostle that the elders of the church be called, and prayer be made for the sick

217. Cf. pp. 186-87.

[Jas. 5:14]. Scarcely one insignificant priest is sent now-adays, although the apostle would have many present, not because of the unction, but because of the prayer. That is why he says: "The prayer of faith will save the sick man, etc." [Jas. 5:15]. I have my doubts, however, whether he would have us understand "priests" when he says "presbyters," that is, "elders." For one who is an elder is not necessarily a priest or a minister. We may suspect that the apostle desired the older, graver men in the church to visit the sick, to perform a work of mercy, and pray in faith and thus heal him. Yet, it cannot be denied that the churches were once ruled by older persons, chosen for this purpose without these ordinations and consecrations, solely on account of their age and long experience.

Therefore I take it that this unction is the same as that practiced by the apostles, of whom it is written in Mark 6 [:13]: "They anointed with oil many that were sick and healed them." It was a rite of the early church by which they worked miracles on the sick, and which has long since ceased. In the same way Christ, in the last chapter of Mark [16:18], gave to believers the power to pick up serpents, lay hands on the sick, etc. It is a wonder that they have not made sacraments of those words also, for they have the same power and promise as these words of James. Therefore this extreme—which is to say fictitious—unction is not a sacrament, but a counsel of James, which anyone who will may follow; and it is derived from Mark 6 [:13], as I have said. I do not believe that it was a counsel given to all sick persons, for the church's infirmity is her glory and death is gain [Phil. 1:21]; but it was given only to such as might bear their sickness impatiently and with little faith, those whom the Lord allowed to remain in order that miracles and the power of faith might be manifest in them.

James made careful and diligent provision in this case by attaching the promise of healing and the forgiveness of sins not to the unction, but to the prayer of faith. For he says: "And the prayer of faith will save the sick man, and the Lord will raise him up; and if he has committed sins, he will be forgiven" [Jas. 5:15]. A sacrament does not demand prayer and faith on the part of the minister, since even a wicked person may baptize and consecrate without prayer; a sacrament depends solely on the promise and institution of God, and requires faith on the part of the recipient. But where is the prayer of faith in our present use of extreme unction? Who prays over the sick one in such faith as not to doubt that he will recover? Such a prayer of faith James here describes, of which he said at the beginning of his epistle: "But let him ask in faith, with no doubting" [Jas. 1:6]. And Christ says of it: "Whatever you ask in prayer, believe that you receive it, and you will" [Mark 11:24].

There is no doubt at all that, even if today such a prayer were made over a sick man, that is, made in full faith by older, graver, and saintly men, as many as we wished would be healed. For what could not faith do? But we neglect this faith which the authority of the apostle demands above all else. Further, by "presbyters"—that is, men pre-eminent by reason of their age and faith—we understand the common herd of priests. Moreover, we turn the daily or temporally unrestricted unction into an extreme unction. And finally, we do not obtain the result promised by the apostle, namely, the healing of the sick, but we render the promise ineffective by doing the very opposite. And yet we boast that our sacrament, or rather figment, is established and proved by this saying of the apostle, which is diametrically opposed[218] to it. O what theologians!

Now I do not condemn this our "sacrament" of extreme unction, but I firmly deny that it is what the apostle James prescribes; for his unction agrees with ours neither in form.

---

218. *bis diapason*. In his *Adagia*, Erasmus explains the intense degree of separation and conflict connoted by this originally Greek phrase. It describes the relationship between two things that are worlds apart, unalterably opposed, and most sharply to be distinguished. *CL* 1, 509 n. 1.

use, power, nor purpose. Nevertheless, we shall number it among those "sacraments" which we have instituted, such as the blessing and sprinkling of salt[219] and water. For we cannot deny that any creature whatsoever may be consecrated by the Word and by prayer, as the apostle Paul teaches us [I Tim. 4:4-5]. We do not deny, therefore, that forgiveness and peace are granted through extreme unction; not because it is a sacrament divinely instituted, but because he who receives it believes that these blessings are granted to him. For the faith of the recipient does not err, however much the minister may err. For one who baptizes or absolves in jest,[220] that is, one who does not absolve so far as the minister is concerned, nevertheless does truly baptize and absolve if the person to be baptized or absolved believes. How much more will one who administers extreme unction confer peace, even though he does not really confer peace so far as his ministry is concerned, since there is no sacrament there! The faith of the one anointed receives even that which the minister either could not give or did not intend to give. It is sufficient for the one anointed to hear and believe the Word. For whatever we believe we shall receive, that we really do receive, no matter what the minister may or may not do, or whether he dissembles or jests. The saying of Christ holds good: "All things are possible to him who believes" [Mark 9:23], and again: "Be it done for you as you have believed" [Matt. 8:13]. But in treating the sacraments our sophists say nothing at all of this faith, but only babble with all their might about the virtues of the sacraments themselves. They will "listen to anybody and can never arrive at a knowledge of the truth" [II Tim. 3:7].

Still it was a good thing that this unction was made the extreme or "last" unction, for thanks to that, it has been abused and distorted least of all the sacraments by tyranny

219. Cf. p. 239 n. 190.
220. Cf. p. 186 n. 132

and greed. This one last mercy, to be sure, has been left to the dying—they may be anointed without charge, even without confession and communion. If it had remained a practice of daily occurrence, especially if it had cured the sick, even without taking away sins, how many worlds, do you think, would not the pontiffs have under their control today? For through the one sacrament of penance and the power of the keys, as well as through the sacrament of ordination, they have become such mighty emperors and princes. But now it is a fortunate thing that they despise the prayer of faith, and therefore do not heal any sick, and that they have made for themselves, out of an ancient ceremony, a brand-new sacrament.

Let this now suffice for these four sacraments. I know how it will displease those who believe that the number and use of the sacraments are to be learned not from the sacred Scriptures, but from the Roman See. As if the Roman See had given these "sacraments" and had not rather received them from the lecture halls of the universities, to which it is unquestionably indebted for whatever it has. The papal despotism would not have attained its present position had it not taken over so many things from the universities. For there was scarcely another of the celebrated bishoprics that had so few learned pontiffs as Rome. Only by violence, intrigue, and superstition has she till now prevailed over the rest. For the men who occupied the See a thousand years ago differed so vastly from those who have since come into power that one is compelled to refuse the name of Roman pontiff to one group or the other.

There are still a few other things which it might seem possible to regard as sacraments; namely, all those things to which a divine promise has been given, such as prayer, the Word, and the cross. For Christ has promised, in many places, that those who pray should be heard; especially in Luke 11 [:5-13], where by many parables he invites us to pray. Of the Word he says: "Blessed are those who hear the Word of God and keep it" [Luke 11:28]. And who can count all the times he promises aid and glory to those who are afflicted, suffer, and are cast down? Indeed, who can recount all the promises of God? Why, the whole Scripture is concerned with provoking us to faith; now driving us with commands and threats, now drawing us with promises and consolations. In fact, everything in Scripture is either a command or a promise. The commands humble the proud with their demands, the promises exalt the humble with their forgiveness.

Nevertheless, it has seemed proper to restrict the name of sacrament to those promises which have signs attached to them. The remainder, not being bound to signs, are bare promises. *Hence there are, strictly speaking, but two sacraments in the church of God—baptism and the bread.* For only in these two do we find both the divinely instituted sign and the promise of forgiveness of sins. The sacrament of penance, which I added to these two,[221] lacks the divinely instituted visible sign, and is, as I have said,[222] nothing but a way and a return to baptism. Nor can the scholastics say that their definition fits penance, for they too ascribe to the true sacrament a visible sign, which is to impress upon the senses the form of that which it effects invisibly. But penance or absolution has no such sign. Therefore they are compelled by their own definition either to admit that penance is not a sacrament and thus to reduce their number, or else to bring forth another definition of a sacrament.

Baptism, however, which we have applied to the whole of life, will truly be a sufficient substitute for all the sacra-

---

221. Cf. p. 132.
222. Cf. pp. 180-81.

ments which we might need as long as we live. And the bread is truly the sacrament of the dying and departing; for in it we commemorate the passing of Christ out of this world, that we may imitate him. Thus we may apportion these two sacraments as follows: baptism may be allotted to the beginning and the entire course of life, while the bread belongs to the end and to death. And the Christian should use them both as long as he is in this mortal frame, until, fully baptized and strengthened, he passes out of this world, and is born into the new eternal life, to eat with Christ in the kingdom of his Father, as he promised at the Last Supper, when he said: "Truly, I say to you, I shall not drink again of this fruit of the vine until it is fulfilled in the kingdom of God" [Matt. 26:29, Mark 14:25, Luke 22:18]. Thus he clearly seems to have instituted the sacrament of the bread with a view to our entrance into the life to come. For then, when the purpose[223] of both sacraments is fulfilled, baptism and bread will cease.

Herewith I conclude this prelude, and freely and gladly offer it to all pious souls who desire to know the genuine sense of the Scriptures and the proper use of the sacraments. For it is a gift of no mean importance, to know the gifts that are given to us, as it is said in I Cor. 2 [:12], and what use we ought to make of them. For if we are instructed with this judgment of the spirit, we shall not mistakenly rely on those things which are wrong. These two things our theologians never taught us; indeed, they seem to have taken pains to hide them from us. If I have not taught them, I certainly managed not to conceal them, and have given occasion to others to think out something better. It has at least been my endeavor to set them both forth. Nevertheless, "not all can do all things."[224] To the

223. *res sacramenti,* cf. p. 137 n. 45.
224. Vergil *Eclogues* viii, 63.

godless, on the other hand, and those who in obstinate tyranny force on us their own teachings instead of God's, I confidently and freely oppose these pages. I shall be completely indifferent to their senseless fury. Yet I wish even them a right understanding. And I do not despise their efforts; I only distinguish them from what is sound and truly Christian.

I hear a rumor that new bulls and papal maledictions are being prepared against me, in which I am urged to recant or be declared a heretic. If that is true, I desire this little book to be part of the recantation that I shall make; so that the arrogant despots might not complain of having acted in vain. The remainder I will publish very soon; please Christ, it will be such as the Roman See has never seen or heard before. I shall give ample proof of my obedience.[225] In the name of our Lord Jesus Christ. Amen.

"Why doth that impious Herod fear
When told that Christ the King is near?
He takes not earthly realms away,
Who gives the realms that ne'er decay."[226]

---

225. The remainder of Luther's "recantation" was *The Freedom of a Christian*. In *An Open Letter to Pope Leo X*, which accompanied it, he gave ample proof of his obedience. See pp. 266-76.

226. The eighth stanza of Coelius Sedulius' *Hymnus acrostichis totam vitam Christi continens* (beginning *A solis ortus cardine*), of the fifth century. Stanzas 8, 9, 11, and 13 were used as an Epiphany hymn, which Luther translated on December 12, 1541—"*Was fürchtst du, Feind Herodes, sehr.*" The above translation is taken from *Hymns Ancient and Modern*, No. 60. Woolf, *op. cit.*, 329, has this translation from *The English Hymnary*:

Why, impious Herod, shouldst thou fear
Because the Christ is come so near?
He who doth heavenly kingdoms grant
Thine earthly realm can never want.

THE FREEDOM
OF A CHRISTIAN

Translated by W. A. Lambert
Revised by Harold J. Grimm

INTRODUCTION

After the Leipzig Debate Luther returned to Wittenberg, where he resumed his heavy responsibilities and at the same time devoted a large amount of time to study and writing. The list of his publications alone was phenomenal. In addition to writing much devotional literature, often at the request of the elector and his court, he produced sermons, lectures, and polemical tracts. Within six months, in 1520, he published three important Reformation tracts which clarified his new evangelical theology for his ever-increasing following.

In *To the Christian Nobility of the German Nation,* on August 18, he attacked the authority of the papacy over secular rulers, denied that the pope was the final interpreter of Scripture, assailed the corruption of the Roman Curia, enunciated his important doctrine of the universal priesthood of believers, and called for a drastic reform of the church. In *The Babylonian Captivity of the Church,* published October 6, he attacked the sacramental system of the church by means of which the ecclesiastical hierarchy had gained its control over all Christians. *The Freedom of a Christian,* published early in November, differed from the preceding two pamphlets in that it was written in a conciliatory spirit. Yet it contained a positive and unequivocal statement of Luther's evangelical theology as applied to Christian life. It owed its origin to a final attempt on the part of Miltitz° to prevent a rift in the church.

° Cf. LW 31, xvii-xix.

Despite the fact that Miltitz' first meeting with Luther had failed to end the indulgence controversy, and animosities had been increased by the Leipzig Debate, Miltitz had a second interview with Luther at Liebenwerda on October 9, 1519, at which time the Reformer agreed to present his case before the archbishop of Trier. This also failed. Miltitz did not, however, give up his attempt to counteract the tactics of Eck, even after the Roman Curia had issued the *Exsurge Domine* on June 15, 1520.[†] On August 28 he attended a chapter meeting of the Augustinians at Eisleben where he conferred with Johann von Staupitz, who retired from his office as vicar general at that time, and Wenceslaus Link, his successor. He persuaded these two to visit Luther and to induce him to write a friendly letter to Leo X, assuring the pope that he had never intended to attack him personally. This they did September 6, and Luther agreed to comply with their wishes. Miltitz, however, wanting to make certain that the letter would be written in the proper spirit, had another interview with Luther on October 12, 1520, this time at Lichtenberg. There Luther agreed to write a conciliatory letter and a devotional booklet to accompany it, and even to date the letter September 6 to indicate that he was not motivated by the publication in Germany of the *Exsurge Domine*.

Luther immediately began writing his open letter to Leo and *The Freedom of a Christian*, both, of course, in Latin. It is not known whether the pope received these two documents. If he did, he must have been shocked by the fact that Luther now wrote him as an equal, offered him advice as though he were the papal father confessor, and expressed his evangelical views without a sign of retraction. Although the tract breathed the spirit of late-medieval mysticism and was favorably commented upon by a number of papal

---

[†] Cf. Carl Mirbt, *Quellen zur Geschichte des Papsttums und des roemischen Katholizimus* (2d ed.; Tübingen and Leipzig, 1901), pp. 183-85.

supporters, it makes clear that a believing Christian is free from sin through faith in God, yet bound by love to serve his neighbor.

Soon after the completion of the open letter to Leo and *The Freedom of a Christian*, Luther made a free translation of the latter into German and sent it to Hermann Mühlphordt of Zwickau. Although this German version is the most widely read, the clearer and more complete Latin text given in *WA* 7, 49-73, and translated into English in *PE* 2, 312-348, is included in this volume with minor revisions. A recent English translation of the German text in *WA* 7, 20-38, is given in Bertram Lee Woolf, *Reformation Writings of Martin Luther*, I, 356-379. The open letter to Leo X was published separately in Wittenberg before November 4, 1520. The translation of it in *PE* 2, 301-311, revised for this volume, was based on the Latin in *WA* 7, 42-49. The most detailed English account of the three important pamphlets of 1520 is that of Mackinnon, *Luther and the Reformation*, II, 222-270.

THE FREEDOM OF A CHRISTIAN

LETTER OF DEDICATION TO MAYOR MUHLPHORDT

To the learned and wise gentleman, Hieronymus Mühl-phordt,[1] mayor of Zwickau, my exceptionally gracious friend and patron, I, Martin Luther, Augustinian, present my compliments and good wishes.

My learned and wise sir and gracious friend, the venerable Master Johann Egran, your praiseworthy preacher, spoke to me in terms of praise concerning your love for and pleasure in the Holy Scripture, which you also diligently confess and unceasingly praise before all men. For this reason he desired to make me acquainted with you. I yielded willingly and gladly to his persuasion, for it is a special pleasure to hear of someone who loves divine truth. Unfortunately there are many people, especially those who are proud of their titles, who oppose the truth with all their power and cunning. Admittedly it must be that Christ, set as a stumbling block and a sign that is spoken against, will be an offense and a cause for the fall and rising of many [I Cor. 1:23; Luke 2:34].

In order to make a good beginning of our acquaintance and friendship, I have wished to dedicate to you this treatise or discourse in German, which I have already dedicated to the people in Latin, in the hope that my teachings and writings concerning the papacy will not be considered objectionable by anybody. I commend myself to you and to the grace of God. Amen. Wittenberg, 1520.[2]

---

1. The given name of Mühlphordt was Hermann, not Hieronymus, as Luther has it.
2. In place of the German version of the treatise which Luther sent to Mühl-phordt, the Latin version dedicated to the pope is used as the basis of the English translation in this volume.

AN OPEN LETTER TO POPE LEO X

To Leo X, Pope at Rome, Martin Luther wishes salvation in Christ Jesus our Lord. Amen.

Living among the monsters of this age with whom I am now for the third year waging war, I am compelled occasionally to look up to you, Leo, most blessed father, and to think of you. Indeed, since you are occasionally regarded as the sole cause of my warfare, I cannot help thinking of you. To be sure, the undeserved raging of your godless flatterers against me has compelled me to appeal from your see to a future council, despite the decrees of your predecessors Pius and Julius, who with a foolish tyranny forbade such an appeal. Nevertheless, I have never alienated myself from Your Blessedness to such an extent that I should not with all my heart wish you and your see every blessing, for which I have besought God with earnest prayers to the best of my ability. It is true that I have been so bold as to despise and look down upon those who have tried to frighten me with the majesty of your name and authority. There is one thing, however, which I cannot ignore and which is the cause of my writing once more to Your Blessedness. It has come to my attention that I am accused of great indiscretion, said to be my great fault, in which, it is said, I have not spared even your person.

I freely vow that I have, to my knowledge, spoken only good and honorable words concerning you whenever I have thought of you. If I had ever done otherwise, I myself could by no means condone it, but should agree entirely with the judgment which others have formed of me; and I should do nothing more gladly than recant such indiscretion and impiety. I have called you a Daniel in Babylon; and everyone who reads what I have written knows how zealously I defended your innocence against your defamer Sylvester.[3] Indeed, your reputation and the fame of your blameless life, celebrated as they are throughout the world by the writings of many great men, are too well known and too honorable to be assailed by anyone, no matter how great he is. I am not so foolish as to attack one whom all people praise. As a matter of fact, I have always tried, and will always continue, not to attack even those whom the public dishonors, for I take no pleasure in the faults of any man, since I am conscious of the beam in my own eye. I could not, indeed, be the first one to cast a stone at the adulteress [John 8:1-11].

I have, to be sure, sharply attacked ungodly doctrines in general, and I have snapped at my opponents, not because of their bad morals, but because of their ungodliness. Rather than repent this in the least, I have determined to persist in that fervent zeal and to despise the judgment of men, following the example of Christ who in his zeal called his opponents "a brood of vipers," "blind fools," "hypocrites," "children of the devil" [Matt. 23:13, 17, 33; John 8:44]. Paul branded Magus [Elymas, the magician] as the "son of the devil, . . . full of all deceit and villainy" [Acts 13:10], and he calls others "dogs," "deceivers," and "adulterers" [Phil 3:2; II Cor. 11:13; 2:17]. If you will allow people with sensitive feelings to judge, they would consider no person more stinging and unrestrained in his denunciations than Paul. Who is more stinging than the prophets? Nowadays, it is true, we are made so sensitive by the raving crowd of flatterers that we cry out that we are stung as soon as we meet with disapproval. When we cannot ward off the truth with any other pretext, we flee from it by ascribing it to a fierce temper, impatience, and immodesty. What is the good of salt if it does not bite? Of

---

3. Sylvester Mazzolini (1456-1523), usually called Prierias after Prierio, the city of his birth, had published three books against Luther. In these he had exaggerated the authority of the papacy.

what use is the edge of a sword if it does not cut? "Cursed is he who does the work of the Lord deceitfully . . ." [Jer. 48:10].

Therefore, most excellent Leo, I beg you to give me a hearing after I have vindicated myself by this letter, and believe me when I say that I have never thought ill of you personally, that I am the kind of person who would wish you all good things eternally, and that I have no quarrel with any man concerning his morals but only concerning the word of truth. In all other matters I will yield to any man whatsoever; but I have neither the power nor the will to deny the Word of God. If any man has a different opinion concerning me, he does not think straight or understand what I have actually said.

I have truly despised your see, the Roman Curia, which, however, neither you nor anyone else can deny is more corrupt than any Babylon or Sodom ever was, and which, as far as I can see, is characterized by a completely depraved, hopeless, and notorious godlessness. I have been thoroughly incensed over the fact that good Christians are mocked in your name and under the cloak of the Roman church. I have resisted and will continue to resist your see as long as the spirit of faith lives in me. Not that I shall strive for the impossible or hope that by my efforts alone anything will be accomplished in that most disordered Babylon, where the fury of so many flatterers is turned against me; but I acknowledge my indebtedness to my Christian brethren, whom I am duty-bound to warn so that fewer of them may be destroyed by the plagues of Rome, at least so that their destruction may be less cruel.

As you well know, there has been flowing from Rome these many years—like a flood covering the world—nothing but a devastation of men's bodies and souls and possessions, the worst examples of the worst of all things. All this is clearer than day to all, and the Roman church, once the holiest of all, has become the most licentious den of thieves

[Matt. 21:13], the most shameless of all brothels, the kingdom of sin, death, and hell. It is so bad that even Antichrist himself, if he should come, could think of nothing to add to its wickedness.

Meanwhile you, Leo, sit as a lamb in the midst of wolves [Matt. 10:16] and like Daniel in the midst of lions [Dan. 6:16]. With Ezekiel you live among scorpions [Ezek. 2:6]. How can you alone oppose these monsters? Even if you would call to your aid three or four well learned and thoroughly reliable cardinals, what are these among so many? You would all be poisoned[4] before you could begin to issue a decree for the purpose of remedying the situation. The Roman Curia is already lost, for God's wrath has relentlessly fallen upon it. It detests church councils, it fears a reformation, it cannot allay its own corruption; and what was said of its mother Babylon also applies to it: "We would have cured Babylon, but she was not healed. Let us forsake her" [Jer. 51:9].

It was your duty and that of your cardinals to remedy these evils, but the gout of these evils makes a mockery of the healing hand, and neither chariot nor horse responds to the rein [Vergil, *Georgics* i. 514]. Moved by this affection for you, I have always been sorry, most excellent Leo, that you were made pope in these times, for you are worthy of being pope in better days. The Roman Curia does not deserve to have you or men like you, but it should have Satan himself as pope, for he now actually rules in that Babylon more than you do.

Would that you might discard that which your most profligate enemies boastfully claim to be your glory and might live on a small priestly income of your own or on your family inheritance! No persons are worthy of glorying in that honor except the Iscariots, the sons of perdition. What do you accomplish in the Roman Curia, my Leo? The

4. An attempt to poison Leo X had been made in the summer of 1517.

more criminal and detestable a man is, the more gladly will he use your name to destroy men's possessions and souls, to increase crime, to suppress faith and truth and God's whole church. O most unhappy Leo, you are sitting on a most dangerous throne. I am telling you the truth because I wish you well.

If Bernard felt sorry for Eugenius[5] at a time when the Roman See, which, although even then very corrupt, was ruled with better prospects for improvement, why should not we complain who for three hundred years have had such a great increase of corruption and wickedness? Is it not true that under the vast expanse of heaven there is nothing more corrupt, more pestilential, more offensive than the Roman Curia? It surpasses beyond all comparison the godlessness of the Turks so that, indeed, although it was once a gate of heaven, it is now an open mouth of hell, such a mouth that it cannot be shut because of the wrath of God. Only one thing can we try to do, as I have said:[6] we may be able to call back a few from that yawning chasm of Rome and save them.

Now you see, my Father Leo, how and why I have so **violently** attacked that pestilential see. So far have I been from raving against your person that I even hoped I might gain your favor and save you if I should make a strong and stinging assault upon that prison, that veritable hell of yours. For you and your salvation and the salvation of many others with you will be served by everything that men of ability can do against the confusion of this wicked Curia. They serve your office who do every harm to the Curia; they glorify Christ who in every way curse it. In short, they are Christians who are not Romans.

To enlarge upon this, I never intended to attack the

5. Bernard of Clairvaux wrote a devotional book, *On Consideration*, to Pope Eugenius III (1145-53), in which he discussed the duties of the pope and the dangers connected with his office. Migne 182, 727-808.

6. Cf. p. 268.

Roman Curia or to raise any controversy concerning it. But when I saw all efforts to save it were hopeless, I despised it, gave it a bill of divorce [Deut. 24:1], and said, "Let the evildoer still do evil, and the filthy still be filthy" [Rev. 22:11]. Then I turned to the quiet and peaceful study of the Holy Scriptures so that I might be helpful to my brothers around me. When I had made some progress in these studies, Satan opened his eyes and then filled his servant Johann Eck, a notable enemy of Christ, with an insatiable lust for glory and thus aroused him to drag me unawares to a debate, seizing me by means of one little word which I had let slip concerning the primacy of the Roman church. Then that boastful braggart,[7] frothing and gnashing his teeth, declared that he would risk everything for the glory of God and the honor of the Apostolic See. Puffed up with the prospect of abusing your authority, he looked forward with great confidence to a victory over me. He was concerned not so much with establishing the primacy of Peter as he was with demonstrating his own leadership among the theologians of our time. To that end he considered it no small advantage to triumph over Luther. When the debate ended badly for the sophist, an unbelievable madness overcame the man, for he believed that it was his fault alone which was responsible for my disclosing all the infamy of Rome.

Allow me, I pray, most excellent Leo, this once to plead my cause and to indict your real enemies. You know, I believe, what dealings your legate, cardinal of St. Sisto,[8] an unwise and unfortunate, or rather, an unreliable man, had with me. When out of reverence for your name I had placed myself and my cause in his hands, he did not try to establish peace. He could easily have done so with a single word, for at that time I promised to keep silent and to

---

7. Thraso, in the original, is the name of a braggart soldier in Terence's *Eunuch*.
8. Cardinal Cajetan, cf. *LW* 31, 264, n. 10.

end the controversy, provided my opponents were ordered to do likewise. As he was a man who sought glory, however, and was not content with such an agreement, he began to defend my opponents, to give them full freedom, and to order me to recant, even though this was not included in his instructions. When matters went fairly well, he with his churlish arbitrariness made them far worse. Therefore Luther is not to blame for what followed. All the blame is Cajetan's, who did not permit me to keep silent, as I at that time most earnestly requested him to do. What more should I have done?

There followed Karl Miltitz,[9] also a nuncio of Your Holiness, who exerted much effort and traveled back and forth, omitting nothing that might help restore the order which Cajetan had rashly and arrogantly disturbed. He finally, with the help of the most illustrious prince, the Elector Frederick, managed to arrange several private conferences with me.[10] Again I yielded out of respect for your name, was prepared to keep silent, and even accepted as arbiter either the archbishop of Trier or the bishop of Naumburg. So matters were arranged. But while this arrangement was being followed with good prospects of success, behold, that other and greater enemy of yours, Eck, broke in with the Leipzig Debate which he had under-taken against Dr. Karlstadt. When the new question of the primacy of the pope was raised, he suddenly turned his weapons against me and completely upset our arrangement for maintaining peace. Meanwhile Karl Miltitz waited. The debate was held and judges were selected. But again no decision was reached, which is not surprising, for through Eck's lies, tricks, and wiles everything was stirred up, aggravated, and confused worse than ever. Regardless of

---

9. Karl von Miltitz had induced Luther to be silent with respect to the indulgence controversy, provided his opponents did likewise. Cf. *LW* 31, 310 and above, pp. 262-63.

10. At Altenburg on January 5 or 6, 1519.

the decision which might have been reached, a greater conflagration would have resulted, for he sought glory, not the truth. Again I left undone nothing that I ought to have done.

I admit that on this occasion no small amount of corrupt Roman practices came to light, but whatever wrong was done was Eck's fault, who undertook a task beyond his capacities. Striving insanely for his own glory, he revealed the shame of Rome to all the world. This man is your enemy, my dear Leo, or rather the enemy of your Curia. From his example alone we can learn that no enemy is more pernicious than a flatterer. What did he accomplish with his flattery but an evil which not even a king could have accomplished? The name of the Roman Curia is today a stench throughout the world, papal authority languishes, and notorious Roman ignorance is in ill repute. We should have heard nothing of all this if Eck had not upset the peace arrangements made by Karl [von Miltitz] and myself. Eck himself now clearly sees this and, although it is too late and to no avail, he is furious that my books were published. He should have thought of this when, like a whinnying horse, he was madly seeking his own glory and preferred his own advantage through you and at the greatest peril to you. The vain man thought that I would stop and keep silent out of fear for your name, for I do not believe that he entirely trusted his cleverness and learning. Now that he sees that I have more courage than that and have not been silenced, he repents of his rashness, but too late, and perceives—if indeed he does finally understand that there is One in heaven who opposes the proud and humbles the haughty [I Pet. 5:5; Jth. 6:15].

Since we gained nothing from this debate except greater confusion to the Roman cause, Karl Miltitz, in a third attempt to bring about peace, came to the fathers of the Augustinian Order assembled in their chapter and sought their advice in settling the controversy which had now grown most disturbing and dangerous. Because, by God's favor, they had no hope of proceeding against me by violent means, some of their most famous men were sent to me. These men asked me at least to show honor to the person of Your Blessedness and in a humble letter to plead as my excuse your innocence and mine in the matter. They said that the affair was not yet in a hopeless state, provided Leo X out of his innate goodness would take a hand in it. As I have always both offered and desired peace so that I might devote myself to quieter and more useful studies, and have stormed with such great fury merely for the purpose of overwhelming my unequal opponents by the volume and violence of words no less than of intellect, I not only gladly ceased but also joyfully and thankfully considered this suggestion a very welcome kindness to me, provided our hope could be realized.

So I come, most blessed father, and, prostrate before you, pray that if possible you intervene and stop those flatterers, who are the enemies of peace while they pretend to keep peace. But let no person imagine that I will recant unless he prefer to involve the whole question in even greater turmoil. Furthermore, I acknowledge no fixed rules for the interpretation of the Word of God, since the Word of God, which teaches freedom in all other matters, must not be bound [II Tim. 2:9]. If these two points are granted, there is nothing that I could not or would not most willingly do or endure. I detest contentions. I will challenge no one. On the other hand, I do not want others to challenge me. If they do, as Christ is my teacher, I will not be speechless. When once this controversy has been cited before you and settled, Your Blessedness will be able with a brief and ready word to silence both parties and command them to keep the peace. That is what I have always wished to hear.

Therefore, my Father Leo, do not listen to those sirens who pretend that you are no mere man but a demigod so that you may command and require whatever you wish. It will not be done in that manner and you will not have such remarkable power. You are a servant of servants,[11] and more than all other men you are in a most miserable and dangerous position. Be not deceived by those who pretend that you are lord of the world, allow no one to be considered a Christian unless he accepts your authority, and prate that you have power over heaven, hell, and purgatory. These men are your enemies who seek to destroy your soul [I Kings 19:10], as Isaiah says: "O my people, they that call thee blessed, the same deceive thee" [Isa. 3:12]. They err who exalt you above a council and the church universal. They err who ascribe to you alone the right of interpreting Scripture. Under the protection of your name they seek to gain support for all their wicked deeds in the church. Alas! Through them Satan has already made much progress under your predecessors. In short, believe none who exalt you, believe those who humble you. This is the judgment of God, that ". . . he has put down the mighty from their thrones and exalted those of low degree" [Luke 1:52]. See how different Christ is from his successors, although they all would wish to be his vicars. I fear that most of them have been too literally his vicars. A man is a vicar only when his superior is absent. If the pope rules, while Christ is absent and does not dwell in his heart, what else is he but a vicar of Christ? What is the church under such a vicar but a mass of people without Christ? Indeed, what is such a vicar but an antichrist and an idol? How much more properly did the apostles call themselves servants of the present Christ and not vicars of an absent Christ.

Perhaps I am presumptuous in trying to instruct so exalted a personage from whom we all should learn and from whom the thrones of judges receive their decisions,

---

11. *Servus servorum* was the usual title of the pope.

as those pestilential fellows of yours boast. But I am following the example of St. Bernard in his book, *On Consideration*,[12] to Pope Eugenius, a book every pope should know
from memory. I follow him, not because I am eager to
instruct you, but out of pure and loyal concern which compels us to be interested in all the affairs of our neighbors,
even when they are protected, and which does not permit
us to take into consideration either their dignity or lack
of dignity since it is only concerned with the dangers they
face or the advantages they may gain. I know that Your
Blessedness is driven and buffeted about in Rome, that
is, that far out at sea you are threatened on all sides by
dangers and are working very hard in the miserable situation so that you are in need of even the slightest help of
the least of your brothers. Therefore I do not consider it
absurd if I now forget your exalted office and do what
brotherly love demands. I have no desire to flatter you in
so serious and dangerous a matter. If men do not perceive
that I am your friend and your most humble subject in
this matter, there is One who understands and judges
[John 8:50].

Finally, that I may not approach you empty-handed,
blessed father, I am sending you this little treatise[13] dedicated to you as a token of peace and good hope. From
this book you may judge with what studies I should prefer
to be more profitably occupied, as I could be, provided
your godless flatterers would permit me and had permitted
me in the past. It is a small book if you regard its size.
Unless I am mistaken, however, it contains the whole of
Christian life in a brief form, provided you grasp its meaning. I am a poor man and have no other gift to offer, and
you do not need to be enriched by any but a spiritual gift.
May the Lord Jesus preserve you forever. Amen.

Wittenberg, September 6, 1520.

---

12. Cf. p. 270 n. 5.   13. *The Freedom of a Christian.*

MARTIN LUTHER'S TREATISE
ON CHRISTIAN LIBERTY

[*The Freedom of a Christian*]

Many people have considered Christian faith an easy thing, and not a few have given it a place among the virtues. They do this because they have not experienced it and have never tasted the great strength there is in faith. It is impossible to write well about it or to understand what has been written about it unless one has at one time or another experienced the courage which faith gives a man when trials oppress him. But he who has had even a faint taste of it can never write, speak, meditate, or hear enough concerning it. It is a living "spring of water welling up to eternal life," as Christ calls it in John 4 [:14].

As for me, although I have no wealth of faith to boast of and know how scant my supply is, I nevertheless hope that I have attained to a little faith, even though I have been assailed by great and various temptations; and I hope that I can discuss it, if not more elegantly, certainly more to the point, than those literalists and subtile disputants have previously done, who have not even understood what they have written.

To make the way smoother for the unlearned—for only them do I serve—I shall set down the following two propositions concerning the freedom and the bondage of the spirit:

A Christian is a perfectly free lord of all, subject to none.

A Christian is a perfectly dutiful servant of all, subject to all.

These two theses seem to contradict each other. If, however, they should be found to fit together they would serve our purpose beautifully. Both are Paul's own statements, who says in I Cor. 9 [:19], "For though I am free from all men, I have made myself a slave to all," and in Rom. 13 [:8], "Owe no one anything, except to love one another." Love by its very nature is ready to serve and be subject to him who is loved. So Christ, although he was Lord of all, was "born of woman, born under the law" [Gal. 4:4], and therefore was at the same time a free man and a servant, "in the form of God" and "of a servant" [Phil. 2:6-7].

Let us start, however, with something more remote from our subject, but more obvious. Man has a twofold nature, a spiritual and a bodily one. According to the spiritual nature, which men refer to as the soul, he is called a spiritual, inner, or new man. According to the bodily nature, which men refer to as flesh, he is called a carnal, outward, or old man, of whom the Apostle writes in II Cor. 4 [:16], "Though our outer nature is wasting away, our inner nature is being renewed every day." Because of this diversity of nature the Scriptures assert contradictory things concerning the same man, since these two men in the same man contradict each other, "for the desires of the flesh are against the Spirit, and the desires of the Spirit are against the flesh," according to Gal. 5 [:17].

First, let us consider the inner man to see how a righteous, free, and pious Christian, that is, a spiritual, new, and inner man, becomes what he is. It is evident that no external thing has any influence in producing Christian righteousness or freedom, or in producing unrighteousness or servitude. A simple argument will furnish the proof of this statement. What can it profit the soul if the body is well, free, and active, and eats, drinks, and does as it pleases? For in these respects even the most godless slaves of vice may prosper. On the other hand, how will poor health or imprisonment or hunger or thirst or any other external misfortune harm the soul? Even the most godly men, and those who are free because of clear consciences, are afflicted with these things. None of these things touch either the freedom or the servitude of the soul. It does not help the soul if the body is adorned with the sacred robes of priests or dwells in sacred places or is occupied with sacred duties or prays, fasts, abstains from certain kinds of food, or does any work that can be done by the body and in the body. The righteousness and the freedom of the soul require something far different, since the things which have been mentioned could be done by any wicked person. Such works produce nothing but hypocrites. On the other hand, it will not harm the soul if the body is clothed in secular dress, dwells in unconsecrated places, eats and drinks as others do, does not pray aloud, and neglects to do all the above-mentioned things which hypocrites can do.

Furthermore, to put aside all kinds of works, even contemplation, meditation, and all that the soul can do, does not help. One thing, and only one thing, is necessary for Christian life, righteousness, and freedom. That one thing is the most holy Word of God, the gospel of Christ, as Christ says, John 11 [:25], "I am the resurrection and the life; he who believes in me, though he die, yet shall he live"; and John 8 [:36], "So if the Son makes you free, you will be free indeed"; and Matt. 4 [:4], "Man shall not live by bread alone, but by every word that proceeds from the mouth of God." Let us then consider it certain and firmly established that the soul can do without anything except the Word of God and that where the Word of God is missing there is no help at all for the soul. If it has the Word of God it is rich and lacks nothing, since it is the Word of life, truth, light, peace, righteousness, salvation, joy, liberty, wisdom, power, grace, glory, and of every incalculable blessing. This is why the prophet in the entire Psalm [119] and in many other places yearns and sighs for the Word of God and uses so many names to describe it.

On the other hand, there is no more terrible disaster with which the wrath of God can afflict men than a famine of the hearing of his Word, as he says in Amos [8:11]. Like-wise there is no greater mercy than when he sends forth his Word, as we read in Psalm 107 [:20]: "He sent forth his word, and healed them, and delivered them from destruction." Nor was Christ sent into the world for any other ministry except that of the Word. Moreover, the entire spiritual estate—all the apostles, bishops, and priests —has been called and instituted only for the ministry of the Word.

You may ask, "What then is the Word of God, and how shall it be used, since there are so many words of God?" I answer: The Apostle explains this in Romans 1. The Word is the gospel of God concerning his Son, who was made flesh, suffered, rose from the dead, and was glorified through the Spirit who sanctifies. To preach Christ means to feed the soul, make it righteous, set it free, and save it, provided it believes the preaching. Faith alone is the saving and efficacious use of the Word of God, according to Rom. 10 [:9]: "If you confess with your lips that Jesus is Lord and believe in your heart that God raised him from the dead, you will be saved." Furthermore, "Christ is the end of the law, that every one who has faith may be justified" [Rom. 10:4]. Again, in Rom. 1 [:17], "He who through faith is righteous shall live." The Word of God can-not be received and cherished by any works whatever but only by faith. Therefore it is clear that, as the soul needs only the Word of God for its life and righteousness, so it is justified by faith alone and not any works; for if it could be justified by anything else, it would not need the Word, and consequently it would not need faith.

This faith cannot exist in connection with works—that is to say, if you at the same time claim to be justified by works, whatever their character—for that would be the same as "limping with two different opinions" [I Kings 18:21], as worshiping Baal and kissing one's own hand [Job 31:27-28], which, as Job says, is a very great iniquity.

Therefore the moment you begin to have faith you learn that all things in you are altogether blameworthy, sinful, and damnable, as the Apostle says in Rom. 3 [:23], "Since all have sinned and fall short of the glory of God," and, "None is righteous, no, not one; . . . all have turned aside, together they have gone wrong" (Rom. 3:10-12). When you have learned this you will know that you need Christ, who suffered and rose again for you so that, if you believe in him, you may through this faith become a new man in so far as your sins are forgiven and you are justified by the merits of another, namely, of Christ alone.

Since, therefore, this faith can rule only in the inner man, as Rom. 10 [:10] says, "For man believes with his heart and so is justified," and since faith alone justifies, it is clear that the inner man cannot be justified, freed, or saved by any outer work or action at all, and that these works, whatever their character, have nothing to do with this inner man. On the other hand, only ungodliness and unbelief of heart, and no outer work, make him guilty and a damnable servant of sin. Wherefore it ought to be the first concern of every Christian to lay aside all confidence in works and increasingly to strengthen faith alone and through faith to grow in the knowledge, not of works, but of Christ Jesus, who suffered and rose for him, as Peter teaches in the last chapter of his first Epistle (I Pet. 5:10). No other work makes a Christian. Thus when the Jews asked Christ, as related in John 6 [:28], what they must do "to be doing the work of God," he brushed aside the multitude of works which he saw they did in great profusion and suggested one work, saying, "This is the work of God, that you believe in him whom he has sent" [John 6:29]; "for on him has God the Father set his seal" [John 6:27].

Therefore true faith in Christ is a treasure beyond comparison which brings with it complete salvation and saves man from every evil, as Christ says in the last chapter of Mark [16:16]: "He who believes and is baptized will be saved; but he who does not believe will be condemned." Isaiah contemplated this treasure and foretold it in chapter 10: "The Lord will make a small and consuming word upon the land, and it will overflow with righteousness" [Cf. Isa. 10:22]. This is as though he said, "Faith, which is a small and perfect fulfillment of the law, will fill believers with so great a righteousness that they will need nothing more to become righteous." So Paul says, Rom. 10 [:10], "For man believes with his heart and so is justified."

Should you ask how it happens that faith alone justifies and offers us such a treasure of great benefits without works in view of the fact that so many works, ceremonies, and laws are prescribed in the Scriptures, I answer: First of all, remember what has been said, namely, that faith alone, without works, justifies, frees, and saves; we shall make this clearer later on. Here we must point out that the entire Scripture of God is divided into two parts: commandments and promises. Although the commandments teach things that are good, the things taught are not done as soon as they are taught, for the commandments show us what we ought to do but do not give us the power to do it. They are intended to teach man to know himself, that through them he may recognize his inability to do good and may despair of his own ability. That is why they are called the Old Testament and constitute the Old Testament. For example, the commandment, "You shall not covet" [Exod. 20:17], is a command which proves us all to be sinners, for no one can avoid coveting no matter how much he may struggle against it. Therefore, in order not to covet and to fulfill the commandment, a man is compelled to despair of himself, to seek the help which he does not find in himself elsewhere and from someone else, as stated in Hosea [13:9]: "Destruction is your own, O Israel: your help is only in me." As we fare with respect to one commandment, so we fare with all, for it is equally impossible for us to keep any one of them.

Now when a man has learned through the commandments to recognize his helplessness and is distressed about
how he might satisfy the law—since the law must be fulfilled so that not a jot or tittle shall be lost, otherwise man
will be condemned without hope—then, being truly
humbled and reduced to nothing in his own eyes, he finds
in himself nothing whereby he may be justified and saved.
Here the second part of Scripture comes to our aid, namely,
the promises of God which declare the glory of God, saying,
"If you wish to fulfill the law and not covet, as the law
demands, come, believe in Christ in whom grace, righteousness, peace, liberty, and all things are promised you. If you
believe, you shall have all things; if you do not believe, you
shall lack all things." That which is impossible for you to
accomplish by trying to fulfill all the works of the law—
many and useless as they all are—you will accomplish
quickly and easily through faith. God our Father has made
all things depend on faith so that whoever has faith will
have everything, and whoever does not have faith will have
nothing. "For God has consigned all men to disobedience,
that he may have mercy upon all," as it is stated in Rom.
11 [:32]. Thus the promises of God give what the commandments of God demand and fulfill what the law prescribes so that all things may be God's alone, both the commandments and the fulfilling of the commandments. He
alone commands, he alone fulfills. Therefore the promises
of God belong to the New Testament. Indeed, they are the
New Testament.

Since these promises of God are holy, true, righteous, free,
and peaceful words, full of goodness, the soul which clings
to them with a firm faith will be so closely united with
them and altogether absorbed by them that it not only will
share in all their power but will be saturated and intoxi-
cated by them. If a touch of Christ healed, how much
more will this most tender spiritual touch, this absorbing
of the Word, communicate to the soul all things that be-

long to the Word. This, then, is how through faith alone without works the soul is justified by the Word of God, sanctified, made true, peaceful, and free, filled with every blessing and truly made a child of God, as John 1 [:12] says: "But to all who . . . believed in his name, he gave power to become children of God."

From what has been said it is easy to see from what source faith derives such great power and why a good work or all good works together cannot equal it. No good work can rely upon the Word of God or live in the soul, for faith alone and the Word of God rule in the soul. Just as the heated iron glows like fire because of the union of fire with it, so the Word imparts its qualities to the soul. It is clear, then, that a Christian has all that he needs in faith and needs no work to justify him; and if he has no need of works, he has no need of the law; and if he has no need of the law, surely he is free from the law. It is true that "the law is not laid down for the just" [I Tim. 1:9]. This is that Christian liberty, our faith, which does not induce us to live in idleness or wickedness but makes the law and works unnecessary for any man's righteousness and salvation.

This is the first power of faith. Let us now examine also the second. It is a further function of faith that it honors him whom it trusts with the most reverent and highest regard since it considers him truthful and trustworthy. There is no other honor equal to the estimate of truthfulness with which we honor him whom we trust. Could we ascribe to a man anything greater than truthfulness and righteousness and perfect goodness? On the other hand, there is no way in which we can show greater contempt for a man than to regard him as false and wicked and to be suspicious of him, as we do when we do not trust him. So when the soul firmly trusts God's promises, it regards him as truthful and righteous. Nothing more excellent than this can be ascribed to God. The very highest worship of God is this that we ascribe to him truthfulness, righteousness, and whatever else should be ascribed to one who is trusted. When this is done, the soul consents to his will. Then it hallows his name and allows itself to be treated according to God's good pleasure for, clinging to God's promises, it does not doubt that he who is true, just, and wise will do, dispose, and provide all things well.

Is not such a soul most obedient to God in all things by this faith? What commandment is there that such obedience has not completely fulfilled? What more complete fulfillment is there than obedience in all things? This obedience, however, is not rendered by works, but by faith alone. On the other hand, what greater rebellion against God, what greater wickedness, what greater contempt of God is there than not believing his promise? For what is this but to make God a liar or to doubt that he is truthful?—that is, to ascribe truthfulness to one's self but lying and vanity to God? Does not a man who does this deny God and set himself up as an idol in his heart? Then of what good are works done in such wickedness, even if they were the works of angels and apostles? Therefore God has rightly included all things, not under anger or lust, but under unbelief, so that they who imagine that they are fulfilling the law by doing the works of chastity and mercy required by the law (the civil and human virtues) might not be saved. They are included under the sin of unbelief and must either seek mercy or be justly condemned.

When, however, God sees that we consider him truthful and by the faith of our heart pay him the great honor which is due him, he does us that great honor of considering us truthful and righteous for the sake of our faith. Faith works truth and righteousness by giving God what belongs to him. Therefore God in turn glorifies our righteousness. It is true and just that God is truthful and just, and to consider and confess him to be so is the same as being truthful and just. Accordingly he says in I Sam. 2 [:30], "Those who honor me I will honor, and those who despise me shall be lightly esteemed." So Paul says in Rom. 4 [:3] that Abraham's faith "was reckoned to him as righteousness" because by it he gave glory most perfectly to God, and that for the same reason our faith shall be reckoned to us as righteousness if we believe.

The third incomparable benefit of faith is that it unites the soul with Christ as a bride is united with her bridegroom. By this mystery, as the Apostle teaches, Christ and the soul become one flesh [Eph. 5:31-32]. And if they are one flesh and there is between them a true marriage—indeed the most perfect of all marriages, since human marriages are but poor examples of this one true marriage—it follows that everything they have they hold in common, the good as well as the evil. Accordingly the believing soul can boast of and glory in whatever Christ has as though it were its own, and whatever the soul has Christ claims as his own. Let us compare these and we shall see inestimable benefits. Christ is full of grace, life, and salvation. The soul is full of sins, death, and damnation. Now let faith come between them and sins, death, and damnation will be Christ's, while grace, life, and salvation will be the soul's; for if Christ is a bridegroom, he must take upon himself the things which are his bride's and bestow upon her the things that are his. If he gives her his body and very self, how shall he not give her all that is his? And if he takes the body of the bride, how shall he not take all that is hers?

Here we have a most pleasing vision not only of communion but of a blessed struggle and victory and salvation and redemption. Christ is God and man in one person. He has neither sinned nor died, and is not condemned, and he cannot sin, die, or be condemned; his righteousness, life, and salvation are unconquerable, eternal, omnipotent. By the wedding ring of faith he shares in the sins, death, and pains of hell which are his bride's. As a matter of fact, he makes them his own and acts as if they were his own and

286

as if he himself had sinned; he suffered, died, and descended into hell that he might overcome them all. Now since it was such a one who did all this, and death and hell could not swallow him up, these were necessarily swallowed up by him in a mighty duel; for his righteousness is greater than the sins of all men, his life stronger than death, his salvation more invincible than hell. Thus the believing soul by means of the pledge of his faith is free in Christ, its bridegroom, free from all sins, secure against death and hell, and is endowed with the eternal righteousness, life, and salvation of Christ its bridegroom. So he takes to himself a glorious bride, "without spot or wrinkle, cleansing her by the washing of water with the word" [Cf. Eph. 5:26-27] of life, that is, by faith in the Word of life, righteousness, and salvation. In this way he marries her in faith, steadfast love, and in mercies, righteousness, and justice, as Hos. 2 [:19-20] says.

Who then can fully appreciate what this royal marriage means? Who can understand the riches of the glory of this grace? Here this rich and divine bridegroom Christ marries this poor, wicked harlot, redeems her from all her evil, and adorns her with all his goodness. Her sins cannot now destroy her, since they are laid upon Christ and swallowed up by him. And she has that righteousness in Christ, her husband, of which she may boast as of her own and which she can confidently display alongside her sins in the face of death and hell and say, "If I have sinned, yet my Christ, in whom I believe, has not sinned, and all his is mine and all mine is his," as the bride in the Song of Solomon [2:16] says, "My beloved is mine and I am his." This is what Paul means when he says in I Cor. 15 [:57], "Thanks be to God, who gives us the victory through our Lord Jesus Christ," that is, the victory over sin and death, as he also says there, "The sting of death is sin, and the power of sin is the law" [I Cor. 15:56].

From this you once more see that much is ascribed to

faith, namely, that it alone can fulfill the law and justify without works. You see that the First Commandment, which says, "You shall worship one God," is fulfilled by faith alone. Though you were nothing but good works from the soles of your feet to the crown of your head, you would still not be righteous or worship God or fulfill the First Commandment, since God cannot be worshiped unless you ascribe to him the glory of truthfulness and all goodness which is due him. This cannot be done by works but only by the faith of the heart. Not by the doing of works but by believing do we glorify God and acknowledge that he is truthful. Therefore faith alone is the righteousness of a Christian and the fulfilling of all the commandments, for he who fulfills the First Commandment has no difficulty in fulfilling all the rest.

But works, being inanimate things, cannot glorify God, although they can, if faith is present, be done to the glory of God. Here, however, we are not inquiring what works and what kind of works are done, but who it is that does them, who glorifies God and brings forth the works. This is done by faith which dwells in the heart and is the source and substance of all our righteousness. Therefore it is a blind and dangerous doctrine which teaches that the commandments must be fulfilled by works. The commandments must be fulfilled before any works can be done, and the works proceed from the fulfillment of the commandments [Rom. 13-10], as we shall hear.

That we may examine more profoundly that grace which our inner man has in Christ, we must realize that in the Old Testament God consecrated to himself all the first-born males. The birthright was highly prized for it involved a twofold honor, that of priesthood and that of kingship. The first-born brother was priest and lord over all the others and a type of Christ, the true and only first-born of God the Father and the Virgin Mary and true king and priest, but not after the fashion of the flesh and the world, for his kingdom is not of this world [John 18:36]. He reigns in heavenly and spiritual things and consecrates them—things such as righteousness, truth, wisdom, peace, salvation, etc. This does not mean that all things on earth and in hell are not also subject to him—otherwise how could he protect and save us from them?—but that his kingdom consists neither in them nor of them. Nor does his priesthood consist in the outer splendor of robes and postures like those of the human priesthood of Aaron and our present-day church; but it consists of spiritual things through which he by an invisible service intercedes for us in heaven before God, there offers himself as a sacrifice, and does all things a priest should do, as Paul describes him under the type of Melchizedek in the Epistle to the Hebrews [Heb. 6-7]. Nor does he only pray and intercede for us but he teaches us inwardly through the living instruction of his Spirit, thus performing the two real functions of a priest, of which the prayers and the preaching of human priests are visible types.

Now just as Christ by his birthright obtained these two prerogatives, so he imparts them to and shares them with everyone who believes in him according to the law of the above-mentioned marriage, according to which the wife owns whatever belongs to the husband. Hence all of us who believe in Christ are priests and kings in Christ, as I Pet. 2 [:9] says: "You are a chosen race, God's own people, a royal priesthood, a priestly kingdom, that you may declare the wonderful deeds of him who called you out of darkness into his marvelous light."

The nature of this priesthood and kingship is something like this: First, with respect to the kingship, every Christian is by faith so exalted above all things that, by virtue of a spiritual power, he is lord of all things without exception, so that nothing can do him any harm. As a matter of fact, all things are made subject to him and are compelled to serve him in obtaining salvation. Accordingly Paul says in Rom. 8 [:28], "All things work together for good for the elect," and in I Cor. 3 [:21-23], "All things are yours whether . . . life or death or the present or the future, all are yours; and you are Christ's. . . ." This is not to say that every Christian is placed over all things to have and control them by physical power—a madness with which some churchmen are afflicted—for such power belongs to kings, princes, and other men on earth. Our ordinary experience in life shows us that we are subjected to all, suffer many things, and even die. As a matter of fact, the more Christian a man is, the more evils, sufferings, and deaths he must endure, as we see in Christ the first-born prince himself, and in all his brethren, the saints. The power of which we speak is spiritual. It rules in the midst of enemies and is powerful in the midst of oppression. This means nothing else than that "power is made perfect in weakness" [II Cor. 12:9] and that in all things I can find profit toward salvation [Rom. 8:28], so that the cross and death itself are compelled to serve me and to work together with me for my salvation. This is a splendid privilege and hard to attain, a truly omnipotent power, a spiritual dominion in which there is nothing so good and nothing so evil but that it shall work together for good to me, if only I believe. Yes, since faith alone suffices for salvation, I need nothing except faith exercising the power and dominion of its own liberty. Lo, this is the inestimable power and liberty of Christians.

Not only are we the freest of kings, we are also priests forever, which is far more excellent than being kings, for as priests we are worthy to appear before God to pray for others and to teach one another divine things. These are the functions of priests, and they cannot be granted to any unbeliever. Thus Christ has made it possible for us, provided we believe in him, to be not only his brethren, coheirs, and fellow-kings, but also his fellow-priests. Therefore we may boldly come into the presence of God in the spirit of faith [Heb. 10:19, 22] and cry "Abba, Father!" pray for one another, and do all things which we see done and foreshadowed in the outer and visible works of priests.

He, however, who does not believe is not served by anything. On the contrary, nothing works for his good, but he himself is a servant of all, and all things turn out badly for him because he wickedly uses them to his own advantage and not to the glory of God. So he is no priest but a wicked man whose prayer becomes sin and who never comes into the presence of God because God does not hear sinners [John 9:31]. Who then can comprehend the lofty dignity of the Christian? By virtue of his royal power he rules over all things, death, life, and sin, and through his priestly glory is omnipotent with God because he does the things which God asks and desires, as it is written, "He will fulfill the desire of those who fear him; he also will hear their cry and save them" [Cf. Phil. 4:13]. To this glory a man attains, certainly not by any works of his, but by faith alone.

From this anyone can clearly see how a Christian is free from all things and over all things so that he needs no works to make him righteous and save him, since faith alone abundantly confers all these things. Should he grow so foolish, however, as to presume to become righteous, free, saved, and a Christian by means of some good work, he would instantly lose faith and all its benefits, a foolishness aptly illustrated in the fable of the dog who runs along a stream with a piece of meat in his mouth and, deceived by the reflection of the meat in the water, opens his mouth to snap at it and so loses both the meat and the reflection.[14]

You will ask, "If all who are in the church are priests, how do these whom we now call priests differ from laymen?" I answer: Injustice is done those words "priest," "cleric," "spiritual," "ecclesiastic," when they are transferred from all Christians to those few who are now by a

---

14. Luther was fond of Aesop's Fables, of which this is one.

mischievous usage called "ecclesiastics." Holy Scripture makes no distinction between them, although it gives the name "ministers," "servants," "stewards" to those who are now proudly called popes, bishops, and lords and who should according to the ministry of the Word serve others and teach them the faith of Christ and the freedom of believers. Although we are all equally priests, we cannot all publicly minister and teach. We ought not do so even if we could. Paul writes accordingly in I Cor. 4 [:1]: "This is how one should regard us, as servants of Christ and stewards of the mysteries of God."

That stewardship, however, has now been developed into so great a display of power and so terrible a tyranny that no heathen empire or other earthly power can be compared with it, just as if laymen were not also Christians. Through this perversion the knowledge of Christian grace, faith, liberty, and of Christ himself has altogether perished, and its place has been taken by an unbearable bondage of human works and laws until we have become, as the Lamentations of Jeremiah [1] say, servants of the vilest men on earth who abuse our misfortune to serve only their base and shameless will.

To return to our purpose, I believe that it has now become clear that it is not enough or in any sense Christian to preach the works, life, and words of Christ as historical facts, as if the knowledge of these would suffice for the conduct of life; yet this is the fashion among those who must today be regarded as our best preachers. Far less is it sufficient or Christian to say nothing at all about Christ and to teach instead the laws of men and the decrees of the fathers. Now there are not a few who preach Christ and read about him that they may move men's affections to sympathy with Christ, to anger against the Jews, and such childish and effeminate nonsense. Rather ought Christ to be preached to the end that faith in him may be established that he may not only be Christ, but be Christ for you and me, and that what is said of him and is denoted in his name may be effectual in us. Such faith is produced and preserved in us by preaching why Christ came, what he brought and bestowed, what benefit it is to us to accept him. This is done when that Christian liberty which he bestows is rightly taught and we are told in what way we Christians are all kings and priests and therefore lords of all and may firmly believe that whatever we have done is pleasing and acceptable in the sight of God, as I have already said.

What man is there whose heart, upon hearing these things, will not rejoice to its depth, and when receiving such comfort will not grow tender so that he will love Christ as he never could by means of any laws or works? Who would have the power to harm or frighten such a heart? If the knowledge of sin or the fear of death should break in upon it, it is ready to hope in the Lord. It does not grow afraid when it hears tidings of evil. It is not disturbed when it sees its enemies. This is so because it believes that the righteousness of Christ is its own and that its sin is not its own, but Christ's, and that all sin is swallowed up by the righteousness of Christ. This, as has been said above,[15] is a necessary consequence on account of faith in Christ. So the heart learns to scoff at death and sin and to say with the Apostle, "O death, where is thy victory? O death, where is thy sting? The sting of death is sin, and the power of sin is the law. But thanks be to God, who gives us the victory through our Lord Jesus Christ" [I Cor. 15:55-57]. Death is swallowed up not only in the victory of Christ but also by our victory, because through faith his victory has become ours and in that faith we also are conquerors.

Let this suffice concerning the inner man, his liberty, and the source of his liberty, the righteousness of faith. He needs neither laws nor good works but, on the contrary,

---

15. Cf. p. 287.

is injured by them if he believes that he is justified by them.

Now let us turn to the second part, the outer man. Here we shall answer all those who, offended by the word "faith" and by all that has been said, now ask, "If faith does all things and is alone sufficient unto righteousness, why then are good works commanded? We will take our ease and do no works and be content with faith." I answer: not so, you wicked men, not so. That would indeed be proper if we were wholly inner and perfectly spiritual men. But such we shall be only at the last day, the day of the resurrection of the dead. As long as we live in the flesh we only begin to make some progress in that which shall be perfected in the future life. For this reason the Apostle in Rom. 8 [:23] calls all that we attain in this life "the first fruits of the Spirit" because we shall indeed receive the greater portion, even the fulness of the Spirit, in the future. This is the place to assert that which was said above, namely, that a Christian is the servant of all and made subject to all. Insofar as he is free he does no works, but insofar as he is a servant he does all kinds of works. How this is possible we shall see.

Although, as I have said, a man is abundantly and sufficiently justified by faith inwardly, in his spirit, and so has all that he needs, except insofar as this faith and these riches must grow from day to day even to the future life; yet he remains in this mortal life on earth. In this life he must control his own body and have dealings with men. Here the works begin; here a man cannot enjoy leisure; here he must indeed take care to discipline his body by fastings, watchings, labors, and other reasonable discipline and to subject it to the Spirit so that it will obey and conform to the inner man and faith and not revolt against faith and hinder the inner man, as it is the nature of the body to do if it is not held in check. The inner man, who by faith is created in the image of God, is both joyful and happy because of Christ in whom so many benefits are conferred upon him; and therefore it is his one occupation to serve God joyfully and without thought of gain, in love that is not constrained.

While he is doing this, behold, he meets a contrary will in his own flesh which strives to serve the world and seeks its own advantage. This the spirit of faith cannot tolerate, but with joyful zeal it attempts to put the body under control and hold it in check, as Paul says in Rom. 7 [:22-23], "For I delight in the law of God, in my inmost self, but I see in my members another law at war with the law of my mind and making me captive to the law of sin," and in another place, "But I pommel my body and subdue it, lest after preaching to others I myself should be disqualified" [I Cor. 9:27], and in Galatians [5:24], "And those who belong to Christ Jesus have crucified the flesh with its passions and desires."

In doing these works, however, we must not think that a man is justified before God by them, for faith, which alone is righteousness before God, cannot endure that erroneous opinion. We must, however, realize that these works reduce the body to subjection and purify it of its evil lusts, and our whole purpose is to be directed only toward the driving out of lusts. Since by faith the soul is cleansed and made to love God, it desires that all things, and especially its own body, shall be purified so that all things may join with it in loving and praising God. Hence a man cannot be idle, for the need of his body drives him and he is compelled to do many good works to reduce it to subjection. Nevertheless the works themselves do not justify him before God, but he does the works out of spontaneous love in obedience to God and considers nothing except the approval of God, whom he would most scrupulously obey in all things.

In this way everyone will easily be able to learn for himself the limit and discretion, as they say, of his bodily castigations, for he will fast, watch, and labor as much as he finds sufficient to repress the lasciviousness and lust of his body. But those who presume to be justified by works do not regard the mortifying of the lusts, but only the works themselves, and think that if only they have done as many and as great works as are possible, they have done well and have become righteous. At times they even addle their brains and destroy, or at least render useless, their natural strength with their works. This is the height of folly and utter ignorance of Christian life and faith, that a man should seek to be justified and saved by works and without faith.

In order to make that which we have said more easily understood, we shall explain by analogies. We should think of the works of a Christian who is justified and saved by faith because of the pure and free mercy of God, just as we would think of the works which Adam and Eve did in Paradise, and all their children would have done if they had not sinned. We read in Gen. 2 [:15] that "The Lord God took the man and put him in the garden of Eden to till it and keep it." Now Adam was created righteous and upright and without sin by God so that he had no need of being justified and made upright through his tilling and keeping the garden; but, that he might not be idle, the Lord gave him a task to do, to cultivate and protect the garden. This task would truly have been the freest of works, done only to please God and not to obtain righteousness, which Adam already had in full measure and which would have been the birthright of us all.

The works of a believer are like this. Through his faith he has been restored to Paradise and created anew, has no need of works that he may become or be righteous; but that he may not be idle and may provide for and keep his body, he must do such works freely only to please God. Since, however, we are not wholly recreated, and our faith and love are not yet perfect, these are to be increased, not by external works, however, but of themselves.

A second example: A bishop, when he consecrates a

church, confirms children, or performs some other duty belonging to his office, is not made a bishop by these works. Indeed, if he had not first been made a bishop, none of these works would be valid. They would be foolish, childish, and farcical. So the Christian who is consecrated by his faith does good works, but the works do not make him holier or more Christian, for that is the work of faith alone. And if a man were not first a believer and a Christian, all his works would amount to nothing and would be truly wicked and damnable sins.

The following statements are therefore true: "Good works do not make a good man, but a good man does good works; evil works do not make a wicked man, but a wicked man does evil works." Consequently it is always necessary that the substance or person himself be good before there can be any good works, and that good works follow and proceed from the good person, as Christ also says, "A good tree cannot bear evil fruit, nor can a bad tree bear good fruit" [Matt. 7:18]. It is clear that the fruits do not bear the tree and that the tree does not grow on the fruits, also that, on the contrary, the trees bear the fruits and the fruits grow on the trees. As it is necessary, therefore, that the trees exist before their fruits and the fruits do not make trees either good or bad, but rather as the trees are, so are the fruits they bear; so a man must first be good or wicked before he does a good or wicked work, and his works do not make him good or wicked, but he himself makes his works either good or wicked.

Illustrations of the same truth can be seen in all trades. A good or a bad house does not make a good or a bad builder; but a good or a bad builder makes a good or a bad house. And in general, the work never makes the workman like itself, but the workman makes the work like himself. So it is with the works of man. As the man is, whether believer or unbeliever, so also is his work—good if it was done in faith, wicked if it was done in unbelief.

But the converse is not true, that the work makes the man either a believer or unbeliever. As works do not make a man a believer, so also they do not make him righteous. But as faith makes a man a believer and righteous, so faith does good works. Since, then, works justify no one, and a man must be righteous before he does a good work, it is very evident that it is faith alone which, because of the pure mercy of God through Christ and in his Word, worthily and sufficiently justifies and saves the person. A Christian has no need of any work or law in order to be saved since through faith he is free from every law and does everything out of pure liberty and freely. He seeks neither benefit nor salvation since he already abounds in all things and is saved through the grace of God because in his faith he now seeks only to please God.

Furthermore, no good work helps justify or save an unbeliever. On the other hand, no evil work makes him wicked or damns him; but the unbelief which makes the person and the tree evil does the evil and damnable works. Hence when a man is good or evil, this is effected not by the works, but by faith or unbelief, as the Wise Man says, "This is the beginning of sin, that a man falls away from God" [Cf. Sirach 10:14-15], which happens when he does not believe. And Paul says in Heb. 11 [:6], "For whoever would draw near to God must believe. . . ." And Christ says the same: "Either make the tree good, and its fruit good; or make the tree bad, and its fruit bad" [Matt. 12:33], as if he would say, "Let him who wishes to have good fruit begin by planting a good tree." So let him who wishes to do good works begin not with the doing of works, but with believing, which makes the person good, for nothing makes a man good except faith, or evil except unbelief.

It is ineed true that in the sight of men a man is made good or evil by his works; but this being made good or evil only means that the man who is good or evil is pointed out and known as such, as Christ says in Matt. 7 [:20], "Thus you will know them by their fruits." All this remains on the surface, however, and very many have been deceived by this outward appearance and have presumed to write and teach concerning good works by which we may be justified without even mentioning faith. They go their way, always being deceived and deceiving [II Tim. 3:13], progressing, indeed, but into a worse state, blind leaders of the blind, wearying themselves with many works and still never attaining to true righteousness [Matt. 15:14]. Of such people Paul says in II Tim. 3 [:5, 7]: "Holding the form of religion but denying the power of it . . . who will listen to anybody and can never arrive at a knowledge of the truth."

Whoever, therefore, does not wish to go astray with those blind men must look beyond works, and beyond laws and doctrines about works. Turning his eyes from works, he must look upon the person and ask how he is justified. For the person is justified and saved, not by works or laws, but by the Word of God, that is, by the promise of his grace, and by faith, that the glory may remain God's, who saved us not by works of righteousness which we have done [Titus 3:5], but by virtue of his mercy by the word of his grace when we believed [I Cor. 1:21].

From this it is easy to know how far good works are to be rejected or not, and by what standard all the teachings of men concerning works are to be interpreted. If works are sought after as a means to righteousness, are burdened with this perverse leviathan,[16] and are done under the false impression that through them one is justified, they are made necessary and freedom and faith are destroyed; and this addition to them makes them no longer good but truly damnable works. They are not free, and they blaspheme the grace of God, since to justify and to save by

---

16. Probably a reminiscence of Leviathan, the twisting serpent, in Isa. 27:1.

faith belongs to the grace of God alone. What the works have no power to do they nevertheless—by a godless presumption through this folly of ours—pretend to do and thus violently force themselves into the office and glory of grace. We do not, therefore, reject good works; on the contrary, we cherish and teach them as much as possible. We do not condemn them for their own sake but on account of this godless addition to them and the perverse idea that righteousness is to be sought through them; for that makes them appear good outwardly, when in truth they are not good. They deceive men and lead them to deceive one another like ravening wolves in sheep's clothing [Matt. 7:15].

But this leviathan, or perverse notion concerning works, is unconquerable where sincere faith is wanting. Those work-saints cannot get rid of it unless faith, its destroyer, comes and rules in their hearts. Nature of itself cannot drive it out or even recognize it, but rather regards it as a mark of the most holy will. If the influence of custom is added and confirms this perverseness of nature, as wicked teachers have caused it to do, it becomes an incurable evil and leads astray and destroys countless men beyond all hope of restoration. Therefore, although it is good to preach and write about penitence, confession, and satisfaction, our teaching is unquestionably deceitful and diabolical if we stop with that and do not go on to teach about faith.

Christ, like his forerunner John, not only said, "Repent" [Matt. 3:2; 4:17], but added the word of faith, saying, "The kingdom of heaven is at hand." We are not to preach only one of these words of God, but both; we are to bring forth out of our treasure things new and old, the voice of the law as well as the word of grace [Matt. 13:52]. We must bring forth the voice of the law that men may be made to fear and come to a knowledge of their sins and so be converted to repentance and a better life. But we must not stop with that, for that would only amount to wounding and not binding up, smiting and not healing, killing and not making alive, leading down into hell and not bringing back again, humbling and not exalting. Therefore we must also preach the word of grace and the promise of forgiveness by which faith is taught and aroused. Without this word of grace the works of the law, contrition, penitence, and all the rest are done and taught in vain.

Preachers of repentance and grace remain even to our day, but they do not explain God's law and promise that a man might learn from them the source of repentance and grace. Repentance proceeds from the law of God, but faith or grace from the promise of God, as Rom. 10 [:17] says: "So faith comes from what is heard, and what is heard comes by the preaching of Christ." Accordingly man is consoled and exalted by faith in the divine promise after he has been humbled and led to a knowledge of himself by the threats and the fear of the divine law. So we read in Psalm 30 [:5]: "Weeping may tarry for the night, but joy comes with the morning."

Let this suffice concerning works in general and at the same time concerning the works which a Christian does for himself. Lastly, we shall also speak of the things which he does toward his neighbor. A man does not live for himself alone in this mortal body to work for it alone, but he lives also for all men on earth; rather, he lives only for others and not for himself. To this end he brings his body into subjection that he may the more sincerely and freely serve others, as Paul says in Rom. 14 [:7-8], "None of us lives to himself, and none of us dies to himself. If we live, we live to the Lord, and if we die, we die to the Lord." He cannot ever in this life be idle and without works toward his neighbors, for he will necessarily speak, deal with, and exchange views with men, as Christ also, being made in the likeness of men [Phil. 2:7], was found in form as a man and conversed with men, as Baruch 3 [:37] says.

Man, however, needs none of these things for his righteousness and salvation. Therefore he should be guided in all his works by this thought and contemplate this one thing alone, that he may serve and benefit others in all that he does, considering nothing except the need and the advantage of his neighbor. Accordingly the Apostle commands us to work with our hands so that we may give to the needy, although he might have said that we should work to support ourselves. He says, however, "that he may be able to give to those in need" [Eph. 4:28]. This is what makes caring for the body a Christian work, that through its health and comfort we may be able to work, to acquire, and lay by funds with which to aid those who are in need, that in this way the strong member may serve the weaker, and we may be sons of God, each caring for and working for the other, bearing one another's burdens and so fulfilling the law of Christ [Gal. 6:2]. This is a truly Christian life. Here faith is truly active through love [Gal. 5:6], that is, it finds expression in works of the freest service, cheerfully and lovingly done, with which a man willingly serves another without hope of reward; and for himself he is satisfied with the fullness and wealth of his faith.

Accordingly Paul, after teaching the Philippians how rich they were made through faith in Christ, in which they obtained all things, thereafter teaches them, saying, "So if there is any encouragement in Christ, any incentive of love, any participation in the Spirit, any affection and sympathy, complete my joy by being of the same mind, having the same love, being in full accord and of one mind. Do nothing from selfishness or conceit, but in humility count others better than yourselves. Let each of you look not only to his own interests, but also to the interests of others" [Phil. 2:1-4]. Here we see clearly that the Apostle has prescribed this rule for the life of Christians, namely, that we should devote all our works to the welfare of others, since each has such abundant riches in his faith that all his other works and his whole life are a surplus with which he can by voluntary benevolence serve and do good to his neighbor.

As an example of such life the Apostle cites Christ, saying, "Have this mind among yourselves, which you have in Christ Jesus, who though he was in the form of God, did not count equality with God a thing to be grasped, but emptied himself, taking the form of a servant, being born in the likeness of men. And being found in human form he humbled himself and became obedient unto death" [Phil. 2:5-8]. This salutary word of the Apostle has been obscured for us by those who have not at all understood his words, "form of God," "form of a servant," "human form," "likeness of men," and have applied them to the divine and the human nature. Paul means this: Although Christ was filled with the form of God and rich in all good things, so that he needed no work and no suffering to make him righteous and saved (for he had all this externally), yet he was not puffed up by them and did not exalt himself above us and assume power over us, although he could rightly have done so; but, on the contrary, he so lived, labored, worked, suffered, and died that he might be like other men and in fashion and in actions be nothing else than a man, just as if he had need of all these things and had nothing of the form of God. But he did all this for our sake, that he might serve us and that all things which he accomplished in this form of a servant might become ours.

So a Christian, like Christ his head, is filled and made rich by faith and should be content with this form of God which he has obtained by faith; only, as I have said, he should increase this faith until it is made perfect. For this faith is his life, his righteousness, and his salvation: it saves him and makes him acceptable, and bestows upon him all things that are Christ's, as has been said above, and as Paul asserts in Gal. 2 [:20] when he says, "And the life I now live in the flesh I live by faith in the Son of God." Although the Christian is thus free from all works, he ought in this

303

liberty to empty himself, take upon himself the form of a servant, be made in the likeness of men, be found in human form, and to serve, help, and in every way deal with his neighbor as he sees that God through Christ has dealt and still deals with him. This he should do freely, having regard for nothing but divine approval.

He ought to think: "Although I am an unworthy and condemned man, my God has given me in Christ all the riches of righteousness and salvation without any merit on my part, out of pure, free mercy, so that from now on I need nothing except faith which believes that this is true. Why should I not therefore freely, joyfully, with all my heart, and with an eager will do all things which I know are pleasing and acceptable to such a Father who has overwhelmed me with his inestimable riches? I will therefore give myself as a Christ to my neighbor, just as Christ offered himself to me; I will do nothing in this life except what I see is necessary, profitable, and salutary to my neighbor, since through faith I have an abundance of all good things in Christ."

Behold, from faith thus flow forth love and joy in the Lord, and from love a joyful, willing, and free mind that serves one's neighbor willingly and takes no account of gratitude or ingratitude, of praise or blame, of gain or loss. For a man does not serve that he may put men under obligations. He does not distinguish between friends and enemies or anticipate their thankfulness or unthankfulness, but he most freely and most willingly spends himself and all that he has, whether he wastes all on the thankless or whether he gains a reward. As his Father does, distributing all things to all men richly and freely, making "his sun rise on the evil and on the good" [Matt. 5:45], so also the son does all things and suffers all things with that freely bestowing joy which is his delight when through Christ he sees it in God, the dispenser of such great benefits.

Therefore, if we recognize the great and precious things

which are given us, as Paul says [Rom. 5:5], our hearts will be filled by the Holy Spirit with the love which makes us free, joyful, almighty workers and conquerors over all tribulations, servants of our neighbors, and yet lords of all. For those who do not recognize the gifts bestowed upon them through Christ, however, Christ has been born in vain; they go their way with their works and shall never come to taste or feel those things. Just as our neighbor is in need and and lacks that in which we abound, so we were in need before God and lacked his mercy. Hence, as our heavenly Father has in Christ freely come to our aid, we also ought freely to help our neighbor through our body and its works, and each one should become as it were a Christ to the other that we may be Christs to one another and Christ may be the same in all, that is, that we may be truly Christians.

Who then can comprehend the riches and the glory of the Christian life? It can do all things and has all things and lacks nothing. It is lord over sin, death, and hell, and yet at the same time it serves, ministers to, and benefits all men. But, alas, in our day this life is unknown throughout the world; it is neither preached about nor sought after; we are altogether ignorant of our own name and do not know why we are Christians or bear the name of Christians. Surely we are named after Christ, not because he is absent from us, but because he dwells in us, that is, because we believe in him and are Christ's one to another and do to our neighbors as Christ does to us. But in our day we are taught by the doctrine of men to seek nothing but merits, rewards, and the things that are ours; of Christ we have made only a taskmaster far harsher than Moses.

We have a pre-eminent example of such a faith in the blessed Virgin. As is written in Luke 2 [:22], she was puri-fied according to the law of Moses according to the custom of all women, although she was not bound by that law and did not need to be purified. Out of free and willing love, however, she submitted to the law like other women that she might not offend or despise them. She was not justified by this work, but being righteous she did it freely and willingly. So also our works should be done, not that we may be justified by them, since, being justified beforehand by faith, we ought to do all things freely and joyfully for the sake of others.

St. Paul also circumcised his disciple Timothy, not because circumcision was necessary for his righteousness, but that he might not offend or despise the Jews who were weak in the faith and could not yet grasp the liberty of faith. But, on the other hand, when they despised the liberty of faith and insisted that circumcision was necessary for righteousness, he resisted them and did not allow Titus to be circumcised Gal. 2 [:3]. Just as he was unwilling to offend or despise any man's weak faith and yielded to their will for a time, so he was also unwilling that the liberty of faith should be offended against or despised by stubborn, work-righteous men. He chose a middle way, sparing the weak for a time, but always withstanding the stubborn, that he might convert all to the liberty of faith. What we do should be done with the same zeal to sustain the weak in faith, as in Rom. 14 [:1]; but we should firmly resist the stubborn teachers of works. Of this we shall say more later.

Christ also, in Matt. 7 [:24-27], when the tax money was demanded of his disciples, discussed with St. Peter whether the sons of the king were not free from the payment of tribute, and Peter affirmed that they were. Nonetheless, Christ commanded Peter to go to the sea and said, "Not to give offense to them, go to the sea and cast a hook, and take the first fish that comes up, and when you open its mouth you will find a shekel; take that and give it to them for me and for yourself." This incident fits our subject beautifully, for Christ here calls himself and those who are his children sons of the king, who need nothing; and yet he freely submits and pays the tribute. Just as necessary and helpful as this work was to Christ's righteousness or salvation, just so much do all other works of his or his followers avail for righteousness, since they all follow after righteousness and are done only to serve others and to give them an example of good works.

Of the same nature are the precepts which Paul gives in Rom. 13 [:1-7], namely, that Christians should be subject to the governing authorities and be ready to do every good work, not that they shall in this way be justified, since they already are righteous through faith, but that in the liberty of the Spirit they shall by so doing serve others and the authorities themselves and obey their will freely and out of love. The works of all colleges,[17] monasteries, and priests should be of this nature. Each one should do the works of his profession and station, not that by them he may strive after righteousness, but that through them he may keep his body under control, be an example to others who also need to keep their bodies under control, and finally that by such works he may submit his will to that of others in the freedom of love. But very great care must always be exercised so that no man in a false confidence imagines that by such works he will be justified or acquire merit or be saved; for this is the work of faith alone, as I have repeatedly said.

Anyone knowing this could easily and without danger find his way through those numberless mandates and precepts of pope, bishops, monasteries, churches, princes, and magistrates upon which some ignorant pastors insist as if they were necessary to righteousness and salvation, calling them "precepts of the church," although they are nothing of the kind. For a Christian, as a free man, will say, "I will fast, pray, do this and that as men command, not because it is necessary to my righteousness or salvation; but that I may show due respect to the pope, the bishop, the com-

---

17. The word "college" here denotes a corporation of clergy supported by a foundation and performing certain religious services.

munity, a magistrate, or my neighbor, and give them an example. I will do and suffer all things, just as Christ did and suffered far more for me, although he needed nothing of it all for himself, and was made under the law for my sake, although he was not under the law." Although tyrants do violence or injustice in making their demands, yet it will do no harm as long as they demand nothing contrary to God.

From what has been said, everyone can pass a safe judgment on all works and laws and make a trustworthy distinction between them and know who are the blind and ignorant pastors and who are the good and true. Any work that is not done solely for the purpose of keeping the body under control or of serving one's neighbor, as long as he asks nothing contrary to God, is not good or Christian. For this reason I greatly fear that few or no colleges, monasteries, altars, and offices of the church are really Christian in our day—nor the special fasts and prayers on certain saints' days. I fear, I say, that in all these we seek only our profit, thinking that through them our sins are purged away and that we find salvation in them. In this way Christian liberty perishes altogether. This is a consequence of our ignorance of Christian faith and liberty.

This ignorance and suppression of liberty very many blind pastors take pains to encourage. They stir up and urge on their people in these practices by praising such works, puffing them up with their indulgences, and never teaching faith. If, however, you wish to pray, fast, or establish a foundation in the church, I advise you to be careful not to do it in order to obtain some benefit, whether temporal or eternal, for you would do injury to your faith which alone offers you all things. Your one care should be that faith may grow, whether it is trained by works or sufferings. Make your gifts freely and for no consideration, so that others may profit by them and fare well because of you and your goodness. In this way you shall be truly good and Christian. Of what benefit to you are the good works which you do not need for keeping your body under control? Your faith is sufficient for you, through which God has given you all things.

See, according to this rule the good things we have from God should flow from one to the other and be common to all, so that everyone should "put on" his neighbor and so conduct himself toward him as if he himself were in the other's place. From Christ the good things have flowed and are flowing into us. He has so "put on" us and acted for us as if he had been what we are. From us they flow on to those who have need of them, so that I should lay before God my faith and my righteousness that they may cover and intercede for the sins of my neighbor which I take upon myself, and so labor and serve in them as if they were my very own. That is what Christ did for us. This is true love and the genuine rule of a Christian life. Love is true and genuine where there is true and genuine faith. Hence the Apostle says of love in I Cor. 13 [:5] that "it does not seek its own."

We conclude, therefore, that a Christian lives not in himself, but in Christ and in his neighbor. Otherwise he is not a Christian. He lives in Christ through faith, in his neighbor through love. By faith he is caught up beyond himself into God. By love he descends beneath himself into his neighbor. Yet he always remains in God and in his love, as Christ says in John I [:51], "Truly, truly, I say to you, you will see heaven opened, and the angels of God ascending and descending upon the Son of man."

Enough now of freedom. As you see, it is a spiritual and true freedom and makes our hearts free from all sins, laws and commands, as Paul says, I Tim. 1 [:9], "The law is not laid down for the just." It is more excellent than all other liberty, which is external, as heaven is more excellent than earth. May Christ give us this liberty both to understand and to preserve. Amen.

Finally, something must be added for the sake of those for whom nothing can be said so well that they will not spoil it by misunderstanding it. It is questionable whether they will understand even what will be said here. There are very many who, when they hear of this freedom of faith, immediately turn it into an occasion for the flesh and think that now all things are allowed them. They want to show that they are free men and Christians only by despising and finding fault with ceremonies, traditions, and human laws; as if they were Christians because on stated days they do not fast or eat meat when others fast, or because they do not use the accustomed prayers, and with upturned nose scoff at the precepts of men, although they utterly disregard all else that pertains to the Christian religion. The extreme opposite of these are those who rely for their salvation solely on their reverent observance of ceremonies, as if they would be saved because on certain days they fast or abstain from meats, or pray certain prayers; these make a boast of the precepts of the church and of the fathers, and do not care a fig for the things which are of the essence of our faith. Plainly, both are in error because they neglect the weightier things which are necessary to salvation, and quarrel so noisily about trifling and unnecessary matters.

How much better is the teaching of the Apostle Paul who bids us take a middle course and condemns both sides when he says, "Let not him who eats despise him who abstains, and let not him whom abstains pass judgment on him who eats" [Rom. 14:3]. Here you see that they who neglect and disparage ceremonies, not out of piety, but out of mere contempt, are reproved, since the Apostle teaches us not to despise them. Such men are puffed up by knowledge. On the other hand, he teaches those who insist on the ceremonies not to judge the others, for neither party acts toward the other according to the love that edifies. Wherefore we ought to listen to Scripture which teaches that we should not go aside to the right or to the left [Deut. 28:14] but follow the statutes of the Lord which are right, "rejoicing the heart" [Ps. 19:8]. As a man is not righteous because he keeps and clings to the works and forms of the ceremonies, so also will a man not be counted righteous merely because he neglects and despises them.

Our faith in Christ does not free us from works but from false opinions concerning works, that is, from the foolish presumption that justification is acquired by works. Faith redeems, corrects, and preserves our consciences so that we know that righteousness does not consist in works, although works neither can nor ought to be wanting; just as we cannot be without food and drink and all the works of this mortal body, yet our righteousness is not in them, but in faith; and yet those works of the body are not to be despised or neglected on that account. In this world we are bound by the needs of our bodily life, but we are not righteous because of them. "My kingship is not of this world" [John 18:36], says Christ. He does not, however, say, "My kingship is not here, that is, in this world." And Paul says, "Though we live in the world we are not carrying on a worldly war" [II Cor. 10:3], and in Gal. 2 [:20], "The life I now live in the flesh I live by faith in the Son of God." Thus what we do, live, and are in works and ceremonies, we do because of the necessities of this life and of the effort to rule our body. Nevertheless we are righteous, not in these, but in the faith of the Son of God.

Hence the Christian must take a middle course and face those two classes of men. He will meet first the unyielding, stubborn ceremonialists who like deaf adders are not willing to hear the truth of liberty [Ps. 58:4] but, having no faith, boast of, prescribe, and insist upon their ceremonies as means of justification. Such were the Jews of old, who were unwilling to learn how to do good. These he must resist, do the very opposite, and offend them boldly lest by their impious views they drag many with them into error. In the presence of such men it is good to eat meat, break the fasts, and for the sake of the liberty of faith do other things which they regard as the greatest of sins. Of them we must say, "Let them alone; they are blind guides." According to this principle Paul would not circumcise Titus when the Jews insisted that he should [Gal. 2:3], and Christ excused the apostles when they plucked ears of grain on the sabbath [Matt. 12:1-8]. There are many similar instances. The other class of men whom a Christian will meet are simple-minded, ignorant men, weak in the faith, as the Apostle calls them, who cannot yet grasp the liberty of faith, even if they were willing to do so [Rom. 14:1]. These he must take care not to offend. He must yield to their weakness until they are more fully instructed. Since they do and think as they do, not because they are stubbornly wicked, but only because their faith is weak, the fasts and other things which they consider necessary must be observed to avoid giving them offense. This is the command of love which would harm no one but would serve all men. It is not by their fault that they are weak, but by that of their pastors who have taken them captive with the snares of their traditions and have wickedly used these traditions as rods with which to beat them. They should have been delivered from these pastors by the teachings of faith and freedom. So the Apostle teaches us in Romans 14: "If food is a cause of my brother's falling, I will never eat meat" [Cf. Rom. 14:21 and I Cor. 8:13]; and again, "I know and am persuaded in the Lord Jesus that nothing is unclean in itself; but it is unclean for any one who thinks it unclean" [Rom. 14:14].

For this reason, although we should boldly resist those teachers of traditions and sharply censure the laws of the popes by means of which they plunder the people of God, yet we must spare the timid multitude whom these impious tyrants hold captive by means of these laws until they are set free. Therefore fight strenuously against the wolves, but for the sheep and not also against the sheep. This you will do if you inveigh against the laws and the lawgivers and at the same time observe the laws with the weak so that they will not be offended, until they also recognize tyranny and understand their freedom. If you wish to use your freedom, do so in secret, as Paul says, Rom. 14 [:22], "The faith that you have, keep between yourself and God"; but take care not to use your freedom in the sight of the weak. On the other hand, use your freedom constantly and consistently in the sight of and despite the tyrants and the stubborn so that they also may learn that they are impious, that their laws are of no avail for righteousness, and that they had no right to set them up.

Since we cannot live our lives without ceremonies and works, and the perverse and untrained youth need to be restrained and saved from harm by such bonds; and since each one should keep his body under control by means of such works, there is need that the minister of Christ be far-seeing and faithful. He ought so to govern and teach Christians in all these matters that their conscience and faith will not be offended and that there will not spring up in them a suspicion and a root of bitterness and many will thereby be defiled, as Paul admonishes the Hebrews [Heb. 12:15]; that is, that they may not lose faith and become defiled by the false estimate of the value of works and think that they must be justified by works. Unless faith is at the same time constantly taught, this happens easily and defiles a great many, as has been done until now through the pestilent, impious, soul-destroying traditions of our popes and the opinions of our theologians. By these snares numberless souls have been dragged down to hell, so that you might see in this the work of Antichrist.

In brief, as wealth is the test of poverty, business the test of faithfulness, honors the test of humility, feasts the test of temperance, pleasures the test of chastity, so ceremonies are the test of the righteousness of faith. "Can a man," asks

Solomon, "carry fire in his bosom and his clothes and not be burned?" [Prov. 6:27]. Yet as a man must live in the midst of wealth, business, honors, pleasures, and feasts, so also must he live in the midst of ceremonies, that is, in the midst of dangers. Indeed, as infant boys need beyond all else to be cherished in the bosoms and by the hands of maidens to keep them from perishing, yet when they are grown up their salvation is endangered if they associate with maidens, so the inexperienced and perverse youth need to be restrained and trained by the iron bars of ceremonies lest their unchecked ardor rush headlong into vice after vice. On the other hand, it would be death for them always to be held in bondage to ceremonies, thinking that these justify them. They are rather to be taught that they have been so imprisoned in ceremonies, not that they should be made righteous or gain great merit by them, but that they might thus be kept from doing evil and might more easily be instructed to the righteousness of faith. Such instruction they would not endure if the impulsiveness of their youth were not restrained.

Hence ceremonies are to be given the same place in the life of a Christian as models and plans have among builders and artisans. They are prepared, not as a permanent structure, but because without them nothing could be built or made. When the structure is complete the models and plans are laid aside. You see, they are not despised, rather they are greatly sought after; but what we despise is the false estimate of them, since no one holds them to be the real and permanent structure.

If any man were so flagrantly foolish as to care for nothing all his life long except the most costly, careful, and persistent preparation of plans and models and never to think of the structure itself, and were satisfied with his work in producing such plans and mere aids to work, and boasted of it, would not all men pity his insanity and think that something great might have been built with what he has wasted? Thus we do not despise ceremonies and works but we set great store by them; but we despise the false estimate placed upon works in order that no one may think that they are true righteousness, as those hypocrites believe who spend and lose their whole lives in zeal for works and never reach that goal for the sake of which the works are to be done, who, as the Apostle says, "will listen to anybody and can never arrive at a knowledge of the truth" [II Tim. 3:7]. They seem to wish to build, they make their preparations, and yet they never build. Thus they remain caught in the form of religion and do not attain unto its power [II Tim. 3:5]. Meanwhile they are pleased with their efforts and even dare to judge all others whom they do not see shining with a like show of works. Yet with the gifts of God which they have spent and abused in vain they might if they had been filled with faith, have accomplished great things to their own salvation and that of others.

Since human nature and natural reason, as it is called, are by nature superstitious and ready to imagine, when laws and works are prescribed, that righteousness must be obtained through laws and works; and further, since they are trained and confirmed in this opinion by the practice of all earthly lawgivers, it is impossible that they should of themselves escape from the slavery of works and come to a knowledge of the freedom of faith. Therefore there is need of the prayer that the Lord may give us and make us *theodidacti,* that is, those taught by God [John 6:45], and himself, as he has promised, write his law in our hearts; otherwise there is no hope for us. If he himself does not teach our hearts this wisdom hidden in mystery [I Cor. 2:7], nature can only condemn it and judge it to be heretical because nature is offended by it and regards it as foolishness. So we see that it happened in the old days in the case of the apostles and prophets, and so godless and blind popes and their flatterers do to me and to those who are like me. May God at last be merciful on them and to

315

us and cause his face to shine upon us that we may know his way upon earth [Ps. 67:1-2], his salvation among all nations, God, who is blessed forever [II Cor. 11:31]. Amen.

Type used in this book
Body, 10 on 12 Caledonia
Display, News Gothic